Unbeatable Résumés

America's Top Recruiter Reveals
What *Really* Gets You Hired

TONY BESHARA

FOREWORD BY DR. PHIL McGRAW

AMACOM AMERICAN MANAGEMENT ASSOCIATION

New York · Atlanta · Brussels · Chicago · Mexico City
San Francisco · Shanghai · Tokyo · Toronto · Washington, D.C.

This publication is designed to provide accurate and authoritative information in regard to the subject matter covered. It is sold with the understanding that the publisher is not engaged in rendering legal, accounting, or other professional service. If legal advice or other expert assistance is required, the services of a competent professional person should be sought.

Library of Congress Cataloging-in-Publication Data

Beshara, Tony, 1948–
    Unbeatable résumés : America's top recruiter reveals what really gets you hired / Tony Beshara ; foreword by Phil McGraw.
        p. cm.
    Includes index.
    ISBN-13: 978-0-8144-1762-1 (pbk.)
    ISBN-10: 0-8144-1762-0 (pbk.)
1. Résumés (Employment)—United States. I. Title.
    HF5383.B4335 2011
    650.14'2—dc22

                                                                    2011006635

About AMA

American Management Association (www.amanet.org) is a world leader in talent development, advancing the skills of individuals to drive business success. Our mission is to support the goals of individuals and organizations through a complete range of products and services, including classroom and virtual seminars, webcasts, webinars, podcasts, conferences, corporate and government solutions, business books, and research. AMA's approach to improving performance combines experiential learning—learning through doing—with opportunities for ongoing professional growth at every step of one's career journey.

Printing number
10 9 8 7 6 5 4

CONTENTS

FOREWORD

On *The Dr. Phil Show*, we strive to bring our guests the best of the best in every category of resource during and after the show. Tony Beshara is just that—the best of the best! Given these tough economic times, more and more of our guests find themselves in social or economic distress, often recently unemployed with the challenge of having to reinvent themselves and find a new career path. Tony is one of the top placement and recruitment specialists in the United States, and with him in your corner you have an incredible advantage. He has developed one of the most successful systems for finding a job or changing careers ever devised. It is specific, action oriented, and above all, "doable."

We asked Tony to intervene with a husband and father, who was out of work for eight months through no fault of his own. Tony began with a dynamic and scientifically based rewrite of his résumé. Within thirty minutes, the transformation had begun. The simple but effective changes that Tony made are here in this book.

The guest implemented Tony's system, including the newly shaped résumé, and despite being in California with its terrible job market, a new job was created. Now, it took nine months of hard job-searching work; it wasn't easy, but it was "doable." There was nothing mystical or magical about what he did—just good, solid, well-executed planning and work.

A résumé is one of the most important tools you can have in a job search.

Tony's first two books, *The Job Search Solution* and *Acing the Interview*, were bestsellers because of Tony's practical, in-the-trenches strategies for how to get a job. He knows what works. Tony taps into everything he knows from decades of job-placement experience when he shows job candidates how crafting their résumés differently can make all the difference in finding a job. When it comes to looking for a job and creating the most effective résumé, Tony's *Unbeatable Résumés* is of the highest standard. Some people are going to get the jobs that are out there. With Tony's system in the mix, your chances are clearly going to go way up. Good luck, and God bless you and your family.

Dr. Phil

ACKNOWLEDGMENTS

Greatest thanks go to Chrissy for her prayers, time, and spiritual support. A great deal of thanks goes to the "team" at AMACOM: Ellen, Erika, Carole, and Kama . . . you all are the best! Thanks also go to Pam Williams, who kept these chapters straight revision after revision, and to Vernelle Fugitt for her research. Thanks to Phil McGraw, his organization, and their spirit of service. And a special thanks to the thousands of candidates I have worked with over the years who contributed to this book's contents.

Dedicated to God's greatest blessings,
My wonderful wife and best friend, Chrissy, and our family.

The Top Ten (BIG) Mistakes of Résumé Writing

I personally *receive* 200 to 300 résumés each week. I personally *use* 200 résumés each week to find people jobs. Being on the front line, in the trenches, when it comes to résumés, I know what works and what doesn't. This isn't theory; this is *truth*. Here are the most common mistakes people make regarding their résumés. In this book, I debunk résumé myths and give you all the inside info you'll need to get the edge in obtaining job interviews.

So, here are the top ten BIG mistakes people make when preparing their résumés:

1. Overestimating the value of a résumé. Suffice it to say, the value of your résumé in getting you a job, let alone an interview, *isn't what* *you think!* Yes, of course there are valuable things to learn about how to craft your résumé, but it's also good to have accurate expectations. I explain in depth the reasons people overestimate the impact of a résumé.

2. Overestimating the attention paid to résumés. The average résumé gets read in ten seconds! Most people imagine that someone will systematically and carefully examine, dissect, and digest the résumé in front of them. The truth is that interviewing or hiring authorities only glance at résumés. They look for companies they recognize, the longevity of jobs held, and maybe a few other things. That's it! They then determine whether to read it in-depth at a later time. If your résumé doesn't grab attention in ten seconds, it's over.

3. Underestimating the odds. People underestimate the number of résumés that interviewing or hiring authorities receive. It is not uncommon for them to receive 200 to 300 résumés for every job opening. With the appearance of the "send" button, these people get overloaded with résumés even when they aren't looking to hire.

4. Overestimating the qualifications of the people who will screen or pass along the résumé. If you think the "right" people are reading your résumé, you're wrong!

5. Including the wrong content. Even the most experienced professionals put the *wrong* content into their résumés. They make the mistake of including material that *they* understand, instead of information that will be understood by the people who matter—the ones who can grant you an interview. If a high school senior, who doesn't know you, has problems reading your résumé and understanding exactly what you have done, who you have done it for, and how successful you were, just imagine what the hiring authorities will think! You have put the wrong content in your résumé! For instance, people routinely list the names of companies they have worked for, without explaining what the companies do. They assume that since they know who their company is and what it does, everyone else does, too. Oh, boy!

6. Using distracting résumé formats. This seems elementary, but most résumés don't get read because of formats that are distracting rather than helpful. Though these graphic formats are often recommended by "professional" résumé writers, they don't work! Now that most résumés are read on a computer screen, you need to take into account the way technology has taught us to read résumés.

7. Overestimating the value of the cover letter. Cover letters are as overrated as résumés. Most of them actually destroy your chances of getting even a good résumé read.

8. Assuming one size fits all. People send the same résumé out to all of the people or job opportunities they are pursuing. No! You should know how to "dumb down" or highlight different parts of your résumé and how to customize it for success in different environments and for different opportunities.

9. Flubbing the basics. It is amazing how often people mess up simple résumé matters such as length, objectives, summaries, dates of employment, and titles. The sheer length of most résumés, for instance, ensures that they will *never* get read. On the vast majority of résumés, including an Objectives statement will *eliminate* candidates right off the bat. And a Summary paragraph can kill your chances of being interviewed.

10. Having the wrong résumé "strategy"—if you have any at all. Ask the average job seeker what his or her strategy is for ensuring the résumé will get attention *and yield an interview*, and you'll get a blank stare. Beyond the "send" button, there's no strategy! Big mistake! There are strategic activities you should do *before* you send your résumé, as well as *after* you send it—and this book will give you the lowdown on each.

I   I   I

This book is going to prevent you from making the mistakes that keep average job seekers from ever getting an interview.

1

Straight Talk About Your Résumé

(From a Guy Whose Living Depends on Using Them)

THIS WEEK I sent 221 résumés of my candidates to different clients and helped three people find jobs. On average, I receive up to 40 résumés a day from people seeking my help in landing a job. I receive a lot of résumés, and I send out a lot of résumés.

I am a professional placement and recruitment specialist, and résumés are the tools I use to help my candidates get interviews. Since 1973, I have reviewed more than 32,000 résumés and have been personally responsible for placing more than 8,500 individuals in jobs, all on a one-on-one basis. That means I picked up the phone, called a hiring authority, got them an interview, helped with subsequent interviews, and negotiated an offer for them—8,500 times.

That's why I know what types of résumés are the most helpful for getting interviews that lead to job offers. In fact, *my livelihood* depends on that knowledge. The truth is that the vast majority of authors who write résumé books and articles have never found anyone a job, nor have they had to justify to prospective employers the quality of good candidates with poor résumés.

Most of the stuff written about résumés reflects those authors' opinions of what they imagine works. Instead, I tell you exactly what *does* work, based on the opinions of the hiring authorities I speak with every day. So, in this book, you're getting proven résumé knowledge about what works in the real world.

Here is a quick example. Some national "personal marketing" firms (i.e., professional résumé services) write résumés for fees of $150 and up. They recommend, and will write, a "functional" résumé for anyone willing to pay their fee. Unlike the traditional chronological résumé, a functional résumé lists all the duties and responsibilities spanning a person's career. Then, at the bottom of the résumé, are the names of companies the person has worked for, along with the corresponding dates. Usually there is little or no explanation of what each company does. Yet, here are the facts: *Most hiring authorities don't like or read these types of résumés.* (Résumé types are discussed in Chapter 3, where you'll also find the results of a survey involving more than 3,000 hiring authorities, which backs up this fact. Indeed, you will learn what they *do want to see* in a résumé.)

Does this mean that no one using a functional résumé ever gets an interview? Or ever gets hired? No, of course not. But it does mean that your chances of getting an interview are better if you *don't* use a functional résumé. And, after all, doesn't it make sense to stack the odds in your favor?

The reason hiring managers don't appreciate functional résumés is that the experience and accomplishments of the candidate are not set in the context of particular companies or job functions. That is, after all, the context in which they are hiring.

A functional résumé crossed my desk a few years ago, in which the candidate had written: "#1 salesperson in the U.S." I went ahead and interviewed the candidate because I recognized the companies he had worked for, listed at the bottom. But I explained that he needed to write a chronological résumé connecting his experiences and successes to each job held. When he did so, it turned out that he had been the "#1 salesperson in the U.S." *10 years ago!* That's why hiring authorities don't like this type of résumé. They hide the details. Unfortunately, this candidate had paid $5,000 to a "consulting firm" that had guaranteed the functional résumé it wrote would land him a job. *Guaranteed?*

The primary reason people spend so much time, money, and effort in writing a résumé is that this is the one activity within the job search that they can control. Instead of picking up the phone and *calling* a prospective employer to ask for a face-to-face interview—risking potential rejection—people agonize over their résumés. It's true that agonizing over a résumé won't get you *rejected*, but spending hours on your résumé doesn't automatically mean it will be successful, either.

Here's the Truth: Nothing you think about your résumé matters unless it helps you get interviews that result in job offers! So, here's what I suggest. If anyone charges you money to write a résumé, tell the person you will *double* the asking price *after* the résumé gets you an interview, let alone a job. Yes, you read that right. Tell the agency or individual you will pay *contingent* upon the résumé's working for you. If the agency truly believes the résumés it produces are as effective as it claims, then it should have no problem taking this deal.

The Real Value of a Résumé

It is rare for someone to get hired by simply submitting a résumé— the purpose of the résumé is to help get you *an interview*. And at the interview, remember that 40 percent of a hiring decision is based on personality. The series of interviews is used to judge the compatibility of your personality with those of people in the company. That is, companies hire people they like; a résumé cannot communicate your personal traits.

It's that simple. Your résumé won't get you hired; rather, your résumé should help you get face-to-face interviews—so that your winning personality can convince your interviewers.

It is possible that you may be lucky and get an invitation to interview strictly by sending your résumé to a hiring authority. But in this market that situation isn't likely. You're going to have to do a lot of other things to secure the interviews, and I tell you what these things are in the chapters of this book.

Résumé Secrets? Résumé Magic? Hogwash

If you Google the words *résumé magic*, you will get over 1.9 million results. If you Google *résumé secrets*, you will get 22.5 million results. What's so absurd about all of this is that there is no *magic*, there are no *secrets* to résumé writing. In fact, the process is not even mysterious. Writing an effective résumé is simple—as long as you have an effective résumé strategy.

You want to write and use the most effective résumé possible so that you can get as many interviews and job offers as you can. It's a simple statistical challenge. But this book will help you learn how to write a résumé that will have a higher probability of helping you get those face-to-face interviews.

Conquering the Biggest Challenge

You've come to the right place. Here, you will learn how to write a simple, straightforward, and *effective* résumé. But that's actually not the hardest part about getting a face-to-face interview. Your biggest challenge is knowing what to do with the résumé after you've written it.

How you use your résumé to secure face-to-face interviews is where the rubber really meets the road. The vast majority of people who call me to complain about their zero job responses think that their problems lie with their résumé. And while for some there may indeed be some résumé kinks, that is not the primary reason they're not getting interviews. Rather, the problem is a lack of technique and strategy.

In Chapters 2 through 7, I show you, step by step, how to write an effective résumé. Then, in Chapters 8 through 10, I coach you on how to use your effective résumé to get results—that all-important golden egg, the face-to-face interview.

2

Surprising Facts About Your Résumé Audience

MOST PEOPLE assume that if they *write* an effective résumé it is going to be *read* by decision makers with great business acumen and experience. And that since these decision makers are so intelligent, they will naturally have the wisdom to interview and hire them. *Nothing could be further from the truth.*

According to the Bureau of Labor Statistics (BLS), there are 7.5 million businesses in the United States with employees, and the average number of employees in those 7.5 million businesses is sixteen. The BLS also tells us that between December 2000 and November 2008, the monthly turnover rate for U.S. companies was 3.3 percent. This means that we are a nation of small companies, with 3.3 percent of our employees coming and going on a monthly basis.

The average job in the United States lasts two and a half to three years. In 2008, *every day* 1,751 companies went bankrupt or closed. And each day they were *replaced* by 1,781 new companies. Even very large companies make poor business decisions and sometimes teeter on insolvency. Most of us are not aware of just how phenomenally erratic businesses are, even in the United States. We tend to think that most businesses are very successful—and that definition of success can be very broad. Yet the U.S. Department of Commerce reports that seven out of ten new employer firms last at least two years but only about half survive five years.

So, businesses expand, contracts are born, and companies die erratically. In 2008, 1.8 million businesses in the United States expanded or opened, creating 7.3 million jobs; meanwhile, 2 million businesses contracted or closed in the same year, eliminating 7.9 million jobs. This means that the hiring authority who might be interviewing you probably hasn't been in that job very long, either. Even "long-term positions" can be short. According to Crist Kolder Associates, roughly half of the CFOs of Fortune 500 and S&P 500 companies are in their jobs for fewer than three years—that's about the average tenure of an NFL running back.

Guess why hiring managers want to know "What can you do for me . . . right now, today?" It's because (1) chances are they won't be there long, and (2) they know they have to perform *now* to keep their jobs into tomorrow.

And with an economy that has been shaky at best, most business-people are operating more out of fear of loss than from a vision of gain. They are afraid of just about everything—especially the economy. They don't know how long this malaise will continue.

When a business is fearful about the future, it's difficult to make hiring decisions, but it's even more difficult for job candidates. With so many candidates to choose from, hiring authorities are compelled to seek out the "perfect" candidate. They feel that they can't afford to make a mistake. And they expect better candidates than they interviewed and hired just a few years ago.

If you are like most candidates, you think your résumé is being perused and considered by intelligent businesspeople who have a genuine sense of appreciation for what you can do for their companies. You imagine a wise hiring authority who is personally reading your perfect résumé. But the truth is, the chances are poor that your résumé will ever get in front of that person, let alone be read by him or her.

I have been a professional recruiter since 1973, and in that time, here's what I have noticed:

- 60 percent of résumés received for a particular opening are *never reviewed* by the hiring authority.

- 70 percent of résumés received for a particular opening are reviewed by a *third party*—that is, a human resources (HR) individual, internal recruiter, or some administrative person—who may or may not be qualified to interview a prospective employee. (A few years ago, we got a call from the CEO of a $40 million manufacturing company. He said he needed to hire a controller and that his daughter was going to do the initial interviewing—while she was home from college over Christmas break.)

- 60 percent of the third parties who review a résumé have *no direct experience* with the job they are recruiting for. Rather, they are relying on information given to them by someone else.

- 40 percent of résumés that are "opened" to be read are deleted because the reader isn't clear about what kind of job the person has done, who the applicant has worked for, and how successful the person has been.

Additionally, most people imagine that companies fill most of their job openings within one to two months. In reality, the average time is more like four or five months.

The average résumé gets read in ten seconds. On top of this, there are at least 100 résumés received for every job posted to the public. Even if a hiring authority decides to read *all* of the résumés him- or herself, the odds of yours surfacing to the top aren't great.

If you have been looking for a job for a while, and you have sent your résumé to many companies, you may have asked yourself, "Why don't those people call me? I am an absolute perfect match for their jobs! What's wrong with them?"

Well, now you know. It is not likely your résumé even got *read*, and it's even less likely that it was read by the *right person*—the person feeling the pain. By "feeling the pain" I mean the person who needs to hire someone because, if someone isn't hired, he has to do the job himself.

Although it is easy to get discouraged when you hear all of this, if you follow the advice in this book you will significantly improve your odds of getting interviews. And, after all, it is better to be aware of what really goes on than to live in a fantasy world and be disappointed.

There's really not much you can do about the chaos that goes on in most companies, especially relating to the hiring process. At least by recognizing the relative mess you will be able to get your expectations in order—and you will realize that "it's not you." And then, having a well-written résumé with a high probability of being read is a good first step toward breaking through that chaos. Of course, it's important to have an effective strategy for *using* your résumé to get an interview—because a great résumé is only as good as your ability to get the interview.

3

The Résumés 3,000 Hiring Authorities Want to See

THIS CHAPTER may be one of the most important things you ever read about getting a job. It translates research findings into practical information that can help you get that job you need.

We surveyed more than 6,000 hiring and interviewing authorities in Dallas/Ft. Worth, Texas. These authorities ranged from first-line hiring managers to CEOs, at companies employing from six people to more than a thousand employees. A full 11 percent of those surveyed were third-party recruiters, such as human resources (HR) managers, while the rest were individuals responsible for managing the persons they would hire. These hiring authorities represented a wide variety of disciplines, including sales, engineering, architecture, administrative support, healthcare (i.e., physicians, nursing, and allied professions), accounting and finance, and information technology.

The Survey

A total of 3,129 people answered our survey. To ensure a good response, we kept the questions short and to the point. Here are the questions we asked:

What are the critical components of a well-written résumé?

When you scan dozens of résumés, what do you look for?

What length of résumé do you prefer?

What are some of the things you see in résumés that you really don't like? What *shouldn't* be on a résumé?

What distinguishes the résumés of candidates you interview from the large number of résumés you ignore?

How many résumés do you personally review—per week? per month? per year? per position you are trying to fill?

How important is a cover letter when you are receiving résumés?

Is it you or your HR department who reviews the résumés first?

When you have a stack of résumés in front of you, how long does it take to initially review each one?

Do you receive or use video résumés?

The Results

Here are the results, with the percentages of respondents specifying the answers given:

What Are the Critical Components of a Well-Written Résumé?

- Reverse chronological order: 98%

- Names of companies, a clear indication of what they do, specific dates, specific job titles, and a clear list of duties: 98%

- Concise evidence of success: 96%

- Quantifiable results and accomplishments: 94%

- No spelling, grammar, or typographical errors: 85%

- Clear, concise articulation of skills and experience: 80%

- Pertinent information that relates to the job being filled: 60%

- Written by the candidate (not professionally written): 48%

- Format that is clear and easy to read: 45%

- Dates of employment with *month* and *year*: 45%

- Résumé tailored to specific job opening ("what can you do for me—now?"): 40%

It's clear that the vast majority of respondents want a *reverse chronological* résumé. As you will see, functional résumés, as well as most Objectives statements and Career Summaries, are not generally appreciated or desired. Clear dates of employment and concise evidence of a person's duties, responsibilities, and accomplishments are important.

Functional résumés are acceptable in some professions, like nursing or healthcare. A nurse is a nurse, no matter if he or she worked at a number of hospitals. A hiring authority would want to know the accomplishments or functions and that, for instance, all of the positions were in nursing. I discuss this, with examples, in Chapter 7.

When You Scan Dozens of Résumés, What Do You Look For?

- Professional experience that relates to what needs to be done: 97%

- The companies an applicant has worked for and whether the duties of those jobs relate to the open job function and skills needed: 95%

- Brevity and clear, well-defined accomplishments: 90%

- Key skills that match the openings: 88%

- Stability: 87%

- Key words, phrases, and acronyms that apply to the job opening: 70%

- Whether there are gaps in employment history: 51%

- Things that set a candidate apart from the rest: 48%

- Progression and continuity of jobs and positions within career: 40%

Résumé readers want clear explanations of what the candidate has done and how that applies to the job being interviewed for. Most résumés are too vague about the kind of work the candidate's prior employers were involved in, and candidates often don't present this information in terms most readers can understand. Not surprisingly, evidence of stability and only minimal gaps in employment are important to the hiring authorities.

What Length of Résumé Do You Prefer?

▪ 1 to 2 pages: 95%

▪ More than 2 pages: 5%

Résumés in healthcare, information technology, and academia can go beyond the two-page rule. Considering the number of résumés most hiring authorities have to review (and with most résumés first read online), it seems that two pages are about all that will get read, even with a more in-depth review. As one respondent wrote, "If a candidate can't tell me what he has done, what he or she can do for me, and why I should interview them in two pages, the candidate isn't concise enough!"

What Are Some of the Things You See in Résumés That You Really Don't Like? What *Shouldn't* Be on a Résumé?

▪ Long, unclear descriptions of present or previous jobs: 98%

▪ Objective or summary statements: 95%

▪ Excessive job descriptions with no factual achievements: 94%

▪ Personal information—photos, church affiliation, marriage, how many kids, hobbies: 90%

▪ Grammatical, spelling, or punctuation mistakes: 90%

▪ Generic competencies that are fluff, such as "dynamic leader," "excellent communication skills," and "effective listener": 90%

▪ Too much information: 88%

▪ Every webinar, seminar, or class the applicant ever attended: 75%

- Personal information: 64%

- "References Available upon Request": 55%

- Anything before college: 50%

- Résumés obviously written by a résumé service: 48%

- Résumés written by copying the published job description: 45%

This question got the longest answers and the most emotional ones. Hiring authorities really feel strongly about what they *don't* like to see in résumés. It is obvious that résumés need to have clear descriptions of exactly what the candidate has done, expressed in terms a prospective employer can identify with (i.e., answering the question, "What is this candidate going to do for me?"). Objectives and summaries are not appreciated unless they apply to the specific position. *Remember this fact!* Summaries and statements of Objectives seem to be popular, and yet the vast majority of employers *don't like them.*

Similarly, personal information is not appreciated on the résumé, so don't include it! One respondent summed it up this way: "Anything that is not relevant to the job I am interviewing for is a waste of time. I won't interview a candidate who can't, succinctly, tell me what he can do for me—now!"

What Distinguishes the Résumés of Candidates You Interview from the Large Number of Résumés You Ignore?

- Accomplishments that qualify the candidate for what is needed: 99%

- Clear, concise information that tells what the candidate has done: 95%

- Job stability: 94%

- Professional layout—not too crammed, with the right amount of white space: 80%

- Easy to compare prior experience to the job to be filled: 78%

- A résumé "customized" to supply needed information: 75%

- Awards and recognitions: 74%

- Attention to detail, such as correct grammar, spelling, and punctuation: 65%

This question got more varied answers than any of the other survey questions. While the above represent answers from the majority of respondents, there were a few other responses that seemed individual:

"Something that catches my eye."

"I only read résumés referred to me by someone I know."

"A local candidate."

"Readability—don't try to be cute."

In sum, clear, concise accomplishments and job stability really make a big splash. Perceptions of job stability are discussed in Chapter 10.

How Many Résumés Do You Personally Review?

- Per week: ranged from 2 to 400, with an average of 65.

- Per month: ranged from 5 to 1,000, with an average of 236.

- Per year: ranged from 10 to 20,000, with an average of 2,429.

- The number of résumés reviewed for each position ranged from 3 to 300, with an average of 60.

The take-away message is that, on average, your résumé is competing with at least *sixty* others each time you apply for a job. So picture yourself sitting down to go through sixty résumés. Maybe even print sixty résumés off one of the job boards and put them in front of you. Now, start reading. How long is your attention span? Does this feel productive? Would you even know what you were looking for? And, how does this exercise make you feel about your own résumé?

How Important Is a Cover Letter When You Are Receiving Résumés?

▪ Not very important: 86%

▪ Important: 14%

The majority of hiring authorities who thought the cover letter was important stated that they read the résumé first. This response typified most: "It is only important to me if the person is of interest. I usually read the cover letter *after* I look at the résumé." Most of the respondents expressed their ambivalence about cover letters by stating that a well-written résumé was more important.

Is It You or Your HR Department Who Reviews the Résumés First?

Note: We did not count respondents from the HR departments in these results.

▪ The HR department screens them first: 39%

▪ The hiring manager reviews them directly: 61%

Comments from hiring authorities about how HR departments screen résumés varied from, "They send me the top three résumés," to "They scan them into a database and eliminate the obviously unqualified ones, then send the rest to me." So, there is tremendous variation in the role played by HR when it comes to reviewing résumés.

These results were a bit surprising. Some HR departments are simply screeners who do lots of other things in the company; others are internal recruiters who spend their day reviewing résumés so the hiring authority won't have too many to review. In spite of this, on average, hiring authorities claim they still have to review sixty résumés for each opening.

When You Have a Stack of Résumés in Front of You, How Long Does It Take to Initially Review Each One?

❙ Less than 1 minute: 56%

❙ 1 to 2 minutes: 21%

❙ 2 to 5 minutes: 13%

❙ More than 5 minutes: 10%

Comments like, "It depends on the number of résumés I have to review" and "It depends on how hard it is to find the kind of candidate I need," accompanied almost every answer. My personal sense is most hiring authorities don't take even 30 seconds to review a résumé unless they see something that they like—performance, accomplishments, recognizable experience, and so on. Most of them don't want to admit that they breeze through these résumés with no real process or plan. In my opinion, this leads them to miss great candidates the majority of the time.

I speak from personal experience on this. Our recruiting and placement firm places close to 800 professionals a year with all types of firms in the Dallas/Ft.Worth area. At least four or five times a month, we place a candidate with a company that had already received the candidate's résumé before, and sometimes two or three times earlier. You know and I know that your résumé does not represent *all* of you and all of your abilities. And it turns out that businesspeople, even hiring authorities, often can't evaluate you from your résumé, either.

This isn't fair, but life is unfair. However, it does reinforce the fact that you have to do everything in your power to get a face-to-face interview; you can't just assume that someone will recognize what a gem you are from your résumé alone.

Do You Receive or Use Video Résumés?

Not one respondent said he or she uses video résumés.

We asked this question to see if any hiring authorities in the "trenches" of average businesses were open to avant-garde or advanced technology as a way of reviewing résumés or applicants. There's increasing hype about video résumés, YouTube résumés, PowerPoint résumés, and other electronic presentations, so we wanted to see whether anyone was considering them. No one seems to be. Traditional résumés are still the norm.

A Summary of Our Findings

Based on our survey, your résumé needs to be written in reverse chronological order and should clearly describe the functions of the companies you have worked for as well as your duties and responsibilities at each of those companies. It must highlight your accomplishments in terms everyone can understand and relate your experience to the job you are applying for. The résumé should communicate longevity in jobs, with specific dates. It must be no more than two pages and it should rarely include an Objective statement or Career Summary—and *only* if it relates to the job you are applying for. Your résumé should feature accomplishments that make you stand out from the crowd (because yours is going to be one of the sixty that make it to the hiring authority's desk).

Keep in mind that you don't need a cover letter. Also, that your résumé has to be good enough to get past the HR screeners and that it is likely your résumé will be read in less than a minute.

4

Key Features of the Most Effective Résumés

YOUR RÉSUMÉ IS not likely to get you hired; rather, its purpose is to get you a face-to-face audience with an interviewing or hiring authority. That is, your résumé is a *sales tool* that says to an interviewing or hiring authority: "You need to interview me because I have been a good employee [or student]. I've been successful before and I will be successful for you." It's that simple.

The rule of thumb is this: As long as your résumé gets you interviews, you can use any format or style you like. But certain contents and formats have the *highest probability* of getting you interviews, based on my thirty-eight years of experience. I begin the chapter with a discussion of some initial considerations—things you should and should not include when preparing to write your résumé. Then I get down to the basics—the reverse chronological format and its elements. And I conclude with a pointed discussion of other ways to put together a winning résumé.

Some Beginning Considerations

Let's get started with some fundamentals.

OVERALL TONE: KEEP IT SIMPLE

Be sure the content of your résumé is on a level any high school senior could understand. In other words, the person looking at your résumé should be able to easily understand exactly who you have worked for, what that company does, what you have done there, how successful you have been, and what you could do for future employers if you were hired. Readers of a résumé will ask themselves, "Why should we interview this person?" And, since the average résumé is read in a matter of seconds, it had better be clear to readers why they need to read a little more deeply.

Similarly, stay away from squishy, meaningless, fluff statements like "Superb written and oral communication skills," "highly motivated," "great mentor," and so on. If you are going to state your "superb written skills," qualify this statement by backing it up with facts; for instance, "Rewrote three training manuals distributed corporate-wide." Or, to document "oral communication skills," you could state that you're responsible for weekly group presentations, training programs, motivational speeches, and so on. *Back up* the broad statements with illustrative *facts*.

THE MEDIUM AFFECTS THE MESSAGE

Probably 99 percent of the résumés you submit will be sent via the Internet, so you need to know how images and information are read differently on-screen than when they are physically held. For example, keep in mind that:

▪ People spend 39 percent less time looking at images and information online than they do when they are printed.

▪ The average person looks first at the center of an online document and then moves around the screen to view other details. One study found that people have a tendency to scan the screen in search of content and that our eyes follow an F-shaped pattern, beginning in the middle, then going to the left, then up the left margin to the top, quickly scanning across text in search of the central nugget of information.

▪ People have a tendency to read "down" a screen rather than across, looking for information.

▪ People's reading online tends to be shallow, with more scanning and skimming. As one researcher put it, "The screen-based reading behavior is characterized by more time spent on browsing and scanning, key word spotting, one-time reading, nonlinear reading, and reading more selectively, while less time is spent on in-depth reading and concentrated reading."

▪ People are interrupted more when reading online and tend to "bounce" from one document or image to another.

▪ Most people print out a résumé only if it looks good to them, and then they read it in more depth in printed form. But the first yes or no decision is made by viewing it online.

▪ Mark Zuckerberg, founder of Facebook, has said that communication on the Web needs to be seamless, informal, immediate, personal, simple, minimal, and short. And with your résumé, it *especially* needs to be seamless, immediate, personal, simple, minimal, and short.

Since your résumé is likely going to be read first online, it needs to be clear and direct. And with research showing that the middle of the screen is the online reader's focal point, position your most compelling information in the center of the "page."

After you write your résumé, ask friends or relatives to read it online, and then check to make sure that it has communicated to them what you want it to communicate.

CAREER SUMMARIES AND OBJECTIVES

I'm not a big fan of the Summary and Objectives sections that appear at the beginning of most résumés. (Obviously, the employers we surveyed feel the same way; see Chapter 3.) Though many résumé writers will tell you that they're a wonderful idea, that's because you're paying them and they're stroking your ego and making you look bigger than life. Unfortunately, these sections will backfire more often than they'll help in getting you an interview. Here are the reasons:

1. Hiring authorities don't care about *your* objectives. They care about *their own* objectives. They care about what you want only if it also gives them what they want. So, in looking to show how you will fill their needs, don't bother telling them what your needs are.

2. A hiring or interviewing authority is generally looking for specific skills to fill a specific position. The vast majority of Objectives and Summary statements are so broad that they don't mean anything.

While there are some exceptions to this caveat (I will get to those in a moment), it's risky to use an Objectives or Summary statement when you can't be sure that it won't annoy the person reading your résumé.

Consider this: One of the résumés that came across my desk recently featured this Objective and Career Summary statement (yes, both):

[Candidate's name] provides profitable return while working in a highly effective environment of success and reward. He is a proven leader with 24 years of experience providing creative information-based solutions in executive management, global

sales leadership, strategic planning, new business unit development, technical management, and operations management. He
has demonstrated the ability and the resolve to develop and
implement strategic business initiatives, initiate innovative solutions to complex problems, and manage high-performance teams
that have significantly contributed to bottom-line results.

This candidate was seeking a sales job. His statements are not
objectives at all, but more like a career summary. Overall, the statement doesn't say anything specific. What does "global sales leadership" mean? What are "strategic business initiatives"? Many hiring
authorities don't think of their organizations as having a "highly effective environment of success and reward." Most are not looking for a
"proven leader" but simply a good "follower" who goes out and does
the job on a daily basis. See my point? Now, how about this Objectives
statement that I recently received:

Seeking a position with an emerging company that possesses
best-of-breed product or service that is looking to rapidly expand
into new markets.

Surely, 99 percent of companies in the United States do not consider themselves "emerging companies." Most of them will not consider themselves to have a "best-of-breed product or service." And
most might well be afraid of a candidate who wants to join only a company "looking to rapidly expand."

I'm sure these Objectives and Summary statements were important to the people who wrote them. But they mean absolutely nothing
(or, nothing good) to a hiring or interviewing authority. It's all fluff.
In fact, that fluff may well keep the candidate from getting an interview. There are, however, occasions when a Career Summary may
work—when it's a *specific description* of what you have accomplished
that would be meaningful to the prospective employer. One example
of this type is:

Offering successful consumer product marketing and product management. Responsible for a successful, first-year, $15 million healthcare product initiative into the Mideast.

Obviously, this kind of Summary statement would be of value only to an organization looking for this type of experience. So, unless your Career Summary or Objectives statement can be that specific, it's best not to write one.

THE INITIAL SCAN

So what *do* hiring authorities initially scan for in the few seconds they have to peruse your résumé?

- The organizations for whom you've worked

- What the companies you worked for did

- How long you were there

- The position(s) you held

- Your accomplishments and successes

The initial scan produces the answers to the *who, what, how long, which,* and *how well* questions. These are the five things that every hiring authority looks for. If the initial scan is palatable, the résumé gets read further, maybe even two or three times. Your best bet, then, is not to distract that hiring authority with a Career Summary or Objectives statement that she may well regard as meaningless.

KEY WORDS AND PHRASES

The use of key words is a relatively recent résumé phenomenon. With the advent of talent-management software used by companies to scan résumés and supposedly catalog them, many so-called authorities recommend a Key Word section. However, the vast majority of companies in the United States do not use applicant-tracking software that scans résumés for these key words. In fact, less than 1 percent of companies actually have this technology, and most of them don't use it. So the importance of including a special section devoted to key words is overrated.

In technical professions such as information technology, healthcare, and engineering, however, using key words may be of value. These key words need to be highly specific, though. I'm sure you're already aware of key words in your profession and in your industry, such as the following:

.net

application development

e-commerce

infrastructure development

Java

Oracle

SAP

SEC

trial balance

UNIX

Windows

Of course, résumés have always included mention of certifications, such as MBA, Ph.D., CNO, and RN.

These new technologies suggest that résumés will be searched for "concepts" instead of key words. For instance, "intelligent search technology" is supposed to overcome the idiosyncratic aspects of résumés and provide more accuracy in locating individuals with applicable talents. Most of the large job boards like Monster and Career Builder are promising this kind of technology for recruiters and subscribers. If it is advantageous to include key words for your profession, such as in information technology or accounting, then do it. I personally don't think you need a section devoted exclusively to key words. These key words will be recognized in the body of your résumé.

Fuzzy key words and phrases should be avoided, in any case. These include *customer oriented*, *excellent communication skills*, *leadership*, *integrity*, and *character*. These fuzzy words and phrases lack meaning and do absolutely nothing to help you get an interview.

The organizations that do pick up on key words are more likely to look for words that refer to titles. Most likely they will retrieve these words from the body of the résumé, rather than from a Key Words section. So, words like *customer service*, *account management*, *controller*, *accountant*, *manager*, and *vice president* may help you there. However, know that one company's "customer service manager" is another company's "client services leader." That variation in terms and titles is the primary challenge in using key words and phrases.

I recently received a résumé that used the words *honesty*, *sincerity*, *character*, *integrity*, and *determined*. Oh, brother! Show me a company that doesn't want these characteristics in its employees. It is senseless to include these words.

A recent book on résumés devotes four pages to a list of key words for inclusion in résumés. The suggested key words include *complex tasks*, *visionary*, *servant leadership*, *creative*, *professional*, and a whole page of "action verbs." Cut it out! What hiring authority is going to respond to this kind of stuff? Visionary? What's that? (The book also suggests designer résumés using clip art and colored boxes.) Oh, no! Please don't go there!

PHOTOS

Get the photos off of your résumé, if you've put them in there. You are looking for a job, not a date. You may think you look wonderful in the photo, but others may not agree! Remember: You are trying to get an interview, and anything that risks getting you eliminated doesn't help your cause. It's too easy for people to draw conclusions from your photo that might eliminate you. For their purposes, you could be too old, too young, too attractive in their opinion, etc. No reason to run that risk!

Writing the Résumé

Here are specific do's and don'ts for writing your résumé.

USE REVERSE CHRONOLOGICAL ORDER

Don't let anyone try to convince you to use any kind of format other than a chronological one. And always use a *reverse* chronological format. That is, you list your present or your most recent job first, and then work backwards. You state the name of the company you work for or have worked for and the dates of your employment—month and year. Then you describe, in detail, what your job function was and how well you performed—again, in terms a high school senior could understand. You don't even have to use full sentences (e.g., you can begin statements with verbs). And each statement should not begin with "I." Just make sure that what you write is short, to the point, and easily understood.

A paragraph format works well. Bulleted lists also work well, as long as they highlight the important points. Bullet points without a descriptive paragraph don't seem to be as effective, though. And too many bullet points can become tedious and make your résumé too long.

Technology has altered the way we read, and so bullet points are common and expected. Quite a few studies have documented how the Internet has changed us from a culture of written media to one of visual media. So bullet points—even bulleted sentences, paragraphs, or short paragraphs—are visual aids for getting the reader's attention.

The bullet points have to communicate *specific, meaningful performance qualities* or else they won't work. After the first few bullet points are read, the rest will be ignored unless there's substantive information given. So, use bullet points to convey information that is:

∎ Specific

∎ Meaningful

∎ Performance based

This seems like a simple concept, but it *isn't that easy to do*. As you will see in the "résumé makeover" section (Chapter 5), many people include fluffy, meaningless material in the body of their résumés. To weed out the fluff, you will have to think, write, and rewrite—many times. Keep what you write simple, but specific and powerful. Remember, you're trying to get the reader to interview you, based on what you say you've done and how successful you say you've been.

DON'T USE A FUNCTIONAL/ACCOMPLISHMENTS FORMAT

Functional/accomplishment résumés are, unfortunately, rather popular. Instead of a reverse chronological listing of prior employment, these list all of the functions a person has fulfilled, and often their accomplishments, in the body of the résumé, without relating them to particular jobs. In fact, most often the functions and accomplishments section takes up the vast majority of space on the résumé. Then, at the very bottom of the document, the companies a person has worked for are listed. (See an example of one of these in Chapter 5.)

Using a functional format immediately communicates that you are trying to cover up something—too many jobs, gaps in your work history, or something else that a chronological format would expose. As a result, a functional/accomplishment format communicates distrust and deception. And with hiring authorities receiving scores of résumés, they quickly look for reasons to weed some out. Most of the time they just reject functional/accomplishment résumés without further review.

Another problem with this format is that, while it communicates what you did and how well you did it, it doesn't do so within the context of *when*, *where*, and *with whom*. Whoever reads the résumé can't associate the accomplishments with particular jobs or companies, and so the information is viewed as useless. (As mentioned in Chapter 3, the hiring authorities in our survey didn't like them, either.)

Here are some statements of accomplishments that appeared on a résumé I recently received. See if you can figure out what these statements mean:

▮ 5-year average of 85% overall CSAT, 94% billable utilization, 97% burn rate while maintaining a 40% up-sell
average

▮ Ranked among the top five account executives, receiving
national achievement for attaining goal; promoted

These statements are meaningless because they exist totally out
of context. Not only do the readers have a problem associating the
functions with the time and place of employment, but they also have
no idea of how the functions and accomplishments relate to what the
companies do.

Some résumé services advise people to use a functional résumé if
they are reentering the workforce, leaving the military, pursuing a different job function, or are seeking their first job. In these instances, it
is possible that a functional résumé may get read. But they will be
more likely to get attention when our economy is booming and when
there are only a few candidates for the jobs available. For now, when
there are too many résumés for each job opportunity, stick to the
reverse chronological format.

YOUR DATES OF EMPLOYMENT

Starting with your most recent position, write the times of your
employment clearly, including both month and year. Do this for every
job that you've had for at least the past fifteen years. Dates, companies,
and functions dating back more than fifteen years can be consolidated.

If you've been out of work for more than three or four months,
or have been between jobs more than twice, record just the years and
omit the months. Be aware that hiring authorities may draw unflatter-
ing conclusions about your using just the years and you run the risk of
being passed over, but putting down the specifics is more likely to call
attention to the gap and get you eliminated from consideration.

If you have changed jobs within the same firm, don't list each job
separately, as though you had changed companies. Often, résumé
readers simply look at the dates of employment; if they see a one-year

stint followed by another year's stint, followed by yet another one-year stint, they may consider you as having had too many jobs. So, if you've had a number of promotions or different jobs with the same company, put the comprehensive dates next to the company name. Then, you can list the dates next to each position within the company, detailing the titles or duties.

YOUR EMPLOYERS AND WHAT THEY DO

Write the complete names of the companies you have worked for. If a company's name would not be easily recognized, also state what it does. If you work for a company whose business is not extremely well known, many résumé readers will dismiss your résumé simply because they aren't familiar with the company!

The point is that you need to be certain the person reading the résumé understands who you have worked for and what that business entails. Even if you worked for a large, well-recognized organization, it doesn't hurt to name and briefly describe the division as well. For example, stating that you worked for IBM is meaningless unless you name the division or group, as well as what you've done.

TITLES AND POSITIONS

You list your job title after the name of the company. If it is not clear from the title exactly what you did, or if the title is in any way confusing, change it to something more consistent with the industry or to a title people might recognize more readily. If you have an oddball title but, for whatever reason, you feel you must use it, put it in parentheses, next to the traditional title. For example, your title of Client Advocate might actually be the same as Customer Service Representative or Account Executive elsewhere. You be the judge, but remember that you want to convey the function of your job at that company.

Titles can be confusing. There are lots of VPs, for example, who are really just sales reps. They are told to use the VP title to help get them in the door of a potential customer. The same goes for Regional Manager, Director, and similar titles. A hiring authority looking for a Salesperson will often immediately dismiss the résumé, thinking *I'm not looking for a VP or Director; I'm looking for a Salesperson!* So, tailor your title, if necessary, to fit the category of work that the hiring authority will recognize.

DESCRIPTIONS OF PRIOR EXPERIENCE

After you've listed the date and title for each job you've had, describe in three or four sentences exactly what you did there. Use language a high school senior would understand, keeping it simple and clear. You may want to devote more space in the résumé to your recent jobs, especially ones that are more applicable to the position you are applying for. However, if you've been in your current position for only one year and have spent fifteen years in your previous position, hiring authorities will likely be more interested in the previous fifteen years than in your past year. The longer you have worked in an organization and the more recent your experience, the more detail you need to provide.

EDUCATIONAL BACKGROUND

Some people leave information on their education for the end of the résumé, while others put it at the beginning. Baccalaureate degrees, especially if you graduated with high honors from a prestigious school, may be worth putting at the beginning. In the business environment, advanced degrees from prestigious schools should probably be noted as well. If you're listing your degrees on the résumé, always include the dates you received them.

If you have a graduate degree, such as a Ph.D., consider preparing one résumé that includes this information and one that omits it. In the business environment, a Ph.D. may communicate that you are overqualified. The academic, scientific, or healthcare environments are different, of course. An undergraduate degree with an MBA is reasonable to report; however, more advanced degrees scare some business employers, who may think, *Why would someone with a Ph.D. want to work here?* (I discuss in more detail in Chapter 6 how having two or three different résumés may be useful for different situations.)

Here is an example of an education statement, placed in the beginning of the résumé because of the prestigious school and the candidate's outstanding athletic success:

Education

U.S. Military Academy, West Point, NY (B.S. Engineering Management 1989)

- 4-year Army Football Varsity Letterman and Senior Captain at Strong Safety

- Awarded Colonel Gillespie Memorial Award for "Leadership, performance, contribution & dedication to the Army Football Program"

- Selected as Graduate Assistant Army Football Coach for first active-duty assignment

- Sun Bowl vs. Alabama, Peach Bowl vs. Illinois, Emerald Isle Classic vs. Boston College

PERSONAL INFORMATION

I never recommend including personal data, and the reason is simple. While what you include in a résumé may work in your favor, it may also work against you. For example, being married with three kids may sound to you like you're a stable, solid citizen, but to a hiring authority looking for someone to travel 60 to 70 percent of the time, that personal information may keep you from being interviewed. Similarly, mentioning that your hobby is golf might communicate to prospective employers that you're going to try to spend two days during the work week playing golf. In short, there's just no good reason to include personal information that may keep you from getting the interview or the job.

Also, forget the ancient history. If you are more than thirty years old, no one cares about your having been an Eagle Scout or having held the high school state record in the high jump.

REASONS FOR LEAVING PREVIOUS JOBS

Never include mention of why you left an organization. That information suggests too many reasons you shouldn't be hired this time. In an interview, when a prospective employer asks for the reason you have left the prior organization, for some reason your *verbal* explanation satisfies the question, whereas a *written* explanation never seems to work in your favor.

A few years ago, I had a candidate who, after each job listed on his résumé, included an explanation of why he had left the job. After four of such explanations, he wrote "Laid off due to downsizing." Now, what do you think a prospective employer will think of that? *When I have to eliminate someone, I will eliminate this guy!* With all those résumés out there, hiring authorities are looking for reasons *not* to interview you as much as they're looking for reasons they *should*. So, it is in your best interest not to explain in your résumé why you have left any organization. Wait for the interview to answer that question.

MONEY MATTERS

Don't *ever, ever* include your past, present, or desired earnings on your résumé. This will automatically eliminate you from too many opportunities.

CONFIDENTIALITY

Any time you e-mail a résumé to a prospective employer, you run the risk of your job search being discovered by your present employer. This matter has become more complicated now that résumés are posted on literally thousands of Internet sites or job boards. No matter how confidential you try to be, if you're looking for a job while you are presently employed, you may be discovered.

If you are worried, and rightfully so, about confidentiality, then you need to send your résumé to specific hiring authorities only after you've spoken with them on the telephone. Unless you are soon to be out of work or don't care if your present employer finds out you're looking for a new job, be careful about where you send your résumé.

Keep in mind that including the word *confidential* on your résumé does *not* help keep it confidential.

Often, candidates state "Employer *confidential* 2006–Present" instead of including the name of the company. Don't do this, either. Potential employers want to know who you have worked for. They have too many other résumés to choose among, and with this missing information, yours won't get read.

REFERENCES AND ENDORSEMENTS

For openings in most traditional business environments, there's no need to include references. With some academic curriculum vitae or political, scientific, and research-oriented résumés, however, it may be appropriate to provide a list of references. It also may be appropriate to just state, "References upon Request." Depending on the situation, you may want to give different references for different positions.

There are exceptions to this guideline, of course. If your references are high-profile people, it could be of value to include those names on your résumé, provided you have checked with the individuals first. Since most of us don't have those kinds of references, it is usually better to leave off any names.

The same advice is true for quotes from people who "endorse" you personally. Unless these quotes are from the president of the United States or someone else who is readily recognizable, it's a waste of space.

Tips for Better Résumés

Here are some tips for better résumé content and format.

STORIES SELL AND NUMBERS TELL

Numbers, statistics, percentages, and the like on a résumé get attention, especially if you put them in bold type. Use truthful statistics on your résumé, and don't go overboard. Statements like **"150% of sales quota," "Increased profit by 28%," "Came under budget by 30%"** get the attention of the reader and communicate performance. Chapter 6 has examples that show how to include meaningful numerical measures of your performance.

As for including stories of your accomplishments, consider brief statements that could prompt questions in the interview that would enable you to tell success stories. People love stories; they humanize the numbers behind your accomplishments and inspire admiration. Stories are particularly effective when they distract from or counter any biases that the hiring authority might have toward certain applicants.

How do you plant in your résumé the seed of a story? A number of years ago, we had a candidate who held an engineering degree from Texas A&M. He was born and raised on a chicken farm, which he noted on his résumé. Subsequently, in interviews, he told stories about his childhood on the chicken farm—how hard the work was, what he learned, and so on. The company that hired him admitted that what made him different from other candidates was that his stories gave them confidence that he would be a hard worker.

TARGET YOUR RÉSUMÉS

Earlier in the chapter I suggested having different résumés for different situations and different employment opportunities. This is a matter of developing targeted résumés, something that is simple to do nowadays with computer word-processing software. Make sure to save each version you create. Chapter 6 has a sample of such résumé variations.

A targeted résumé is simply one that is customized to stress the relevancy of its content to the specific job you are applying for. If you find a particularly narrow job posting that your experience fits very well, add to your résumé the terminology used in the posting. For instance, if a posting reads something like, "Manage a staff of six senior accountants and four junior accountants," and your résumé reflects that you have managed an accounting department, you may want to alter your résumé to reflect the number of accountants, both junior and senior, that you managed. Try to be as specific as you can.

Similarly, if you're an engineer with both design and quality control in your background, and you're applying for an engineering position with a major emphasis on quality control, you can emphasize the quality-control experience in the résumé you send. Likewise, if you're a bookkeeper who has worked for a comptroller where you used Great Plains software, you may not want to put that information on your master résumé, but paste it into the résumé when applying for positions where knowledge of Great Plains will set you apart from other candidates.

Customize your targeted résumé with anything you might know to be of value to a particular employer. For example, if you are an HR professional and you read about a company that is fending off union organization, you could emphasize that you have helped your previous employer defeat attempts at union organization. In short, the more precisely you customize, the better off you are.

GET THE PARTICULARS

For information about jobs, don't simply rely on the ads posted on the Internet. Those ads are usually quite generic, and most of the time they are not written by the person actually feeling the pain (the one needing the person to be hired). Use any specific insights you might have regarding a particular position or any information you might have gleaned from someone else. If you speak to the hiring authority before you forward your résumé, you may collect excellent information to customize your résumé.

You might even try investigating the opportunity with someone in the organization other than the hiring authority. For instance, a company looking for someone to manage a group of purchasing agents or a purchasing department has subordinates for the job in question whom you may want to talk to. Subordinates can give you lots of information about what is needed. The more specifics you get, the better targeted your résumé will be.

Caution! Sometimes people put different spins on their basic résumé. In fact, they sometimes go overboard with so many different résumés they forget which one they use for which situation.

DUMBED-DOWN RÉSUMÉS

People sometimes confuse selling *themselves* with selling a consumer product. I call this "presenting yourself in an all-galactic fashion." That is, many times candidates will "oversell" themselves in their résumés, thereby coming across as overqualified and acing themselves out of good, solid job opportunities.

Of course, if you get laid off from being VP of finance for a multimillion-dollar Fortune 500 banking firm, it doesn't matter how "all world" you are; there are damned few positions out there for which you will be hired. That's regardless of how wonderful your experience is, how much responsibility you had, how many millions of dollars you have managed, or how many hundreds of people you've supervised. No one can do anything about the availability—or, should I say, lack of availability?—of those kinds of jobs. So, in a case like that, it's best to have a couple of different résumés: one that's "all world" and one that's "dumbed down."

Sometimes you need to adjust your résumé so you can reasonably apply for opportunities that require less responsibility or experience than you have. For example, if you were an engineering manager of a hundred-million-dollar company with a staff of five, you may want to have one résumé that reflects the full-blown aspects of your job, where you describe every bit of leadership you've shown and every accomplishment that you ever achieved, and you would have another résumé that might downplay the extent of your leadership experience and focus instead on your engineering responsibilities.

In recent years, I've personally placed numerous VPs of sales, sales managers, and directors of sales in front-line sales jobs. In a difficult market, the level of management positions that most of these people were seeking simply wasn't available, and they found alternative solutions. Sometimes the earnings often are not much less than those of higher level managers. Only you can judge the viability of earnings relative to the job you have or no longer have. Most people would agree it's better to be an employed accountant than an unemployed controller.

SIMPLE FORMAT, CLEAN WHITE PAGES

Avoid the fancy-schmancy layout, font, and other special effects. Once in a while, I get a résumé written on colored paper, paper with a cutesy background, maybe with yellow balloons; others are printed in italics, with some nontraditional script, or with flowers in the margins. Please don't do this! Unless you are in an artistic field, where appearance is pertinent, an unusual presentation may amuse the recipient but will likely eliminate your résumé automatically.

Stick to the traditional font of Times New Roman (or maybe Ariel), 9 to 12 point size, black type against a white background. You might want to vary the type size for your name, the companies you have worked for, and perhaps your titles. But try to be consistent. Too many variations in type size make the résumé look cluttered. Also, allow a reasonable amount of white space on each page. Some résumés are so "crowded" that they would never get read. Your résumé needs to be pleasing to the eye, whether printed out or on a computer screen.

Especially, go easy on the boldface type, italics, and underlining. Tables, text boxes, icons, and graphs on your résumé might impress you, but often they get messed up or eliminated when you e-mail your résumé. So keep the graphics to a minimum, if you use them at all. When a résumé can't easily be read online, it will likely be passed over in favor of the 100 other résumés that are easier to view online.

Do not place your résumé in a table format or use a template, especially if you are planning to give it to a placement service. Recruiters or placement services will always submit résumés with their logo at the top and a disclaimer on the bottom. When résumés come with a table/template format, they become distorted or lose their formatting if placed within the placement service's own template. Similarly, when you e-mail a résumé formatted in a table or template, your lines will show if the recipient's computer has the "show gridlines" button turned on. Just prepare your résumé in a simple Word format that can easily be viewed on most computers.

TRUTH, NOT LIES AND MISREPRESENTATIONS

An unacceptable form of "spinning" the facts on a résumé is to take credit for successes that weren't all yours. I have had candidates claim on their résumés that they were individually responsible for megadollar sales deals. Often, though, a reference is checked and it turns out that the candidate inherited the sale or was part of a team that made the sale. The candidate *embellished* by taking credit for something that wasn't all his own doing.

Think that you wouldn't embellish—or even lie—on your résumé? A large number of studies show that many people do embellish or even outright lie at least once every time they rewrite their résumés. Lies on a résumé run the gamut from statements of expanded duties and responsibilities, to factual matters of job titles, degrees, or length of time in a position. The most common lie is made to cover up a job or jobs that, for whatever reason, a person doesn't want to include on the résumé. Candidates simply extend the dates of employment for other jobs and hope the difference will never be discovered. Admittedly, these fabrications are the most difficult to detect or discover. Nevertheless, don't do this!

Another common lie is to expand on successes. As I mentioned previously, this involves taking credit for more than is reality—for example, claiming an innovation that was the product of a team. Don't do this!

One of the most common lies is declaring to have a baccalaureate degree when that's not the case. I've never quite understood why people will lie about having a degree. It's so easy to verify this information. There are even clearinghouses that perform this task for hiring organizations. Don't do this!

If you lie on your résumé and it is discovered beforehand, it is unlikely that you will be hired. If you lie and it is discovered *after* you are hired, you will likely be fired. Many companies verify a candidate's dates of employment, especially the most recent employment, *after* the individual is hired. So if you put on your résumé "2007 to Present," and you left that job six months prior to being interviewed, you'd best correct the dates before you accept the job. If you don't and it is discovered, you may well be fired.

In spite of our preaching about truth, at least twice a month we have candidates lose out on an opportunity because they lied on their résumés. Five or six times a year, we have a candidate get fired *after* they were hired because a lie on their résumé was discovered. Don't lie!

5

The Basic Résumé and Some Résumé Makeovers

YOU WANT YOUR résumé to explain clearly what you have done, who you have done it for, and how successful you have been. It should be written in simple terms a high school senior can understand. This chapter offers a basic annotated example of what a résumé should look like for most professional job searches. Then, there are four examples of weak résumés and the corresponding makeovers to show you how to fix common problems, such as not sufficiently stressing your strengths and accomplishments or having a résumé that's too long or too detailed.

Standard Résumé Format

The following sample shows information organized in a way that employers will expect to see it presented in a standard résumé.

YOUR NAME
Your Address
Home phone number   Cell number   E-mail address

EXPERIENCE

April 2008–Present   Name of Company
[Short explanation of what the company does or explanation of the division of a large company, so that anyone can clearly understand its function]

Title: [Make sure the title is commonly understood; if not, explain it in common terms]

[A specific, understandable explanation of your duties and responsibilities, and highlighted specific *accomplishments*. Remember, the résumé is to communicate why you should be interviewed. Write all the way from one margin to another so that you can get as much information on one page as possible. Write *no more* than a three- or four-sentence paragraph that a high school senior could understand.]

January 2003–April 2008   Name of Company [Same as above]

Title: [Same as above. If your title is "odd," you may want to change it to make it resonate better: Just be sure to explain to an interviewing or hiring authority what you have done during the interview.]

- Remember, *numbers* and *statistics* get recognized and paid attention to. So if you can "quantify" what your successes and accomplishments have been, do so.

- Percentages of sales quota, cost savings, size of a department, even amounts of budgetary responsibility, are noticed. Highlight or boldface any outstanding "numbers" that will set you apart from other candidates.

August 2000–January 2003   Name of Company [Same as above]

Title: [Same as above]

The further back you go in your job history, the less you have to explain about what you did and how you did it. But of course you'll want to mention any outstanding accomplishments.

How to Handle Previous Experience: If your experience goes back more than fifteen years, you could summarize all of it in two or three sentences. You may want to highlight the names of the companies and the success you had with them, if it's appropriate to do so.

EDUCATION

[College or University, type of degree, beginning with the graduate degree first and year of graduation. If no degree was conferred, simply put the years of attendance. Any honors such as high grade point average, or scholarships, should be noted. Any formal school less than college doesn't need to be reported. Any continuing education (such as certifications, sales courses, or negotiation courses) could be mentioned here. Stay away from any "personal growth" programs that might be religious or political—mention nothing controversial.]

Note that if you want to include an Objectives statement, use only general terms such as *sales, accounting, engineering, production, administration,* and so forth. Make sure that what you say *means something* to the reader.

Writing your résumé is that simple. Make sure anyone can understand everything about your résumé.

A Short-Version Résumé

One way of having a "quick" résumé, one that you can hand out when the opportunity arises, is to have a business card printed up with your name, contact information, and a line of copy about yourself. When you are actively looking for a job, you can give these to anybody you might run into. When I say anybody, I mean absolutely anybody—the barista at Starbucks, your barber, your doctor, anyone who might be able to get you an interview with someone who might have a job opening or know of one.

Here is the "business card" Terry McDonald had printed. Terry was one of the guests on *The Dr. Phil Show* whom I helped get a job. You will see his original résumé later in the chapter, but notice his abbreviated, "card" résumé. He gave one of these to just about anyone he ran into.

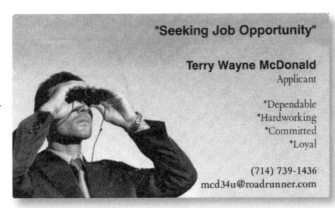

FRONT

"Seeking Job Opportunity"

Terry Wayne McDonald
Applicant

*Dependable
*Hardworking
*Committed
*Loyal

(714) 739-1436
mcd34u@roadrunner.com

BACK

State Farm Ins.	**1993 to Present**

Increased agency residual by 30%

Grew agency renewable household count by 200

Developed rewards program for the referral of new business

Wrote most Health Policies in the district

MetLife Healthcare	**1986–1993**

Promoted 3 times during tenure

Supervised and trained 5–12 person staff of dept

1988 to 1992 University of XXXXXXXX, Honors Graduate

Terry's card is unique. It gets people's attention. It communicates a "visionary." Even the descriptive words "dependable, hardworking, committed, and loyal" have a good effect. A way of improving it might be to write a brief and compact résumé of the last few years on the back:

'05–'09 State Farm Insurance, Brea, CA
Sales—Increased agency residual by 30%

'93–'04 State Farm Insurance, Long Beach, CA
Office Manager—#1 agent of health policy sales in the district

'86–'93 MetLife Healthcare Network, Long Beach, CA
Membership Representative—promoted three times

This kind of thing would easily fit on the back of the card and be a little more meaningful than what Terry had there.

A similar approach is to fold your résumé into a packet the size of a business card that has your name and contact information, along with any graphics on the front and an abbreviated résumé on the two inside faces of the card.

Again, you can give this mini résumé to anyone who might help to get you an interview.

FRONT

NAME

address   e-mail address   phone #

A passionate, committed, successful sale professional

INSIDE

ABC Company 2006 to Present Sold enterprise software—never less than 130% of quota every year.

LMN Company 2000 to 2006 Sold data communications equipment and services . . . never less than 110% of quota every year.

PQR Company 1996 to 2000 Sold business forms. #1 sales person in the region all four years.

LOWER
INSIDE
FACE

XYZ Company 1992 to 1996 Entry-level sales of copiers and office equipment. #1 rookie!

1988 to 1992 University of XXXXXXXX, Honors Graduate

Résumé Makeover #1

Once you get the hang of doing a résumé makeover, rewriting almost anyone's résumé (especially your own) will be easy to do.

Terry McDonald, one of the guests on *The Dr. Phil Show*, is a really good guy. Using my techniques—the ones I teach on my Web site, www.thejobsearchsolution.com—he found a job. It took him eight months after he got laid off, and it wasn't easy in the California economy, with unemployment at 12 percent at the time; nevertheless, he was successful. However, the résumé he started out with was pretty poor. (You can view a video clip of our on-air résumé critique at www.tonybeshara.com.) Here is what Terry's original résumé looked like:

Terry Wayne McDonald

Address   Cell #   E-mail

OBJECTIVE:

To provide personal dedication to the common cause of profitability and retention of a dynamic team.

QUALIFICATIONS:

Supervisory Experience	Proactive and Goal Driven	Adaptable
Integrity	Problem Solving Skills	Team Player
Public Communications	Sharp Customer Service	Proficient Computer Skills
Relationship Building	Strong Organization Skills	Works Well Independently

EXPERIENCE:

State Farm Insurance 2005–2009

Business Insurance Representative

Production Manager, Producer, and Team Leader

Initiated agency marketing strategies

Created new households and business referral program

Field underwriter for Commercial and Personal Lines

State Farm Insurance 1993–2004

Office Manager-Marketing Coordinator

Managed work flow and supervised insurance representative team

Generated overall profitability with multi-line sales and service techniques

Established and maintained exceptional customer service relations

MetLife Healthcare Network 1986–1993

Sr. Membership Accounting Representative

Supervised and trained department team

Made underwriting decisions with letter notification

Administrated and input new group contracts and mass group terminations

CREDENTIALS:

CA Department of Insurance, Licenses 1996–Present
 • Accident and Health
 • Fire and Casualty Broker-Agent
 • Life-Only

State of California 2005–Present
 • Notary Public

CRITIQUE

A brief look at Terry's résumé is very revealing. First, the Objectives statement says absolutely nothing. Second, his Qualifications? Integrity . . . Adaptable . . . Public Communications.

What do those words mean? Really, they don't say anything. Essentially, Terry did not emphasize his sales ability. His function was as much sales and increasing business as it was administration; unfortunately, his résumé did not emphasize that.

Now, look at the revised résumé. With a few minor changes and by emphasizing Terry's percentage of *increase* in business as well as his *profitability*, he communicates being a top contributor. Again, *numbers tell*. Increasing profitability 35 percent, being the number-one agent of health policy sales, and having been promoted three times are facts that say: "This is what I've done in the past for others and therefore this is what I will do for you." Pretty simple!

Here's Terry's revised résumé:

Terry Wayne McDonald

Address　Phone #　Cell #　E-mail

EXPERIENCE

December 2005–January 2009　State Farm Insurance (Agency Sales & Service), Brea, CA
Business Sales Representative

- Increased agency residual *by 30%*

- Grew agency renewable household count *by 20%*

- Lowered single-line household ratio *23%* by writing additional policies to existing book

- Developed rewards program for the referral of new business that *increased business 25%*

- Had company authority to write claims checks directly to clients

- Suggested target marketing ideas that were implemented and *increased profit by 35%*

May 1993–September 2004　State Farm Insurance (Agency Sales & Service), Long Beach, CA
Office Manager / Sales Coordinator

- Created sales promotions to motivate team and increase office production

- Annually achieved corporate Life Insurance sales goals *105%*

- *#1 agent* of Health policy sales in the district

- Oversaw sales and customer service work flow of 2–4 person staff

- Educated clients of underwriting requirements and insurance policy interpretation

September 1986–March 1993　MetLife Healthcare Network (Corporate HMO), Long Beach, CA
Sr. Membership Representative

- *Promoted three times during tenure*

- Administrated employer health insurance contracts and individual health insurance cards

- Supervised, trained, and doubled the size of the membership accounting staff

- Made underwriting exceptions for those seeking coverage outside the eligibility period

- Provided customer service to employers, members, physicians, and their contracted groups

LICENSES

California Department of Insurance

- Accident and Health

- Fire and Casualty Broker-Agent

- Life-Only

State of California

- Notary Public

Résumé Makeover #2

Some résumés are simply too long. Let's analyze and rework the résumé of a candidate I have known for many years. When Rex first wrote his résumé, it was nine pages long. That's right, nine pages! Here are just four of the nine pages.

REX THOMPSON TEACHENOR
Address   Cell #   E-mail

Seeking senior executive assignments in Management and Leadership / Research & Development / Strategic Planning / Sales and Marketing / Business Development / Product & Program Management / Customer Service in a growth-oriented innovative high-technology organization. 16 years selling IT in Oil & Gas Industry.

CAREER ABSTRACT

• An astute and result-oriented professional with over 28 years of experience in the sales and marketing operations across industries such as Oil and Gas, Petroleum Industries, High Technology, R&D, and Information Technology within the Information Technology, Computer, Data Communications, Storage, and Telecommunications Industries, supporting hardware and software-based products and solutions. *Distinction of working with IBM for 15 years.*

Core Competencies	
• Research & Development	• Key Account Management
• Strategic Planning	• Client Relationship Mgmt
• P&L Management	• Financial Management
• Strategic Alliances	• Mergers and Acquisitions
• Sales and Marketing	• People Management
• O&G Niche Marketing	• Training and Development
• Business Development	• Quality
• Product Launch/Promotions	• Contract Management
• Public Relations	• Product Development
• Distribution Management	• New Technology Development
• Supply Chain Management	• Productization

• Strong business acumen with the ability to execute a wide range of marketing strategies to establish market presence and increase revenues and profitability.

• A proactive planner and leader with expertise in market plan execution, key account management with skills in competitor/ market analysis.

• Extensive experience in networking with channel partners, resulting in deeper market penetration and reach.

• Successful at building and leading world-class sales and marketing teams for various organizations. Excel at building sales channel.

• Well versed with the various finance/accounting practices (Sarbanes-Oxley) and principles.

• Possess excellent team-building, leadership, relationship management, and analytical skills.

Selected Accomplishments

• Experience in subsidiaries, alliances, spin-offs, partnerships, incorporations, start-ups, VC funding, investment banking, IPOs, mergers, reverse mergers, and acquisitions/divestitures derived from the establishment of four high-tech start-up companies.

• *Entrepreneurship experience in building 4 high-technology companies.*

• Achieved a sales volume of $500M and attained as high as 500% in revenue growth in one year at an 85% gross margin.

• *Managed 80 Program Managers supporting 5 worldwide plants and more than 200 customers.*

Business Skills

• Identifying and developing new streams for long-term revenue growth and maintaining relationships with customers to achieve repeat/referral business.

• Evaluating marketing budgets periodically, including manpower planning initiatives and adherence to planned expenses.

• Performing sales presentations to prospects, negotiating contracts, and closing new business deals.

- Negotiating and placing orders with the principals for the regular business and for any large deals.

- Planning the yearly budgets of promotional activities with the principal companies.

- Recruiting, training, and providing guidance and support to the front-line team/ channel sales team through target setting and reviewing measures.

Career Highlights

Since August 2008 to present, SATYAM COMPUTER SERVICES LTD., Houston, TX, Energy & Utilities Industry Vertical, specialized on strategic Oil & Gas Majors, Business Development Head and Enterprise Executive to ExxonMobil. (http://www.satyam.com)

Satyam is a 27-year-old global leader in computer & IT services, staffing, managed services & hosting, professional & engineering services, and business processes consulting with revenues approaching $3 billion and 52,000 worldwide employees and having 28 global delivery centers spread across USA & Canada, Latin America, Europe, Africa, Middle East, and Asia. World's 3rd largest Oracle Eco-Systems Integrator. Ranked among the Top 5 SAP Practices in the World. Ranked as largest overall ERP practice by AMR Research. Largest Microsoft Oil & Gas Competency Center. Largest Business Intelligence and Data Warehousing Competency Practice. Ranked 1st consistently in recent years in Product Engineering Services. Leader in Providing Integrated Enterprise Mobility, worldwide listed on the NYSE: SAY. Ranked #4 in Global Outsourcing Vendor for Energy & Utilities. Providing fully integrated and comprehensive solutions for Upstream, Midstream, Downstream needs to over 31 principal O&G companies worldwide.

> **Principal responsibilities:**
> Provide leadership and help strengthen client relationships with strategic clients in the Energy & Utility Industry and build Satyam engagements as a Partner and strive to achieve a dominant position in the industry. Enterprise Executive to ExxonMobil. A Specialist in selling Integrated Engineering Services and projects in addition to all full-service IT solutions and services.
>
> - Build Satyam engagements as a Strategic Partner.
>
> - Global Enterprise Executive to ExxonMobil. Won 2 large five-year global staff augmentation contracts. ExxonMobil's Global Corporate Information Services for over 250 Satyam professionals on three continents for SAP & ERP support, total revenue potential up to $220M/5 years.
>
> - Specialist in marketing Knowledge Retention and Knowledge Acquisition Solutions to the Energy Industry.
>
> - Worked with Satyam's Energy vertical and Indian-based course and solutions developers to bring to market viable and timely KR/KA offerings.

January 2007 to present, Principal Consultant, BRAIN TRUST CORPORATION, Richardson, TX, High Tech Sales & Marketing Consulting Company. (http://www.braintrust.name)

Details of recent consulting engagements, titles, and responsibilities:

> **Dec 2007 to Aug 2008 with SOUTHWEST RESEARCH INSTITUTE, San Antonio, TX, Oil & Gas Vertical, IT Marketing & Business Development Senior Consultant to the Information Systems Engineering Department.** (http://www.swri.org)
>
> The Southwest Research Institute (SwRI) is among the most highly respected national applied research and development (R & D) institutions in the United States and a Texas-based icon. SwRI was founded 60 years ago as a not-for-profit company; it remains a

trusted 3rd-party source of technology development, applied science, and solutions innovation. SwRI is headquartered in San Antonio with over 3,600 scientists, engineers, and staff on a 1,200-acre campus housing 170 buildings with 2 million square feet of space. Total sales exceeding US$550,000,000 in 2008. SwRI is composed of 14 principal departments of which I represent the Information Systems Engineering Department as their only Marketing and Business Development Consultant, working remotely out of Richardson, Texas.

Principal solutions marketed:
Knowledge transfer/retention process reengineering • networks & cyber security • real-time & embedded systems • image & signal processing • radar & remote sensing • information technology • reconfigurable communications • lean manufacturing • automated inspection • machine design • machine vision • network modeling & simulation • cooperative vehicle technologies • control systems • green efficient manufacturing • aerospace networks • MEMS & micro-fluidics • embedded & application security • immune-fluorescence detection • control center software • automation & robotics • intelligent transportation systems • automated instrument & test systems • wireless sensor networks • intelligent vehicle systems System architecture - legacy systems in North Sea Drilling Software • System and Software requirements elicitation • Workflow Engine • Data Visualization • eCommerce • Software Development and Physical Sciences • Rotating Machinery and Collaboration Environments • Infinite element, solver coupling, mixed modules and WITSML • Rotating machinery • Optimization package • Control Systems on Corporate Network (security issue) • Georeferencing Data Warehouse – Metadata • Master Wellhead Database • Bottom-hole Pressure Database • Database Development • Outsource programming/software development for existing O&G projects • Outsource web development—SQL and .NET • Collaboration in Co-proposals for O&G efforts WITSML/WITS initiatives • PRODML production optimization initiative • Data Mining Merging and updating legacy Geophysical databases

Jan 2007 to Nov 2007 with TEXAS INSTITUTE OF SCIENCE, INC., Richardson, TX, as Vice President of Sales (http://www.txis.us/PressRelease3.html)
The Institute facilitates, builds, and manages global R&D projects & teams for Oil & Gas companies using its highly developed project management system and an extensive and exclusive network of over 18,000 Ph.D.-level scientists, researchers, and engineers located in 109 world-class universities within Eastern Europe, Russia, and China. The Institute's clients further benefit by retaining all ownership of the Intellectual Property (IP) and patents that were contracted. The Institute's second principal line of endeavor provides for Intellectual Property Harvesting of Pre-patentable Discoveries and funneling of potentially 30,000 new innovations per year, firstly to client under a special retainer basis and then on to the general marketplace.

Key milestones:
- Opened up and concentrated on the acquisition of new accounts principally in the Oil & Gas, Energy, and Petroleum Industries including upstream, midstream, downstream exploration production companies and equipment suppliers from the very large global conglomerate to regional small to mid-tier oil patch companies.

- Sales hunter bringing in the bounty—Responsible for getting start-up companies successfully launched and into a sustained financially sound orbit in only 6 months, selling all inaugural customers *producing $11M in pipeline, 33 projects, and $2M in short-term cash . . . making company profitable in year zero.*

Contributed actively in:

‣ *Merging Global Optimization Technology* with other technologies several times within a product cycle from early stage of Intellectual Property (IP) to serial production.

‣ *Harvesting the discoveries and inventions of participants* in the TxIS network of 18,000+ engineers and scientists.

‣ Identifying thousands of IPs, distilling most mature and relevant into hundreds of marketable IPs and patents per year.

‣ *Leading the way for 1/3 of the world's scientists and solving the problems of client companies with practical innovation and solutions.*

‣ *Being the pioneer in the global R&D outsourcing and human capital arbitrage.*

Oct 2005 to Jan 2007 with TTI TELECOM, Richardson, TX, as Director—Global Enterprise Executive to AT&T (www.tti-telecom.com)

TTI Team Telecom International Ltd. (TTI Telecom) is a leading provider of next-generation Operations Support Systems (OSSs) to communications service providers (CSPs) worldwide. For incumbent and emerging CSPs spanning fixed, mobile, and cable markets, we provide a robust OSS platform that helps manage their networks and services effectively.

Role:

‣ Managing the entire business operations encompassing sales, marketing, customer service, and channel development activities for southwestern US.

‣ Selling advanced modular and integrated hardware and software products and services for Telecommunications Operations Support Systems (OSS) and Business Support Systems (BSS) to telecom service providers.

Key Milestones:

‣ *Oversaw the company's largest worldwide customer, AT&T, producing $14M* in volume in 2006. Supported the strategic goals and immediate needs of AT&T as a principal and longtime supplier.

‣ Handled a team of over 60 individuals across the country.

‣ Managed accounts such as New AT&T (SBC, Cingular, AT&T LD, AT&T Local & Enterprise, AT&T Labs, & BellSouth) and calling on all C-level executives.

CRITIQUE

Rex is a very intelligent guy. He has excellent qualifications, and has a great mix of technical and business skills. He is a very good job candidate. However, you can imagine how difficult it would be for an interviewing or hiring authority to read his résumé—all *nine* pages. Here are the major problems with Rex's original résumé:

∎ Way too long. Rex is trying to sell the "whole enchilada." Remember, your résumé is simply to sell the reader on the idea of interviewing you.

▪ "Rex Thompson Teachenor." That's way too pretentious and stuffy sounding—simply "Rex Teachenor" will do.

▪ Way too much detail. Some of these statements just don't say anything to the reader.

▪ Confusing statements, such as "Jan 2007 to Present, Principal Consultant, Brain Trust Corporation, Richardson, TX, High Tech Sales & Marketing Consulting Company." Does Rex still work for this firm? It appears he is still working there. How can that be? He has worked for two other people at the same time.

In reality, Rex hired himself out to the companies he worked for on a consulting basis. Admittedly, it is easier to explain short stops on one's résumé in this manner, but it isn't a good idea to do so. Companies do not want to hire someone as a full-time employee if he considers himself a consultant. "Consultant" communicates the idea that the candidate will leave and go to work for the highest bidder. As you will see, we did not include this title on his final résumé. Now, if Rex wants to have both a consulting-type résumé and a full-time employee type résumé, that's another matter.

A hiring authority would take one look at his nine-page résumé and almost certainly throw it away. So, we edited Rex's résumé down to two pages and here is what we came up with:

Rex Teachenor
Address   Cell #   E-mail

Satyam Computer Services Ltd (Satyam), Houston, TX   **Aug 2008–Present**
4th largest Indian-based IT & Engineering Services Company

    Sales—Energy & Utilities Industry Vertical
- 250% of yearly quota.

- Global Enterprise Executive to Exxon Mobil. **Won 2 large five-year global staff augmentation contracts.** Exxon Mobil's Global Corporate Information Services for over 250 Satyam professionals on three continents for SAP & ERP support, total revenues potential up to $220M/5Y.

- Specialist in marketing Knowledge Retention and Knowledge Acquisition Solutions to the Energy Industry.

- Worked with Satyam's Energy vertical and Indian-based course and solutions developers to bring to market viable and timely KR/KA offerings.

Southwest Research Institute (SwRI), San Antonio, TX   **Dec 2007–Aug 2008**
SwRI is a national applied R & D institution

    Business Development Consultant & Enterprise Executive to AT&T
- On-Shore Engineering Services and IT Services business development.

- Sold the largest knowledge retention and customer training initiative ever at AT&T.

- Sold knowledge retention projects to BP, Chevron, NASA, and Social Security Administration.

- Created and developed all marketing materials.

Texas Institute of Science, Inc (TxIS), Richardson, TX   **Jan 2007–Nov 2007**
TxIS builds, manages, delivers global R&D projects

    Vice President of Sales—400% of quota
- Created and developed all marketing materials & literature, brochures, PowerPoints, press releases, articles, training materials, contracts, and related business planning.

- Opened up and concentrated on the acquisition of new accounts principally in the Oil & Gas, Energy, and Petroleum Industries.

- **Produced $11M in pipeline, thirty-three projects and $2M in short-term cash, making company profitable in year zero.**

TTI Telecom, Richardson, TX   **Oct 2005–Jan 2007**
TTI Telecom is a leading provider of next-generation Operations Support Systems (OSSs) to communications service providers

    Director—Global Enterprise Executive to AT&T—140% of quota
- Managed the company's business operations encompassing sales, marketing, customer service, and channel-development activities for southwestern US.

- Sold advanced modular and integrated hardware and software products and services for Telecommunications Operations Support Systems (OSS) and Business Support Systems (BSS) to telecom service providers.

Global Communication Technologies, Dallas, TX   **Jul 2004–Apr 2005**
GLOBAL is a worldwide manufacturer of full-service, turnkey programmable telecommunications hardware and software solutions to telecom carriers

    Executive Director, Global Operations—Sales, Marketing, & Product Management
(http://www.globaltech-us.com)

‣ Oversaw the entire business operations encompassing sales, marketing, product development & research, customer service, and business-development activities for a global telecommunications Softswitch, converged TDM & IP VoIP platform.

‣ **Won $115M** contract to rebuild the Iraqi telecommunication infrastructure.

Distributed Software Engineering Tools (DSET) Corporation and spin-offs
(Trigon Technology Group & Advanced Storage Array Products), Dallas, TX   Sept 1996–Jul 2004
Company is leading provider of Network Management Systems, Storage Management Systems, Operations Support System software & Business Support Systems

Positions: Director, Vice President, Executive Vice President of Sales, Marketing & Business Development—700% of quota
‣ **Top sales performer in all years, both in gross sales and gross profit.**

‣ Established a small start-up company and converted to a publicly traded and listed company.

‣ Established go-to-market strategies and handled key clients such as Direct, ISP, ISVs, ASP, SSPs, Systems Integrators, Distributors, Resellers, OEM, and Large Enterprise Accounts.

‣ Established, created, and marketed the new concept of UBT (Ubiquitous Bus. Technology) for interconnecting Business Management Systems to Service Management Systems, Service Management Systems to Network Management Systems. Achieved initial sales of $2.5M 1st year and obtained a sales growth of **200% in 2001.**

‣ Strategically led company into 3 new dynamic markets by instigating new marketing initiatives.

‣ GR-303. Sold the first multimillion-dollar GR-303 Projects (Seiscor) and started SBU.

‣ Sold the first major OEM partnership (Alcatel), produced $30,000,000 in sales.

‣ Sold Off-Shore and On-Shore full turnkey fixed-price outsourced projects.

Sanmina-SCI Corporation, Carrollton, Texas   Jun 2003–Feb 2004
Sanmina-SCI is a $9B company, one of the world's premier Global Electronic Manufacturing Services companies sold to the contract manufacturing services industry

Director, Worldwide Program Management & Customer Service (Inside Sales)
‣ Managed a staff of 120 employees in five plants in 4 counties; Monterrey, Mexico; Greenock, Scotland; Kunshan, China; San Jose, California; and Dallas, Texas.

‣ Oversaw the acquisition and absorption of customer needs of a $60M cables business, with customer business from acquisition of a primary competitor, FCI Cables Systems, approximately valued at $15M.

‣ Managed the entire business operation encompassing marketing and product management functions including additional Customer Support, Customer Service Delivery, Customer Training & Education, and Customer Order Fulfillment.

EDUCATION
Doctor of Management—IS & Technology, 2011 (pursuing)
University of Phoenix (GPA 3.5/4.0)
Master of Management, Telecommunications, 1996
University of Dallas—Irving, Texas (GPA 3.7/4.0)
M.B.A., International Management, 1992
University of Dallas—Irving, Texas (GPA 3.8/4.0)
BS Economics
University of Oregon—Eugene, Oregon (GPA 2.9/4.0)

CRITIQUE

The résumé is still a bit busy and compact, but it communicates what Rex has done. Notice that we made some of the titles more directly "sales," and we made specific references to his *quota success*. Remember, the point of the résumé is to convince a hiring authority to interview you.

Résumé Makeover #3

The initial résumé of Dominic Coletto followed a functional format instead of the reverse chronological format. Dominic is a friend of mine and a first-class manager in the software and talent-management systems arena.

DOMINIC COLETTO
Address   Phone #   Cell #

SALES LEADER & STRATEGIST

Strategic sales mindset with Bottom-line focus and Top-line alignment + Over 18 years of both strategic and tactical experience in all facets of Sales Management + Excellent communicator and business-minded analyst

AREAS OF EXPERTISE

· Strategic/Business Planning · Sales Strategy Development/Execution · Sales Process Mapping

· Forecasting/Pipeline Management · CRM Deployment · Organizational/Territory Development · Brand Management

· Process Improvement · Market Research · Needs Assessment · Proposal Preparation · Contract Negotiations

· Project Management · Training/Mentoring · Performance Management · Motivation/Recognition/Retention

· Change Management · Total Rewards/Compensation Management · Succession Planning

· HRIS Systems · Metrics & Analysis · Talent Acquisition & Employment Development

EMPLOYMENT & EDUCATION

Absolute Inc. . . . . Vice President		MBA—
The Elements . . . . Vice President Sales		Executive Program, TEC
Salespeople.com. . . . . Director of Professional Services		BA Marketing—
Activant . . . . Vice President Global Sales		North Central College
Achieve Performance. . . . . Regional Vice President		
Kinetic . . . . Sr. Account Manager		
GBC . . . . Sales Executive		

PROFESSIONAL OBJECTIVE

Positions:	Location:	Industries:	Revenues/Employees:
Director/VP of Sales	Dallas	All	$20MM to $500MM
Director/VP of Services	Chicago		100 to 5000 employees
Director/VP of Sales Operations	New York		

ACCOMPLISHMENTS

Start-up
· Launched a sales team, which generated $114 million in revenue in the first year, surpassing projection by 200%.

Channel Management
· Guided a new business-development team in growing sales 35% the first year and 48% the second.

· Established a strategic-alliance program that produced $45 million in revenue the first year.

Change Management
· Repositioned a company to attain $1.3 million in profit in year one and $5.3 million in profit in year two.

· Executed a new marketing campaign that increased new client sales 22%.

Sales Leadership
- Directed a mid-market sales team in contributing over 28% of overall region sales at a 45% lower cost.
- Developed client team strategies that fueled a 38% increase in existing client sales.
- Personally sold and negotiated new contracts for a total contract value of $35 million.
- Ranked #2 of six regions in revenue attainment in 2007.
- Earned President Circle of Excellence award for 2007 performance.

Process Improvement/CRM Deployment
- Led a task force challenged to create an integrated sales force automation to support the sales strategy.
- Led the sales leadership team, which established and enforced compliance with national sales policies and strategies to facilitate goal attainment within the region.
- Appointed to a task force challenged to create an integrated marketing and sales plan following the merger.

Contact Negotiations
- Sold and negotiated a four-year, $23 million contract with Verizon Communications.
- Led strategy development and contract negotiations for an $8.7 million contract with State Farm Insurance.

ACADEMIC AND PROFESSIONAL CREDENTIALS

Executive Master of Business Administration Program, sponsored by the Executive Business Council

Bachelor of Arts in Marketing, North Central College, Naperville, IL

Instructor Certification in Sales, Leadership, and Customer Service, Achieve Performance

Instructional Design Certification, Langevin

Project Management Professional (PMP), Project Management Institute

Certified Professional Sales Coaching, Achieve Performance; Activant Corp.

CRITIQUE

There is no doubt that Dominic is a top performer, but this functional-type résumé doesn't help him. His accomplishments are not associated with the companies he has worked for. Although he has had excellent performance, it is too hard to tell in what context he performed. This is the major problem with all functional-type résumés. If the reader doesn't know who Absolute or The Elements or Salesforce.com are, he or she won't appreciate Dominic's ability.

Dominic rewrote the résumé to make sure the duties and accomplishments he listed were associated with the companies that he had worked for. Much, much better! However, he still did not identify what the companies do, so it was still not possible for any reader to realize how good he really is. Here is the second attempt.

DOMINIC M. COLETTO

Address   Cell #   E-mail

Qualifications for Sales Leadership

Dynamic, results-oriented Sales Leader with experience in sales management, marketing, business development, and P&L responsibility. An assertive leader with a track record of guiding top-performing sales teams in executing annual sales action plans, consistently overachieving sales targets. Astute decision maker capable of making sound judgments to drive the attainment of start-up, turnaround, and growth objectives. Motivated by challenge and dedicated to cultivating positive work environments. Exhibits outstanding presentation skills and highly proficient in closing high-level sales, establishing strategic alliances, and fostering positive client relations. Extensive background in community/volunteer organizations.

Areas of expertise include:

Strategic Sales Planning	Sales Strategy Execution	Sales Process Mapping
Forecasting/Pipeline Management	Territory Development	Process Improvement
Market Research	Needs Assessment	Proposal Preparation
Contract Negotiations	Project Management	Training/Mentoring
Recruiting Interviewing/Hiring	Performance Management	Motivation/Recognition/ Retention

CAREER TRACK

ABSOLUTE INC.

Vice President   **2008 to 2009**

- Developed three new territories that increased new client sales 18%.

- Launched a new product into a new market in six months and generated a 3.7 M pipeline.

- Managed 4 global accounts and increased existing revenue 12%.

THE ELEMENTS

Vice President Solution Sales   **2007 to 2008**

- Ranked #2 of six regions in revenue attainment in 2007.

- Earned President Circle of Excellence award for 2007 performance.

- Sold and negotiated new contracts with Accor NA, Verizon Communications, FedEx Kinko's, Harrah's Entertainment, and Charles Schwab. Total contract value of $35 million.

- Led the sales leadership team, which established and enforced compliance with national sales policies and strategies to facilitate goal attainment within the regions.

- Led a task force challenged to create an integrated sales force automation project to support the sales strategy.

SALESPEOPLE.COM

Professional Services Director   **2005 to 2007**

- Achieved 118% of annual sales revenue goal in first year and 112% in second year.

- Directed a mid-market sales team in contributing over 28% of overall region sales at a 45% lower cost.

ACTIVANT CORP.

Vice President of Global Sales   **2002 to 2005**

• Reversed a negative revenue and profit trend, boosting sales 11% while cutting direct sales expenses 35%.

• Attained 110% of revenue plan and 107% of profit plan in 2003.

ACADEMIC AND PROFESSIONAL CREDENTIALS

Executive Master of Business Administration Program, sponsored by the Executive Business Council

Bachelor of Arts in Marketing, North Central College, Naperville, IL

Instructor Certification in Sales, Leadership, and Customer Service, Achieve Performance

Instructional Design Certification, Langevin

Project Management Professional (PMP), Project Management Institute

Certified Professional Sales Coaching, Achieve Performance; Activant Corp.

CRITIQUE

Better, but still not as good as it could be. By adding what the companies do to the résumé and boldfacing some of his accomplishments, the third version of Dominic's résumé is about as good as a functional résumé could be. Most important, it invites people to interview Dominic.

DOMINIC M. COLETTO
Address   Phone   Cell   E-mail

Qualifications for Regional Sales Manager

Dynamic, results-oriented Sales Leader with experience in sales management, marketing, business development, and P&L responsibility. An assertive leader with a track record of guiding top-performing sales teams in executing annual sales action plans, consistently overachieving sales targets. Astute decision maker capable of making sound judgments to drive the attainment of start-up, turnaround, and growth objectives. Motivated by challenge and dedicated to cultivating positive work environments. Exhibits outstanding presentation skills and highly proficient in closing high-level sales, establishing strategic alliances, and fostering positive client relations. Extensive background in community/volunteer organizations.

Areas of expertise include:

Strategic Sales Planning	Sales Strategy Execution	Sales Process Mapping
Forecasting/Pipeline Management	Territory Development	Process Improvement
Market Research	Needs Assessment	Proposal Preparation
Contract Negotiations	Project Management	Training/Mentoring
Recruiting Interviewing/Hiring	Performance Management	Motivation/Recognition/ Retention

CAREER TRACK

Absolute Inc. A global leader in business process and information technology services.

Vice President   **2008 to 2009**

- Developed three new territories that **increased** new client sales **18%**.

- Launched a new product into a new market in six months and generated a 3.7 M pipeline.

- Managed 4 global accounts and **increased existing revenue 12%**.

The Elements A leader in the Web-based training industry, specializing in consulting and training in the areas of IT, Leadership Development, Compliance and Custom e-learning solutions.

Vice President Solution Sales   **2007 to 2008**

- **Ranked #2** of six regions in revenue attainment in 2007.

- Earned President Circle of Excellence award for 2007 performance.

- Sold and negotiated new contracts with Accor NA, Verizon Communications, FedEx Kinko's, Harrah's Entertainment, and Charles Schwab. Total contract value of $35 million.

- Led the sales leadership team, which established and enforced compliance with national sales policies and strategies to facilitate goal attainment within the regions.

- Led a task force challenged to create an integrated sales force automation project to support the sales strategy.

Salespeople.com A leader in the Customer Relationship management software that assists companies in accelerating sales and enhancing client relationships through the deployment of CRM technologies and delivery of effective services.

Professional Services Manager   2005 to 2007
  · Achieved 118% of annual sales revenue goal in first year and 112% in second year.

  · Directed a mid-market sales team in contributing over 28% of overall region sales
    at a 45% lower cost.

Activant An industry leader specializing in consulting and skills training in the areas of sales and sales leadership.

Vice President of Global Sales   2002 to 2005
  · Reversed a negative revenue and profit trend, **boosting sales 11%** while
    cutting direct sales expenses 35%.

  · Attained **110% of revenue plan** and **107% of profit plan in 2003.**

ACADEMIC AND PROFESSIONAL CREDENTIALS

Executive Master of Business Administration Program, sponsored by the Executive Business Council

Bachelor of Arts in Marketing, North Central College, Naperville, IL

Instructor Certification in Sales, Leadership, and Customer Service, Achieve Performance

Instructional Design Certification, Langevin

Project Management Professional (PMP), Project Management Institute

Certified Professional Sales Coaching, Achieve Performance; Activant Corp.

Résumé Makeover #4

Here is an example of a résumé that is just too full, too long. It is not likely to get read. What would you cut to bring this down to two pages? Remember, you need to keep your information concise and easy to understand.

JOYCE LINDEN
Address   Cell #   E-mail

Senior Executive specializing in technology solution sales and consulting services to both large public and small private corporations. Strong history of significantly exceeding desired revenue, company, and client goals.

Documented history of developing and implementing growth strategies, including short-term and long-term tactical planning, market analysis, and expansion programs. Achievements and emphasis on creating, developing, training, executing, and monitoring existing and new strategic products and offerings. Excel in developing new market approaches for existing and new client targets to further expand and grow, while monitoring and evaluating the competitive landscape for further market penetration.

Experienced leader of sales professionals who inspires teamwork and loyalty within the organization as well as customer loyalty. Have led sales teams, up to 29 sales professionals, with both regional and national territories. Natural communicator with exceptional motivational skills. Ability to manage priorities, people, and deadlines in a rapidly changing and dynamic environment. Over twenty years of top-flight negotiation and complex consultative selling skills used to develop professional sales team and direction for C-level sales. Special analytical expertise and understanding of market trends and client goals, empowering enterprise sales professionals to develop responses that meet the progressive needs of customers.

CONSTELLATION CONSULTING SERVICES   **2005–PRESENT**
Vice President of Client Development & Marketing
Recruited by CEO to create and restructure a new litigation discovery solution sales strategy. The sales and technology focus was to broaden and increase the targeted law firm and corporate client base. The aggressive and entrepreneurial rebranding and approach for national and international sales by the organization was instrumental for revenue gains. Firm revenue increased six-fold since 2005, with revenue for 2006–2009 equal to $57.1 million while also ensuring growth in market penetration.

The organization has expanded to become an end-to-end consulting firm across the EDRM model offering forensics acquisitions and collections; compliance, records management; and best-of-breed complex technology solutions in the electronic discovery arena with AMLAW 100 and Fortune 500 clientele. The revenue performance and growth qualified the organization as one of the private companies awarded Inc5000 Fastest Growing Companies (2007 & 2008).

As Key Leader on Executive Team for Sales, Marketing, and Business Development areas continue to be the visionary involved with the company's direction, continuing to achieve overall growth and objectives for the firm. Responsible for business and competitive intelligence gathering as well as identifying trends and potential new partners. Participate and direct the evaluation of new products that are being considered to enhance the firm's offerings and strategic direction in the areas of cloud computing, electronic discovery, compliance, forensics, and ESI consulting offerings to meet the desired client base.

Developed processes as well as tools for client engagement as new products, service offerings, and workflows are offered. Ensure profitability of existing and ever-changing landscape of firm's offerings. Prepare monthly reports for budget meetings to manage cash flow and profitability of firm as well as revenue performance reporting for internal and external clients.

At the request of the CEO, handled additional Executive Team strategic goals for operations by authoring and delivering a client-centric-culture firm-wide training program. Also developed the implementation and Award & Recognition programs for all employees, which enhanced the company culture and met with the CEO's vision.

Business Awards & Accomplishments while at CCS
- Drove revenue growth in 2007 and 2008 that qualified CCS to qualify on Inc5000 of "Fastest Growing Companies"
- Grew Company Revenue from ~ $3.8M in 2005 as follows through 2009
- 2006—Grew Company Revenue 25% over 2005–$5.8M
- 2007—Grew Company Revenue 51% over 2006–$11.8M
- 2008—Grew Company Revenue 49% over 2007–$19.3M
- 2009—Grew Company Revenue 5% over 2008–$20.2M
- Promoted from Client Development Director to Vice President of Client Development & Marketing.

GUARDIAN CORP.   **1992–2005**
National Sales Manager 2001–2005
Throughout the years at Guardian, held various positions selling primarily to the large law-firm marketplace. Managed $21 million technology law firm business among AMLAW 250 Firms. Awarded LexisNexis Region and Manager of the Year in 2002. Nine years awarded Circle of Excellence recognition, Top 5% of Sales Organization Annual Award.

While in Sales Manager roles, recruited, developed, and directed the sales team to over-achieve revenue quotas. Consulted with C-level executives, law firm partners, and administrators on improved methods of litigation management, cost recovery, client development, and the use of technology in the practice of law. Created cost-recovery strategy for CFO focus for entire national sales organization. Rolled out cost-recovery strategies to national sales organization.

Established and cultivated long-term relationships to build loyalty and secure revenue base. Managed key account strategies, negotiations, and resources for the territory and negotiations with CFOs, Managing Partners, Executive Directors, Litigation/Practice Support Managers, IT Managers, Partners (Section Heads) and Librarian Directors. Led and set vision, as well as served as coach and mentor, for a team of up to 29 sales representatives across five states while covering two regions (law firms and law schools), 1996–1998.

Positions and Promotions while at Guardian
National Sales Manager (2001–2005)

Senior Regional Sales Manager (2000–2001)

Regional Sales Manager (1996–2000)

Account Manager (1993–1996)

Account Representative (1992–1993)

Business Awards & Accomplishments while at Guardian
- Guardian National Region and National Manager of the Year—2002
- Promoted to National Sales Manager—2001
- Managed revenue performance of Region as Number One (#1) Western Market Area for four straight years—1998–2001
- Promoted to Senior Regional Sales Manager—2000
- National Circle of Excellence Award Winner—1996, 1997, 1999, 2001, 2002, & 2003
- Exceeded revenue goals in 1996, 1997, 1999, 2001, 2002, & 2003
- Promoted to Regional Sales Manager—1996

- National Circle of Excellence Award—1993, 1994, and 1995
- Promoted to Account Manager in 1993
- As Account Manager—Exceeded revenue goals in 1993, 1994, & 1995

BURROUGHS, INC.   **1983–1991**
Sales Representative 1988–1991
Joined Burroughs to become a member of the professional services office solution team. As Customer Support Analyst (1983–1986), activities included demonstration and installation of software and systems, as well as front line on 800 technical support. Promotion to Systems Consultant in 1986 (1986–1988) and became a member of the professional services division; focused sales division selling to legal and accounting firms. In this role, responsibilities included pre-sales technical and marketing support for software/hardware solutions as well as RFP and pricing responsibility, demonstrations, consulting and implementation planning of accounting/billing and office automation technology, as well as client installation.

Promoted to Sales Representative in 1988 and performed as Sales and Account Manager for law firms marketing Wang's full product line. Formulated strategic marketing and sales plans for law firm, corporate, and top accounting client base. In 1990, exceeded revenue goal, $1.75 million on $1 million goal, which was Top 1% of Worldwide Sales. In early 1991, Wang went through dramatic downsizing and this is when a move was made to another employer to continue career aspirations.

Positions and Promotions while at Burroughs:

- Sales Representative (1988–1991)
- Systems Consultant (1986–1988)
- Customer Support Analyst (1983–1986)

Business Awards & Accomplishments while at Burroughs:

- Chairman's Club—Top 1% Worldwide at 174% of Goal in 1990
- Outstanding Regional Consultant Q1'88 and Q2'88, MVP Club 1988
- Outstanding Customer Support Analyst Q2'86 and Promoted to Systems Consultant
- Promoted to Systems Consultant in 1986
- Promoted to Sales Representative in 1988

6

Sample Traditional Résumés

HERE IS THE HEART of this book—dozens of sample résumés representing a range of positions in several major industries and professions. These sample résumés start with an entry-level position; the résumé template for a military transition to civilian work and a sample; and four variations on a single résumé, targeting different skills, to show how to prepare multiple résumés for different jobs. Then, the chapter presents some résumés in the fields of banking, human resources, sales, administration, accounting, various technologies, architecture, operations, and production management. These are applicable for additional kinds of jobs that may not be covered here.

Start by looking over the résumés that pertain most directly to your field of work, but don't overlook the résumés that fall outside of your job experience because they offer excellent ideas that you can adapt to your particular circumstances. Complementing this chapter's selection of résumés is the chapter that follows, with its samples of nontraditional résumés for yet other types and levels of work.

The Entry-Level Résumé

Direct and sincere, entry-level résumés need to be both simple and powerful. Hiring authorities recognize that the candidate is relatively inexperienced, so they're not expecting a ten-year history. However, the information needs to be presented in a clean, crisp format and be to the point. The primary message of an entry-level résumé is: "These were my successes in and during school. I will be just as diligent and successful in my work [for you] as I was during my school years."

The relevant points to emphasize in an entry-level résumé are:

∎ Good grades

∎ Working your way through college and paying for it yourself

∎ Athletic competition and successes

∎ Good grades

∎ Extracurricular participation, especially leadership positions (i.e., officer in fraternity, sorority, club, or organization)

∎ Summer leadership programs, internships, and the like

∎ Summer jobs

∎ Good grades

∎ Graduating either cum laude or summa cum laude, with honors

▪ Academic or leadership recognition

▪ Good grades

You'll notice that I mentioned good grades often. Despite my own Ph.D., my undergraduate grade point average was only 2.8. I had a blast as an officer in my fraternity, worked two or three jobs at a time to earn money, and devoted tons of time to playing rugby. I know now that these are lousy excuses for achieving less than what I was capable of in the grades department. Kinda sad! However, the greatest blessing I received from undergraduate school was meeting my wife, Chrissy. But . . . I still could have and should have studied harder.

If you are still a student, the most important thing you can do toward getting a good job is to become *smarter* and *work harder*. The best companies (in fact, all companies) want to hire hard-working, smart people. In fact, very few things beat being smart—but working hard *can* outrun being smart. Of course, if you are both hard-working and smart, life will be easier. Right or wrong, hiring authorities speculate on how smart you are by looking at your grade point average. If your grades are good, emphasize that. Don't try to defend lousy grades, but do offset them with mention of work or leadership positions.

The following résumé is of our son, James, which he prepared when he was graduating from Wake Forest University in 2008. He takes after his mother, getting good grades as well as demonstrating leadership.

JAMES BESHARA

Address	Cell Phone #	E-mail Address

EDUCATION   2004–2008

Wake Forest University

B.A. Economics   Graduation: May 2008 **cum laude**   Overall GPA: 3.77   Major GPA: 3.83

- Received a qualitatively and quantitatively broad, economic and liberal arts education

- Primary Subjects:
  Economics—Macro, Advanced Micro, Public Finance
  Spanish—Advanced Studies in Madrid, Spain (Fall '06)
  Math—Calculus, Statistics, Advanced Topography

- Activities and Honors: Dean's List every semester, Donald Bauer Scholar, International Studies Scholarship, Sigma Chi Fraternity Executive Committee in the positions of Secretary, Alumni Chair, Publications Chair, Rush Chair, and Social Chair, Intramural Basketball and Football, Samaritan Inn Homeless Shelter Volunteer

Graduated with Honors, Highland Park High School (Dallas, TX)   2004

- Activities and Honors: Honors Program, National Honor Society, Student Council, Principal's Advisory Committee President and Co-Founder, Treasurer of Feed My Starving Children, Rotary Youth Leadership Award and Scholarship, Varsity Track and Basketball, Habitat For Humanity, Tutoring in Mathematics

WORK EXPERIENCE

May 2008–Aug 2009   Saturn Learning Solutions, Dallas, TX   *Associate*
                           (online training company)

- Part-time (along with a class at Southern Methodist University)

- Developed and implemented sales process of online insurance pre-licensing program for national insurance clients

- Worked with software programmers in development of user-friendly interface

- Provided real-time process management and learning solutions to key institutional customers

May 2004–Aug 2004   Allen Edmonds Dress Shoes, New York, NY   *Sales Associate*

- Part-time (along with a class at New York University)

- Designed a personal strategy to meet my monthly goals of sales

- Managed customer service

- Met all personal goals and superseded all company goals for part-time employees

May 2004–Sept 2004   Individual After School Tutoring, Dallas, TX   *Peer Tutor*

- Tutored fellow high-school students in areas from chemistry to mathematics, specializing in calculus

Summer 2002/2003   Direct Connect Computer Services, Dallas, TX   *Technician*

- Serviced, repaired, and networked personal and corporate computer systems

SKILLS

Microsoft Word, PowerPoint, Excel; computer systems; highly organized and detail-oriented; approaching Spanish fluency; great communication and personal skills

OTHER ACTIVITIES AND INTERESTS

Balfour Leadership Training Workshop (Summer 2005), Rotary Youth Leadership Award (2004)

The Military Transition Résumé

Transitioning from the military to the private sector is more difficult to do when unemployment is high and the economy is challenging. As with other types of job candidates, people leaving the military need to be able to communicate to a prospective employer what they can do for that employer better than anyone else. Thanks go to Dan McCall and his company, The Lucas Group, for providing the résumé examples for this section. The Lucas Group Military Division specializes in placing military professionals planning a transition to a corporate career.

For transitioning military personnel, it's very important to communicate your experience in terms that are meaningful to the private employer. There's a tendency for long-term military personnel to describe their work and themselves in military terms rather than civilian terms. Remember, the hiring authority wants to know, "What can you do for me, *right now!*" Your résumé is among hordes of others. It has to have obvious implications to catch attention and get you the interview. That means translating military terminology into civilian terminology. "Combat readiness" will have a different meaning to a hiring authority than it will to your commanding officer.

The following is a standard format we recommend you use as a guide when you create a chronological résumé in the Lucas format.

NAME
Street address
City, State, Zip code
Home # Cell #
[If stationed outside continental US, phone/address
where you can be reached during the interviewing process]
E-mail address(es)

EDUCATION

BS/BA Major, year completed   MS/MA Emphasis, year completed
University   University

ACTIVITIES

College: [Include any community or civic activities, as well as the number of hours of part-time work you did in college. It is *very important* to submit as much information in the Activities section as possible. This information can weigh heavily.]

EXPERIENCE

[List the most recent position first; give date and title of each position held. Then, using 2–6 typed lines, give information about the *specific* responsibilities, supervisory duties, number and type of people supervised, amount and *specific* type of equipment used and/or responsible for. Then list *significant accomplishments* while in each position. Accomplishments can be military and/or personal goals attained or exceeded. Include collateral duties, but only as a minority portion of your comments. Have all time periods accounted for with no gaps between months. Use complete sentences, and list several accomplishments per job. Keep the entire résumé to *one* page. Focus on *marketable* skills that include leadership, maintenance, engineering, language skills, logistics, material management, scheduling.] For example:

United States Army Officer   **06/08 to Present**
Captain, Field Artillery
    Executive Officer

- Increased operational readiness rate from 75% to 95%

- Recognized for having the "best platoon" in the battalion, #1 of 12 units

- Maintained project status on time despite a 55% cut in budget funding

- Reduced payroll discrepancies from 23% to 2% in 3 months

- Awarded Division's "McArthur Leadership Award"

[Also list all civilian work—dates worked, positions held (even family business without pay), duties involved, and company worked for (if applicable). Give short job description (1 or 2 lines is enough). Include any co-op experience.]

ADDITIONAL INFORMATION:

[List language skills, computer programs, hobbies, interests, sports, and other pertinent information.]

Additionally, if you have worked for a civilian firm before and/or after the military, describe your civilian experience along with your military experience.

Here's how this format looks as an actual résumé:

JOE BAILEY

Address   Phone #   Cell #   E-mail

EDUCATION AND TRAINING

Civilian

University of Rhode Island Graduate School, Kingston, RI   2002–2003
  Master's of Business Administration Degree Program
United States Military Academy, West Point, NY   1990–1994
  Bachelor of Science, Environmental Science

CIVILIAN EXPERIENCE

Frito-Lay North America
  Fleet Manager, Killingly Traffic Center, Dayville, CT   8/2003–Present
  - Implemented program to eliminate all trailer rentals and reduce tractor rental costs by over 50%
  - Reduced garage staffing by over 30% and maintained same production efficiency
  - Oversaw installation of new on-board computer tracking system for all assets (317)
  - Reduced inventory storeroom value by over $25,000
  - Managed operating budget of $1.8 million
  - Responsible for DOT regulatory compliance, scored 92% on audit
  - Mentored, directed, and coached garage staff of 10 personnel and one fleet administrative

MILITARY EXPERIENCE

United States Army, University of Rhode Island Army ROTC   8/1999–2/2002
  Executive Officer, Recruiting Operations Officer, Assistant Professor of Military Science
  - Processed and maintained all cadet applications and records; scored 100% on Command Inspection
  - Achieved 150% scholarship utilization and increased the caliber of enrolled cadets
  - Responsible for Battalion marketing action plan that increased cadet enrollment by over 25%
  - Increased utilization of National Guard and Reserve scholarship program at URI
  - Managed $15K annual marketing budget for advertisement in local media

United States Army, Aviation Support Battalion, Camp Zama, Japan
  Commander of the Headquarters and Headquarters Detachment (JJD)   1997–1998
  Battalion Personnel Officer (S1)   1996–1997
  Platoon Leader, Helicopter Flight Section   1995–1996
  - Created autonomous administrative section that received Fully Mission Ready rating on first inspection
  - Implemented and supervised policies to raise Command Inspection scores to 100%
  - Obtained operational readiness rates in excess of the Department of the Army Standard of 80%
  - Responsible for aircraft and ground support equipment valued in excess of $12M

Same Person, Four Different Résumés

Sarah Addison is looking for a job in writing, research, teaching, or administrative work. The following four résumés highlight her different skills and experiences, applied to each of these job types. Note: The same jobs and positions she has held are present on all four targeted résumés but *different skills* are listed in the job descriptions. These individual skills are further emphasized by the targeted Experience summary at the beginning of each résumé. The overall picture is of an experienced person with solid skills in each particular job area.

TARGETED RÉSUMÉ #1: WRITER

Sarah Addison
Address | Phone Number | E-mail Address

SUMMARY INFORMATION
- Outstanding writing, editing, proofreading, and computer skills
  - Over ten years of writing, proofreading, and editing experience
  - Expert at English composition and scientific writing
  - Advanced use of Microsoft Office Suite
  - Published author; currently working on another book
- Have worked with diverse populations through formal education and past work experiences
- Multitask efficiently and have great interpersonal skills
- Excellent communication and teaching ability
  - Preparing and implementing classroom materials and lectures
  - Breaking down difficult or complex topics in ways that enable the student to understand
  - Bringing in real-world stories and discoveries to make more abstract concepts easier to understand

EDUCATION

University of East Texas, Texarkana, TX   2005–2008
  Master's in Biomedical Sciences
  Area of Research: Microbiology
  Dissertation Topic: Toll-like Receptors and Their Role in Pathogen Interactions

University of Texas at Austin, Austin, TX   2002–2005
  B.S. in Biology
  Minor: English

WRITING, EDITING, AND PROOFREADING EXPERIENCE

E Texas Publishing, Inc.
  Freelance Writer   2010–Current
  Write, edit, and proofread presentation, term paper, and scientific report samples for college students; résumé writing and editing

  Toll-like Receptors and Their Role in Pathogen Interactions
    Published by University of East Texas   2008

University of East Texas, Texarkana, TX
  Graduate Research Assistant   2005–2009
  Wrote, edited, and proofread student posters, presentations, manuscripts, and scientific reports; edited grant proposals

  Falling Upside Down
    Published by Publish America Corporation   2006

University of Texas at Austin, Austin, TX
    Student   **2002–2005**
    Wrote, proofread, and edited manuscripts, presentations, and school newspaper

    Member of the East Texas Writer's Guild and   **2002–Current**
       East Texas Writer's Network

    Writer   **1998–Current**

RESEARCH

Windell Staffing, Cool, TX
    Researcher   **2010–Current**
    Research candidates and job openings for recruiters; provide support
    for executive assistants as needed

UT Eastern Medical Center, Texarkana, TX
    Research Assistant   **2009–2010**
    Area of Research: Human Growth and Development
    Laboratory experiments focus on working with mouse obesity paradigms

University of East Texas, Texarkana, TX
    Graduate Research Assistant   **2005–2009**
    Areas of Research: Microbiology, Neuroscience, and Pharmacology
    Laboratory experiments included both *in vitro* and *in vivo* study of *E. coli*
    and *in vivo* studies using the rat model of multiple sclerosis

TARGETED RÉSUMÉ #2: RESEARCH SCIENTIST

Sarah Addison
Address | Phone Number | E-mail Address

SUMMARY INFORMATION
- Excellent GLP
- Proven track record of organizational, interpersonal, and multitasking skills
- Outstanding writing, editing, and proofreading skills
- Exceptional communication, teaching, and supervising ability
- Great computer skills
- Superb animal handling/surgery dexterity
- Great aseptic technique
- Have worked with diverse populations through formal education and past work experiences

EDUCATION

University of East Texas, Texarkana, TX   **2005–2008**
    Master's in Biomedical Sciences
    Area of Research: Microbiology
    Dissertation Topic: Toll-like Receptors and Their Role in Pathogen Interactions

University of Texas at Austin, Austin, TX   **2002–2005**
    B.S. in Biology
    Minor: English

RESEARCH

Windell Staffing, Cool, TX
    Researcher   **2010–Current**
    Research candidates and job openings for recruiters; provide support for executive assistants as needed

UT Eastern Medical Center, Texarkana, TX
    Research Assistant   **2009–2010**
    Area of Research: Human Growth and Development
    Laboratory experiments focus on working with mouse obesity paradigms

University of East Texas, Texarkana, TX
    Graduate Research Assistant   **2008–2009**
    Areas of Research: Pharmacology and Neuroscience
    Laboratory experiments included *in vivo* studies of axonal transport and tissue differences in the rat model of multiple sclerosis; helped organize and start up lab; tested combinational therapeutics in disease paradigm; revised protocols for experiments; supervised personnel

University of East Texas, Texarkana, TX
    Graduate Research Assistant/Master's Student   **2005–2008**
    Areas of Research: Microbiology
    Laboratory experiments included both *in vitro* and *in vivo* study of *E. coli*; revised protocols; responsible for data collection and analysis; troubleshooted unexpected results, experimental design, and equipment failure

Professional Presentations

"Toll-like Receptors and Their Role in Pathogen Interactions"
Poster presented at the Research Appreciation Day, Texarkana, TX   **2007**

"Stress Susceptibility in Murine E. coli Infections"
Poster presented at the Research Appreciation Day, Texarkana, TX   **2006**

"Lipoprotein Characterization of Transposon Mutants of E. coli."
Poster presented at the Departmental Retreat, Irving, TX   **2006**

WRITING, EDITING, AND PROOFREADING EXPERIENCE

E Texas Publishing, Inc.

Freelance Writer   **2010–Current**
Write, edit, and proofread presentations, term papers, and scientific
report samples for college students; résumé writing and editing

Toll-like Receptors and Their Role in Pathogen Interactions   **2008**
Published by University of East Texas

University of East Texas, Texarkana, TX

Graduate Research Assistant   **2005–2009**
Wrote, edited, and proofread student posters, presentations, manuscripts,
and scientific reports; edited grant proposals

Falling Upside Down   **2006**
Published by Publish America Corporation

University of Texas at Austin, Austin, TX

Student   **2002–2005**
Wrote, proofread, and edited manuscripts, presentations, and school newspaper

Member of the East Texas Writer's Guild and   **2002–Current**
    East Texas Writer's Network

Writer   **1998–Current**

TARGETED RÉSUMÉ #3: TEACHER

Sarah Addison
Address | Phone Number | E-mail Address

SUMMARY INFORMATION

▪ Excellent communication and teaching ability
  - Preparing and implementing classroom materials and lectures
  - Breaking down difficult or complex topics in ways that enable the student to understand
  - Bringing in real-world stories and discoveries to make more abstract concepts easier to understand
  - Having the experience and education to teach in both a lab and classroom setting

▪ Outstanding writing, editing, proofreading, and computer skills

▪ Have worked with diverse populations through formal education and past work experiences

▪ Multitask efficiently and have great interpersonal skills

EDUCATION

University of East Texas, Texarkana, TX   2005–2008
  Master's in Biomedical Sciences
  Area of Research: Microbiology
  Dissertation Topic: Toll-like Receptors and Their Role in Pathogen Interactions

University of Texas at Austin, Austin, TX   2002–2005
  B.S. in Biology
  Minor: English

TEACHING EXPERIENCE

University of East Texas, Texarkana, TX
  Graduate Research Assistant   2005–2009
  Prepared presentations to colleagues and students, taught and fielded
  questions on my areas of research; organized classroom material to lead
  study groups; trained other students and personnel on lab techniques

University of Texas at Austin, Austin, TX
  Microbiology Lab Assistant/Teacher   2004
  Prepared and set up materials for student experiments; taught, created test
  questions, and graded assignments and tests; worked with students on
  equipment problems, analyzing data, and troubleshooting unexpected results

Kaplan, Austin, TX
  MCAT proctor   2004
  Administered practice exams

Equine Riding Instructor, Austin, TX   2003
  Taught techniques and practices in horseback riding, emphasizing basics and
  safety, Austin Independent School District

Teach and Tutor 2001–2009

Planned, prepared, and implemented lesson plans; worked with both junior high and high school students in both the classroom setting and one-on-one

WRITING, EDITING, AND PROOFREADING EXPERIENCE

E Texas Publishing, Inc.

Freelance Writer 2010–Current

Write, edit, and proofread presentations, term papers, and scientific report samples for college students; résumé writing and editing

Toll-like Receptors and Their Role in Pathogen Interactions

Published by University of East Texas 2008

University of East Texas, Texarkana, TX

Graduate Research Assistant 2005–2009

Wrote, edited, and proofread student posters, presentations, manuscripts, and scientific reports; edited grant proposals

Falling Upside Down

Published by Publish America Corporation 2006

University of Texas at Austin, Austin, TX

Student 2002–2005

Wrote, proofread, and edited manuscripts, presentations, and school newspaper

Member of the East Texas Writer's Guild and 2002–Current
East Texas Writer's Network

Writer 1998–Current

RESEARCH

Windell Staffing, Cool, TX

Researcher 2010–Current

Research candidates and job openings for recruiters; provide support for executive assistants as needed

UT Eastern Medical Center, Texarkana, TX

Research Assistant 2009–2010

Area of Research: Human Growth and Development
Laboratory experiments focus on working with mouse obesity paradigms

Graduate Research Assistant 2005–2009

University of East Texas, Texarkana, TX
Areas of Research: Microbiology, Neuroscience, and Pharmacology
Laboratory experiments included both *in vitro* and *in vivo* study of *E. coli*

TARGETED RÉSUMÉ #4: ADMINISTRATIVE WORK

Sarah Addison
Address ǀ Phone Number ǀ E-mail Address

SUMMARY INFORMATION

• Multitask efficiently and have great interpersonal skills

• Excellent customer service ability

• Outstanding communication, writing, editing, proofreading, and computer skills
  - Superb in Microsoft Word, PowerPoint, and Excel

  - Experience in transcription, dictation, and data entry

  - Telephone, calendar, and budget experience

  - Fast and accurate typist

• Have worked with diverse populations through formal education and past
  work experiences

EDUCATION

University of East Texas, Texarkana, TX   2005–2008
   Master's in Biomedical Sciences
   Area of Research: Microbiology
   Dissertation Topic: Toll-like Receptors and Their Role in Pathogen Interactions

University of Texas at Austin, Austin, TX   2002–2005
   B.S. in Biology
   Minor: English

ADMINISTRATIVE/SECRETARIAL EXPERIENCE

Windell Staffing, Cool, TX
   Researcher   2010–Current
   Research candidates and job openings for recruiters; provide support
   for executive assistants as needed

University of East Texas, Texarkana, TX
   Graduate Research Assistant   2005–2008
   Maintained experiment and presentation calendar; wrote, proofread,
   and edited manuscripts and presentations; advanced use of Microsoft Word,
   PowerPoint, and Excel; manned laboratory phones; transcribed protocols
   and lab notebooks; experience in data entry

University of Texas at Austin, Austin, TX
   Student   2002–2005
   Wrote, proofread, and edited manuscripts and presentations; expert use
   of Microsoft Word, PowerPoint, and Excel; transcribed minutes and class
   notes; experience with dictation through lectures and letter writing

Texas Aquaculture, Austin, TX
   Office Clerk/Customer Service   2005
   Updated and organized company files; data entry

WRITING, EDITING, AND PROOFREADING EXPERIENCE
E Texas Publishing, Inc.

Freelance Writer	2010–Current

Write, edit, and proofread presentations, term papers, and scientific
report samples for college students; résumé writing and editing

Toll-like Receptors and Their Role in Pathogen Interactions

Published by University of East Texas	2008

University of East Texas, Texarkana, TX

Graduate Research Assistant	2005–2009

Wrote, edited, and proofread student posters, presentations, manuscripts,
and scientific reports; edited grant proposals

Falling Upside Down

Published by Publish America Corporation	2006

University of Texas at Austin, Austin, TX

Student	2002-2005

Wrote, proofread, and edited manuscripts, presentations, and school newspaper

Member of the East Texas Writer's Guild and	2002–Current

East Texas Writer's Network

Writer	1998–Current

BANKING: BANK EXECUTIVE

Great résumé; excellent layout.

BOBBY DUKE, CPA

Address   Phone #   Cell #   E-mail

EXPERIENCE

Texas Enterprise Bank   2006–Present

- Worked with organizers during the last 6 months before bank opened—
  developing policies, procedures, purchasing equipment, training on and
  preparing for computer conversion (setup), raising capital, and hiring staff.

- Serve as CFO & COO for the bank.

Independent Contract Work   2005–2006

- Worked as interim CFO / Operations Review at two banks in the Dallas area

- Worked in Bryan, TX, since November at a De Nova Organization—developing
  policies, working with regulators, raising capital, finishing out the facility,
  interviewing / hiring staff members, purchasing furniture and equipment,
  preparing for the computer processing conversion, and other tasks as necessary

Jefferson Bank, Dallas, Texas   2003–2005
A $170 Million Asset Institution

EVP, CFO, & COO

- Hired as CFO, assumed the position of COO when that became vacant

- Responsible for management reporting (budgeting, asset/liability
  and interest rate risk analysis)

- Served as liaison between bank and external auditors

- Served as senior management's representative on the internal audit committee

- Developed Excel spreadsheets to quickly prepare management reports

- Developed policies / procedures for operations

- Coordinated branch openings

- Staff development (evaluating, training, & assigning)

- Problem solver

First Savings Bank, Arlington, Texas   2001–2003
A $500 Million Asset Institution

CFO

- Responsible for management reporting (budgeting, asset/liability,
  and interest rate risk analysis)

- Prepared Subsidiary portion for SEC reporting

- Served as liaison between bank and external auditors

- Developed Excel spreadsheets to quickly prepare management reports

- Established / maintained G/L reconciliations

Orange Savings Bank, SSB, Orange, Texas   1995–2001
A $175 Million Asset Institution

Controller

- Responsible for management reporting (budgeting, asset/liability, and interest rate risk analysis)
- Served as liaison between bank and external auditors
- Developed Excel spreadsheets to quickly prepare management reports
- Established / maintained G/L reconciliations
- Headed bank's IT Committee, served on Fiserv's User Committee

Dewey's Foods, Inc., Harlingen, Texas   1995
A Distributor of Frozen Foods

Controller

- Responsible for management reporting (A/P, A/R, BS, Income, Cash Flow)
- Established / maintained G/L reconciliations
- Supervised the office staff, consisting of four employees

Harlingen National Bank, Harlingen, Texas   1992–1994
A $170 Million Asset Commercial Bank

Senior Vice President & CFO

- Responsible for management reporting (budgeting, asset/liability, and interest rate risk analysis)
- Established / maintained G/L reconciliations
- Served as liaison between bank and external auditors
- Supervised eight supervisors and 70 employees in four branch locations
- Reorganized and consolidated the Loan Operations Department
- Headed an IT team in the selection and successful conversion of the data processing function from a facilities management company to an in-house system
- Evaluated a failed bank's operations, securities, accounting, personnel, and deposits; and developed a successful bid for the purchase of the bank, which was reopened as a branch. Because of the prudent purchase price, the branch proved to be extremely profitable.
- Assisted in the design, bidding and building of two branch offices, including the equipment, which came in under budget
- Hired and trained staff for two new branch offices
- Purchased and enhanced an Asset and Liability Management Program that has assisted in the continued profitability of the bank

EDUCATION

MBA Finance and Economics and **BBA** Banking and Finance,
   Delta State University, Cleveland, MS

CPA, State of Texas, 1986

SOFTWARE

Excel for Windows and Word
Asset / Liability / Budgeting programs: Plansmith's Compass, Farin & Associates' SAM

BANKING: TELLER/NEW ACCOUNTS REPRESENTATIVE

Excellent explanations of positions held and what candidate gained from each of these positions.

ASHLEY WARNER
Address   Phone #   Cell #   E-mail

New Accounts Rep. / Teller   4/2007–Present

Bank of the Ozarks, Frisco, TX

- Opened new accounts while performing everyday teller functions
- Cross-sold products (not required)
- Prepared reports to send to back office/cash management
- Sent wires
- Made banking transactions
- Found products to suit each individual customer
- Balanced the ATM daily
- Balanced vault daily
- Made changes to customer information (on request)
- Ordered checks
- Ordered debit cards (and other products on request)
- Prepared official checks
- Sent branch logs and MIL logs to BSA officer monthly

While working at Bank of the Ozarks, I have learned how to open new accounts and learned how to find the right accounts to meet the individual needs of each customer, including IRAs.

Teller   10/2006–3/2007

Park Cities Bank, Dallas, TX

- Made banking transactions
- Found products to suit each individual customer
- Balanced the ATM daily
- Made changes to customer information (on request)
- Ordered checks
- Ordered debit cards (and other products on request)
- Prepared official checks
- Exchanged foreign currency

This work experience taught me some things that I had never encountered while working in the banking industry, such as encoding and filming both my work and my co-workers'.

Teller   5/2006–9/2006

    Bank of Texas, Plano, TX

- Met and exceeded monthly sales quota
- Prepared official checks
- Prepared money orders
- Handled customers' transactions
- Balanced the ATMs weekly
- Ordered debit cards (and other products on request)
- Made changes to customer information (on request)
- Helped with new concepts and ideas to endorse current promotions

Working for Bank of Texas was a great experience. While I was there I had Monthly Sales quotas that I had to meet. This was my first time learning key points in cross-selling banking products to potential clients. I met my goals and exceeded my monthly goals with the help of a great leadership team.

Teller   11/2004–5/2006

    Century Bank, Dallas, TX

- Ordered checks
- Ordered debit cards (and other products on request)
- Balanced the ATMs weekly
- Prepared official checks
- Handled customers' transactions
- Balanced the coin counter daily

In my first opportunity in the banking industry I learned how to do so many functions, including how to build great rapport with my customers and cross-sell other products (even though not required).

Customer Service Rep I and II   10/2003–4/2005

    Best Buy, Plano, TX

- Handled customer transactions. Added tag on sales for current promotions that Best Buy was offering.

EDUCATION

Collin County Community College, Plano, TX

Plano East Senior High, Plano, TX

High School Diploma

CERTIFICATIONS

Notary Public for the state of Texas

BANKING: UNDERWRITER

Excellent explanations of duties and credentials.

Wade Fisher

Address   Cell #   E-mail

PROFESSIONAL EXPERIENCE

Commercial Real Estate and Commercial Banking Professional with over 14 years of experience with a proven background in Commercial Real Estate and Banking Analysis and Management, including financial/risk analysis, financial statement, operating statement and cash flow modeling, projection and forecasting strategies, acquisitions, dispositions, and capital expenditure.

MAJOR PROJECTS

Portfolio Acquisition Associate—Beal Bank   **10/08–Present**

- Responsible for commercial real estate loan portfolios to identify, assess, and quantify risk; and to capture the data required to determine the salient characteristics, analyzing market data to determine value of the loans including the collateral, related lien priority, assessment of loan documents, and collateral valuations to report to Senior Management so they could bid for purchase of portfolios from FDIC.

- Negotiated with borrowers on nonperforming loans to compromise and settle debt based on loan action plans.

- Successfully won over $200 million in loans that I presented to senior management as good loans to bid on.

Sr. Underwriter/Asset Manager–Commercial Mortgage Backed
Securities/Balance Sheet Lending—GE Capital Real Estate   **10/05–09/08**

- Responsible for credit quality through timely and accurate credit recommendations. Made sound recommendations based on financial analysis, risk assessment, Argus analysis, analyzing market data, loan structure development, and adherence to credit policies.

- Underwrote over $800 million in deals during stay at GE.

- Was mentor to more junior underwriters.

- Underwriter on 40 multifamily deals, Fannie Mae, Freddie Mac, FHA.

- Conducted site visits as part of underwriting and asset management.

- Asset managed all property types, with emphasis on multifamily and office, until CMBS deals were sold and balance sheet deals were either refinanced or effectively disposed of.

- Assigned over 50 multifamily deals to asset manage once credit crunch hit market.

Sr. Asset Manager/Underwriter III,
Multifamily Lending—Washington Mutual Bank   **06/04–09/05**

- Responsible for commercial real estate portfolios with an average load of 20–30 multifamily assets located in the west, northwest, and mountain regions of the United States; Fannie Mae, Freddie Mac, FHA.

- Underwrote new financing totaling over $110 million.

- Managed a staff of 6 people in portfolio management.

- Monitored portfolio risk, identified, assessed, quantified, and mitigated to report results to head of Risk Management.
- Conducted site visits as part of asset management and underwriting process.

Sr. Credit Underwriter–Middle Market
Commercial Banking—Compass Bank 05/02–06/04

- Responsible for credit quality through timely and accurate credit recommendations. Made sound recommendations based on financial analysis, risk assessment, analyzing market data, loan structure development, and adherence to credit policies.
- Performed detailed credit analysis, due diligence, and review of documents for new transactions and monitored/managed ongoing performance/risk of accounts within assigned portfolio under limited direction of senior staff.
- Underwrote over $80 million in commercial and SBA loans.
- Mentor to more junior underwriters and the banking division's credit analysts.

Credit Portfolio Manager/Jr. Asset Manager–Private
Banking Group—Northern Trust 10/00–05/02

- Responsible for managing credit product risk and profitability for large portfolio of real estate clients, focused on high net worth clients.
- Portfolio consisted of 15 multifamily and several strip malls with an aggregate real estate value of $200 million.
- Underwrote large residential construction homes that totaled $50 million for 30 homes.

Underwriter–Middle Market Commercial Banking—Bank of America 05/95–10/00

- Primarily responsible for ensuring the timely delivery of technically accurate financial, industrial, and economic credit analysis.
- Completed formal credit training program with Bank of America.
- Performed detailed credit analysis, due diligence, and review of documents for new transactions and monitored/managed ongoing performance/risk of accounts within assigned portfolio under limited direction of senior staff.
- Performed credit reviews for 16 credit facilities per month and underwrote 8 new deals a month.

BANKING: MORTGAGE BROKER

Good layout of responsibilities and job descriptions.

CAROLYN MASTERS
Address   Cell #   E-mail

QUALIFICATIONS

- Extensive experience in the mortgage/banking industry.
- Experienced in all phases of commercial, residential, and consumer lending.
- Qualified in all operational aspects of a commercial/retail bank.
- Broad managerial ability to work effectively with all levels of management, ownership, employees, and community and customer relationships.
- Comprehensive knowledge in regulatory compliance and operational auditing.
- Thorough commitment to product implementation and delivery, including customer call programs.

WORK HISTORY

City Mortgage   **April 2005 to Present**
Owner/Broker

- Originate, process, and close residential and commercial mortgages.
- Responsible for the operations of a 2-person full-service mortgage brokerage company.
- Specialize in land financing, retail financing, residential financing, and commercial financing.
- Received the state's highest compliance rating for safety and soundness of operations.

Clausen Home Mortgage   **April 2003–March 2005**
Senior Loan Officer/Branch Manager

- Responsible for the mortgage branch operation in Midlothian, TX, overseeing 3 LOs and a receptionist.
- Originated and closed on average $1,000,000 in new mortgages per month.

Keller Custom Homes   **May 2001–April 2003**
Owner/President/General Contractor

- Estimated job costs on commercial and residential new construction.
- Negotiated all customer and subcontractor contracts.
- Responsible for the oversight of all aspects of design, development, and construction.

Century 1st Mortgage   **January 1999–March 2001**
Senior Correspondent/Sales Account Executive

- Responsible for the mortgage management of 5 Coldwell Banker Residential Brokerage offices (National Realty Trust) and 4 federal credit unions.
- Top producer of mortgage leads and closings with the Dallas/Fort Worth Metropolitan National Realty Trust.

- Trainer, facilitator, and trouble-shooter for 258 real estate agents.

- Attained "President's Club" status April 2000 by placing number 16 nationally out of 300 account executives.

- Successfully developed and managed the nation's 2nd highest mortgage lead–producing Century 21 office. Century 21 office management received national recognition.

- Awarded "Rookie of the Year" in 1999 for the Midwest region, generating over $18,000,000 in new loans closed.

Texas Bank & Trust   **1997–1998**
President and Chief Executive Officer

- Developed and submitted new bank charter application to the Office of the Comptroller of the Currency, Dallas. Received preliminary approval.

- Implemented protocol for the private solicitation of qualified investors.

- Coordinated and set up all operational aspects of the bank.

Texas Securities Banking   **1985–1996**
President

- Forecasted, budgeted, and operated a $22,000,000 profitable bank operation.

- Effectively managed a 21-employee bank operation.

- Built and managed $11,000,000 diversified loan portfolio, maintaining a delinquency ratio under 1%.

- Consistently top producer, commanding 67% of total loans originated and closed.

- Developed and implemented profitable second lien wholesale division within the bank, which generated $150,000 net profit the first year of operation.

- Developed and implemented all internal policies, procedures, and training.

- Directed all bank security and regulatory compliance affairs, consistently receiving satisfactory regulatory compliance reviews.

EDUCATION

- **Bachelor of Science in Business Administration,** Texas State University, 1977, with concentrations in finance and economics.

- **Graduate School of Commercial Lending,** Plano, TX.
  Basic and Standard Certificates (Dallas American Institute of Banking).

- **Certified Finance Specialist** designation.

- Continuing education courses in real estate at the University of Texas at Arlington.

BANKING: BRANCH MANAGER

This is a great résumé because of the bullet points. This woman had
several years' experience at a credit union, and she showed her
advancement in each area of the credit union. The bullet points make
it easy for a quick read.

TIFFANY WHITTLE

Address   Phone #   Cell #   E-mail

SUMMARY

Over nine years' experience in a financial sales and customer-service–oriented environment
Strong interpersonal skills   Accomplished public speaker   Outstanding verbal and written communication   High level of professionalism   Highly organized and accurate   Strong analytic and presentation abilities   Proven successful sales technique   Track record for meeting timelines and
exceeding expectations

PROFESSIONAL EXPERIENCE

Jefferson Bank—Rockwall, TX

    Branch Manager, AVP   **Sept. 2008–Present**

- Manage the daily operations of the branch and employees while ensuring bank policies
  and procedures are followed and customers are served professionally and promptly

- Implement, coordinate, and oversee the adherence of all branch operational responsibilities, including all updates to bank policies and procedures

- Maintain the department's employee morale to ensure a positive and friendly work
  environment for customers and other employees

- Provide staff frequent monitoring, follow-up, and feedback to enhance or correct activities related to achievement of goals

- Monitor branch security and perform cash audits, security meetings, and branch assessments to ensure adherences to established bank policies and procedures

- Attend regular branch manager meetings and involved in Corporate Culture
  Committee to create Jefferson Bank new Mission Statement and internal employee culture statement

- Open new accounts as needed; branch primarily attracts IRAs, Trust Accounts, and
  Certificates of Deposit

- Assist in daily banking activities as needed such as teller line, ATM, and vault duties, as
  well as opening and closing branch duties

- Manage CIP exceptions list, CIP/scanning/filing/reviewing employee CIP, daily NSF
  reports, and banking function decisions such as customer sign-offs, overrides, and holds

- Analyze monthly performance analysis and expense reports in order to better manage
  daily banking activities

- Interact with customer base through Chamber events, including new business ribbon
  cutting and Business After Hours events

Advancial Federal Credit Union—Dallas, TX

Member Service Center Manager — Dec. 2005–Sept. 2008

- Promoted to transform a call center into a complete phone branch, including the full training of loan processing and sales procedures and techniques

- Directly managed 7 employees

- Reported directly to AVP Branch Operations

- Facilitated weekly staff sales meetings

- Responsible for the interviewing, hiring, and training of employees; planning, assigning, and directing work; appraising performance; rewarding and disciplining employees; addressing complaints and resolving problems

- Monitored call volume and hold times to ensure abandon calls were at a minimum and member inquiries were answered quickly

- Developed and implemented a call-monitoring program to identify training needs and MSR abilities, as well as an incentive program to rate and reward MSR daily duties

- Continually backed up my department when shorthanded by answering phones, opening new accounts, and processing loans as needed

- Track record for catching suspicious activity, such as fraudulent checks and kiting accounts

- Completed core conversion experience; responsible for the full training of my employees; one of a three-person team to customize a new account workflow for MSRs from bottom up and creation of all new account membership forms for Jack Henry-Symitar; one of a committee of ten to audit data transferred from Custar to Symitar

- As Security Committee member, met monthly to discuss security issues involving the credit union. Met on as-needed basis to research and vote on fraudulent fees being reimbursed to members and whether high-risk accounts should be shut down

- As Back office/Front office Barriers Committee member, met monthly to discuss specific situations to improve morale between the branches and the corporate office to keep them working together effectively

- One of five to brainstorm ideas to better the company intranet, purchase a new system, and implement the ideas

- One of five given authority to access highly secure documents on customers and given ability to review and do maintenance on employee accounts

ACKNOWLEDGMENTS

Advancial President's Circle Award 2007

One of four out of the entire company elected by upper management and co-workers for incorporating unusually creative ideas on the job, providing the highest quality of work, and being known to have a team-oriented philosophy. This group worked directly with the President and CEO to come up with innovative solutions for 2007.

EDUCATION

Collin County Community College
Some Courses Completed

CONTROLLER

This résumé is concise and easy to read.

ROBERT CONRAD
Address   Phone #   Cell #   E-mail

PROFESSIONAL EXPERIENCE

Randal Bank, Frisco, Texas   **May 2007–Present**

Randal Bank is a $130 million single-location community bank based in Frisco, Texas. Hired in May 2007 as Vice President–Controller. Responsibilities include call report preparation, internal financial statements and financial performance reporting for Board of Directors. Play an integral role in the annual budget preparation process. Management of the bank's investment portfolio and interest rate risk. Manage the bank's information technology systems and compliance. Oversee fixed asset accounting, accounts payable, and bookkeeping areas of the bank. Serve as Secretary to the Board and manage the shareholder accounting function. Human resources liaison between the bank and its P.E.O.

Citywide Bank, N.A., Dallas, Texas   **June 2005–May 2007**

Citywide is a $70 million, 3-location community bank based in the Lakewood area of Dallas. Began June of 2005 as Vice President of Operations. My responsibilities included managing the IT and telecommunications systems of the bank, as well as being responsible for managing and marketing the bank's treasury-management applications and development of new products within treasury management. Implemented ACH origination, lockbox, zero balance accounts, online wire transfer origination, and remote deposit capture. A member of the bank's technology committee and involved in all technology-related projects.

Security Bank, Garland, Texas   **May 1997–June 2005**

(Acquired by First Bank of Bryan in December 2003.) Security Bank is a $180 million commercial community bank; First Bank of Bryan is a $3.5 billion Texas-based institution and a global banking institution.

Assistant Vice President—First Bank of Bryan

Appointed in August 2004 as Commercial Lender to manage a $15 million loan portfolio and to build commercial banking relationships. Responsibilities included business development, exception management, monitoring past dues, and monthly renewals.

Appointed in January 2004 as Cash Management Representative for the Garland market. Primary responsibilities included establishing cash-management customer relationships and managing the conversion of the Security Bank cash-management customers to First Bank of Bryan's system. Assisted loan officers in calling efforts for cash-management services and provided comparisons of bank charges for new customers.

Assistant Vice President—Security Bank

Supervised back-office operations and item processing for our in-house system. Responsibilities included daily processing of the bank's data-processing system for 5 branches, which involved exception-item processing, ATM processing, ACH processing, Wire Transfers, and proof operations. Prepared monthly board meeting packages. Managed the Internet Banking, VRU, and Cash Management systems. Worked with CFO to manage the bank's investment portfolio and was a member of the bank's ALCO committee. Also, was a member of the bank's technology steering committee, OFAC, BSA, and new product development committees.

- Led the data-processing conversion from Security Bank's system to First Bank of Bryan's system.
- Coordinated all of Security Bank's data-processing conversion from McCoy Myers to Sparak.
- Installed and implemented Bisys Document Solutions check imaging and power proof system.
- Coordinated and implemented Free Checking and Overdraft Privilege programs.

Credit Analyst—Security Bank

Assisted loan officers in underwriting commercial credits. Performed financial statement spreads, fixed-charge coverage analysis, and A/R aging spreads. Prepared loan packages for Officer Loan Committee meetings and Board Loan Committee meetings. Provided loan officers with portfolio reports, including past dues, maturing loan reports, exception reports, and portfolio tracking. Worked with Senior Credit Analyst to perform loan reviews on the bank's loan portfolio.

Bookkeeping / Data Processing Clerk—Security Bank

Performed daily back-office duties, which included exception-item processing, ACH processes, ATM processing, and cash letter file processing. Other duties would include proof operator and night update processor.

EDUCATION

B.S. Business Administration, 2001, University of Texas at Dallas; concentration in Finance

BANK PRESIDENT

A clear, concise, bulleted résumé.

LUKE LIVELY

Address   Phone #   Cell #   E-mail

PROFESSIONAL EXPERIENCE

Lively Consulting Services (January 2007 to Present), Southern Pines, NC
Owner

- Conduct sales, service, and leadership reviews for banks, insurance firms, software, and Internet businesses
- Deliver seminars with emphasis on company-directed initiatives
- Provide programs and training to improve sales, service, and problem-resolution efforts
- Assist financial service providers in selling services to banks

BB&T (May 2005 to August 2006), Pinehurst, NC
Regional Retail Banking Manager II & Senior Vice President

- Responsible for leadership and management of retail banking region in South-Central North Carolina, involving over 480 employees, 38 direct report managers and 42 offices in eleven-county area
- Managed retail loan portfolio ($2.5 billion) and deposit portfolio ($2.6 billion)

BB&T (October 2003 to May 2005), Johnson City, TN
Regional Retail Banking Manager I & Senior Vice President

- Responsible for leadership and management of retail banking region in West Virginia, Southwest Virginia, and Northeast Tennessee, involving over 500 employees, 36 direct report managers, and 40 offices in three-state area
- Managed retail loan portfolio ($1.1 billion) and deposit portfolio ($1.6 billion)

First Vantage Bank (July 2001 to October 2003), Johnson City & Bristol, TN
Chief Administrative Officer & President, Board of Directors

- Responsible for leadership and management of all areas in a multi-state bank with 33 offices
- Served on executive committees in corporate bank structure, creating sales/service initiatives and problem-resolution program for holding-company member banks

First Virginia Bank–Mountain Empire (October 1997 to July 2001), Wise, VA
Chairman, President, & Chief Executive Officer

- Responsible for leadership and management of all areas in one of the most profitable member banks of First Virginia Banks, Inc.
- Served on executive committees in corporate bank structure, creating sales/service initiatives and problem-resolution programs for all member banks

Premier Bank–Central, NA (July 1995 to October 1997), Honaker, VA
President, Chief Executive Officer, & Vice Chairman

- Responsible for leadership and management of all areas in the most profitable and largest member bank of Premier Bankshares Corporation, Inc.

∙ Served on executive committees in corporate bank structure, creating sales/service initiatives and problem-resolution program for Premier member banks

Premier Bankshares Corporation (January 1994 to July 1995), Salem, VA
Vice President & Chief Administrative Officer

∙ Responsible for leadership and management of human resources, corporate and bank compliance, secondary market mortgage, credit analysis (duties of corporate credit officer), proprietary credit card portfolio, and coordination of mergers/acquisitions

∙ Conducted stock analyst meetings, corporate board of director meetings, and primary contact in pre-merger discussions with target acquisitions

Premier Bank, NA (January 1990 to January 1994), Salem, VA
Senior Vice President, Senior Lending Officer, & Regional Manager

∙ Responsible for leadership and management of commercial and retail lending functions in flagship bank of Premier Bankshares Corp.

∙ Managed credit card operations and electronic banking

Greenbrier Valley National Bank (April 1984 to January 1990), Lewisburg & Alderson, WV
Vice President, Commercial Lender, Compliance Officer

∙ Primary commercial lender for one of largest banks in West Virginia

∙ Served in other positions, including compliance officer, regional manager, and branch manager

Flat Top National Bank (January 1983 to April 1984), Bluefield, WV
Commercial Lender, Credit Card Officer, & Electronic Banking Supervisor

∙ Served as commercial lender for one of larger independent banks in West Virginia

∙ Served in other positions, including credit card officer and electronic banking supervisor

CIT Financial Services (August 1981 to January 1983), Beckley, WV
Assistant Manager, Management Trainee

∙ Hired as management trainee responsible for all areas of office management, including lending, collection, solicitation of new business, and compliance

EDUCATION, RELATED ACTIVITIES, & ACCREDITATIONS

Graduate Banking Degree, 1989, Stonier Graduate School of Banking, University of Delaware; Thesis was "Survival of Community Banks in West Virginia"

Bachelor of Arts (pre-law with major in History and minor in Political Science), 1981, Concord University, Athens, WV; academic honors include cum laude and Dean's List each semester, with 3.5 GPA (3.9 in major/minor fields)

Associate Degree in Business Administration and Associate in Arts, 1979, Mountain State University, Athens, WV; honors include Dean's List each semester of full-time attendance

National Speaker's Association. Active member, conducting motivational, sales/service seminars for businesses, nonprofits, governmental agencies, and Chambers of Commerce.

Banking schools attended include ABA Commercial Lending and Compliance; served as instructor for BAI classes and AIB classes for many years

BANKING: VICE PRESIDENT/LOAN OFFICER

All the necessary information in a quick, easy-to-read format.

Donna Honea

Address   Phone #   Cell #   E-mail

Highlights of Qualifications Progressive Bank Management and Loan Operations Experience, Excellent Communication Skills, Proven Organizational Skills, and Exceptional Leadership Ability

Comerica Bank, Austin, TX   **2006 to Current**

Vice President, National Documentation Manager—Texas Market

- Manage regional multi-state loan operations for commercial and personal loans
- Oversee 20 direct reports in production and audit of commercial and personal loans
- Direct high-performance team in high-volume loan preparation environment
- Manage budget expenditures, capacity model, and staffing needs
- Participate in creation of enhanced efficiency processing software system
- Ensure due diligence collected and compliance with applicable laws, regulations, and credit policy
- Evaluate benchmarking survey to improve processes for higher efficiencies

Town Center Bank, Austin, TX   **2004 to 2006**

Vice President, Loan Manager

- Founding officer for community de novo bank
- Developed, documented, and established internal loan policies and procedures
- Attended training for loan operational systems and acted as trainer to staff
- Established/tested parameters in implementation of loan system and document preparation system
- Coordinated and negotiated contracts with vendors for new bank systems setup
- Responsible for loan operations, loan preparation, funding, loan booking, adjustments
- Post-loan audit review, including assessment and tracking of credit and collateral exceptions
- Control of promissory notes, collateral files, negotiable collateral, and credit files

Colonial Bank, Clemens, TX   **2002 to 2004**

Vice President, Regional Loan Manager

- Managed a $16 billion Texas regional loan operations staff with 15 direct reports
- Managed loan preparation, collateral, payment processing, customer service
- Liaisoned between staff, branch personnel, and management to ensure workflow
- Adherence to bank credit policy, state and federal regulatory compliance

First American Bank, Centerville, TX   **2001 to 2002**

Assistant Vice President, Commercial Product Manager

- Supervised the commercial/consumer loan staff of 6 direct reports for $30 billion Dallas LPO
- Assisted in the formulation and implementation of department's lending operations procedures

- Oversaw the preparation of all commercial, construction, and consumer loan documentation
- Monitored the staff in the closing, renewing, funding, servicing, and posting review
- Maintenance of syndications, participations, rollovers, pay downs, and multiple rate change loans
- Supervised the handling of ongoing financial transactions, payments, advances
- Ensured excellent customer service was provided to internal and external customers

Bank of Texas, Centerville, TX　　　　　　　　　　　　　　　　1999 to 2001
Assistant Vice President, Loan Coordination Manager
- Managed 12 direct reports for $41 billion operation
- Created and established loan operation procedures for newly created department
- Managed the relocation project of loan department to new location
- Worked with system conversion analyst to ensure proper conversion
- Conducted training of staff during acquisition and merger of new banks and conversions
- Traveled to branch for onsite visits to assist Loan Coordinators as necessary
- Interfaced with lenders, attorneys, and division and compliance managers, ensuring quality work flow

Texas Bank, Waco, TX　　　　　　　　　　　　　　　　　　1996 to 1999
Banking Officer, Branch Loan Closer
- Handled daily branch loan operations for $40M branch
- Responsible for documentation, collateral, customer service
- Coordinated the preparation, closing, funding, and servicing of all loans
- Handled commercial real estate builder lines, advances, pay down, lot releases
- Acted as a liaison between lenders, attorneys, title companies, and customers
- Handled paid loans, terminated UCC filings, and executed release of liens on real estate and auto loans

Bank of America, Waco, TX　　　　　　　　　　　　　　　　1986 to 1996
Banking Officer, Portfolio Servicing Officer
- Servicing officer for $50MM portfolio representing 60% of department totals
- Prepared, closed, funded, and serviced commercial, construction, and builder lines loans
- Verified documentation to ensure adherence with credit policy and regulations
- Received Bank of America employee STAR award

Lending Assistant
- Handled credit application with consumer customers and obtained credit reports
- Created loan memorandums and loan documentation; handled direct customer service
- Prepared departmental pipeline and production reports

EDUCATION
North Texas Central College: Accounting
Texas Bankers Association: Principles of Banking, Real Estate Compliance, Leadership Development, Advanced Real Estate Lending

BANKING: CHIEF INFORMATION OFFICER/ CHIEF TECHNOLOGY OFFICER

This is an excellent CIO/CTO résumé because it clearly describes the two major functions of a CIO—increased performance and lower cost.

Jason Drake
Address   Cell #   E-mail

SUMMARY

Recognized business leader with over 20 years of experience, including C-level IT accomplishments in companies ranging from early-stage start-ups to fast-growth Fortune 1000 corporations. Deep industry expertise in banking, software product development, technology services, financial services, and IT management. Performance with abilities in building and managing organizations and operations. **History of increasing IT Department performance as well as lowering costs.**

PROFESSIONAL EXPERIENCE

Vice President/CIO, Everest Bank Holding   Oct 2008–Present

Currently responsible for both the IT strategic vision and tactical support for all corporate IT functions in 20 locations, across several states, for Everest Bank, Salute Bank KC, and Center Mortgage, a subsidiary of Everest Bank, with assets approaching $500 million.

Significant Measurable Accomplishments

Reduced IT costs, resulting in a bottom-line profit of **over 10%** to the bank.

Deployed a Windows 2003 Server-based Citrix infrastructure.

Consolidated multiple banks and **data centers** into one primary and secondary data center.

Deployed an enterprise-wide MPLS & Cisco VOIP telecommunications system.

Developed and deployed an entire set of corporate IT policies and procedures.

Deployed new Mortgage, Internet Banking, Mobile Banking, and Bill Payment systems.

Managed acquisition of Salute Bank, valued at $62 million in assets.

Managed acquisition of Wells State Bank, valued at $69 million in assets.

Received **exceptional ratings** from both FDIC and OCC on all IT-related audits.

IT Management: Responsible for the establishment of corporate IT strategic plans and objectives. Direct and control the activities of broad functional areas through the management team within the company having overall responsibility for planning, budgeting, implementing, and maintaining costs, methods, and employees. Increase operating efficiency and effectiveness and reduce total cost of ownership.

Operational Services: Provide optimal operation and readiness of the technology infrastructure and applications. Responsible for infrastructure availability, capacity management, change control, service level measurement, computer operations, storage management, applications processing, voice and data communications, and network and print services.

Chief Technology Officer, Metropolitan Bank Holdings   Apr 2004–Oct 2007

Responsible for the day-to-day direction, support, business, and technical operations of corporate IT, supporting a financial holding company and several community banks managing 500-plus million dollars in assets. Managed a multi-location entity comprising employees, independent contractors, and related parties, all of whom have complex communication, technology, and security requirements. Reported to the CEO and board of directors.

Significant Measurable Accomplishments

Year 1: Reduced IT costs 30% annually by deploying a Win. 2003 Server/Citrix based architecture. Consolidated multiple operations sites to create redundant primary and secondary data centers.

Year 2: Reduced WAN costs by over $250,000 by deploying a modern MPLS solution. **Reduced IT** and DP staffing headcount **over 30%** as a result of using more efficient technology.

Year 3: Reduced IT costs by over $2M by implementing a digital "Check21" image processing system. Saved additional expense by implementing a "paperless office" document imaging system.

Private Consultant   Jan 2002–Mar 2004

Served in various capacities as a consultant while delivering information technology-related project work and business related consulting for private companies and individuals.

Manager, KPMG LLP   Feb 2001–Dec 2001

As a member of the senior management team, primary role was to deliver the firm's suite of risk-mitigation products targeted at information technology users.

- Successfully managed engagements; delivered risk- and security-based products to key clients
- Identified and qualified leads; developed and presented proposals
- Planned, organized, and deployed the Dallas-area marketing and sales strategy for our practice

Consulting Manager, LANTE   Mar 1999–Nov 2000

Founded Lante office in Dallas; served as a manager in the delivery management practice that specialized in helping clients to define and build e-markets. Successful IPO.

- Successfully managed and delivered $20M+ of services for southern region
- Provided guidance and direction for e-business strategy and e-commerce consulting
- Responsible for business development, client executive role, contract negotiation, recruiting

Consulting Manager, Tensor Information Systems   Sept 1998–Mar 1999

Served as technical sales manager for the hardware and software integration and delivery practice.

- Responsible for business development, client executive role, contract negotiation, recruiting
- Achieved both sales and revenue targets of $4.6M in sales and revenue of $2.3M
- Company held spot (176) on Inc. 500 fastest-growing consulting firms

EDUCATION

Northeastern State University of Oklahoma, BS in Collegiate Study (Computer Science, Business Management)

HUMAN RESOURCES: CORPORATE TRAINER

This candidate uses a paragraph style, with all the necessary information in an easy-to-read format.

GAYLE G. ELLEVEN

Address   Phone #   Cell #   E-mail

PROFESSIONAL EXPERIENCE

PlainsCapital Corporation, Dallas, Texas   2003–Present

A $3 billion financial services company with 1500 employees and more than 100 offices nationwide

Corporate Training Manager 2004–Present

Responsible for implementing company-wide training initiatives geared toward integrating and retaining employees, performance improvement, customer service, and development of managers and supervisors. Supervise two full-time training and organizational development specialists; manage corporate training budget; oversee coordination of annual corporate culture events.

HR Generalist 2003–Present

Serve as a resource for employees and management, providing assistance with employee questions concerning all aspects of human resources. In addition to providing ongoing customer service, key projects include redesigning employee handbook; designing and writing content for the human resources section of employee intranet site; developing officer evaluation process; working with director to develop goal-setting process for tracking defined incentives.

Bimbo Bakeries USA, Fort Worth, Texas   2002–2003

A $1.2 billion baking company with over 9000 employees throughout the U.S.; a division of Grupo Bimbo, an international leader with a presence in 14 different countries

Manager of Professional Development

Managed corporate training initiatives for central region of organization; facilitated supervisor training program for mid-level management; coordinated and delivered change management training and initiatives; managed employee communications committees.

Carter & Burgess, Inc., Fort Worth, Texas   2000–2002

A $300M national architecture / engineering / construction management firm with 2500 employees in 34 offices nationwide

HR Consultant—Employee Relations & Training

Designed, developed, and delivered training to employees at all levels within the organization: conducted training needs assessments; consulted subject-matter experts in the design and delivery of process training; evaluated training effectiveness and determined ROI; interfaced with external training providers and coordinated off-site training programs; implemented compliance training. Coached supervisors and HR field managers on areas of management, company policy and procedures; analyzed HR processes and made recommendations for improvement.

- Partnered with executive management to develop project-management training for architects and engineers.

- Worked with supervisor to revise employee handbook.

Daydots International, Fort Worth, Texas   1998–2000
A $22 million manufacturer and distributor of food safety products

Training Specialist/Human Resource Representative

Designed, developed, and delivered company training initiatives to incorporate comprehensive new employee orientation program, monthly supervisor training, employee safety program, and team-based employee work-skills program. Also coached supervisors in areas of corrective action, professional development, and human resource policies; interpreted and enforced company policy; tracked employee attendance; and administered monthly recognition program.

- Collaborated with supervisor to develop and implement three-tiered performance appraisal process.
- Introduced and spearheaded 360° review process for upper management.
- Became certified ServSafe trainer, a food safety training program geared toward the food-service industry; customized the program to deliver internally in an effort to reinforce the mission of the organization.

The University of North Texas, Denton, Texas   1996–1997
The fourth largest university in the state of Texas

Assistant Director for Student Employment Services

Coordinated off-campus jobs for UNT's student population of 25,000, acting as a liaison between students and area employers.

- Organized four part-time job fairs throughout the academic year.
- Managed four-hour, customer service training program, CASA (Creating a Student Attitude), for student employee population of 3,800; supervised and mentored eleven CASA trainers; marketed program to supervisors, tracked employee participation; provided customized classes upon request.

COMMUNITY INVOLVEMENT

Leadership Arts Program, North Texas Business Community for the Arts, 2005–2006
Member, American Society for Training & Development, Fort Worth Chapter, 2000–2003
Guest Speaker, Student Leadership Excellence Program, TCU, April 1999
Team Building Facilitator, National Association of College and University Food Professionals, August 1998
Keynote Speaker, Resident Assistant Fall Training, Texas A&M University, August 1998
Putting Your Best Foot Forward: A Course on Business Etiquette & Interpersonal Skills, June 1997

EDUCATION AND TRAINING

Master of Science, Applied Technology, Training & Development, May 1996
    University of North Texas
Bachelor of Arts, Journalism, Marketing & Communication Studies, May 1993
    University of North Texas
PHR Certification, Society for Human Resource Management, December 2000–December 2003
UNT Service Advantage Facilitator & Trainer, 1994–1997

HUMAN RESOURCES MANAGER

The bullet-point style here is so easy to glance at and get a summary view in 15 to 20 seconds. Also, the candidate shows great longevity in her jobs, which is important to employers.

NANCY HUFFMAN, SPHR
Address   Phone #   Cell #

HUMAN RESOURCES PROFILE

HR professional with a proven track record of contributing to organizational improvement. Meets strategic and operational objectives utilizing experience in banking/financial services, hands-on HR experience, strong management skills, and effective relationships established across all levels of the organization.

CORE COMPETENCIES

Recruitment/Retention Practices • Benefits and Compensation • Performance Evaluation Communication Strategies • Employee Relations • Compliance (EEOC / FLSA / FMLA)

PROFESSIONAL EXPERIENCE

Town North Bank, Dallas, TX

TNB Card Services / TNB Nevada

$1 billion financial institution in the Dallas/Ft. Worth Metroplex, which consists of two divisions: an independent bank and a nationwide credit/debit card processor with offices in Texas and Nevada.

Human Resources Manager   2005–Present

- Interact with business units (bank, mortgage warehouse, card services, IT, and investments) to align their business objectives with HR deliverables (i.e., staffing, training, and employee relations)

- Collaborate with Executive Management, serving as a member of the Strategic Planning Committee responsible for defining corporate goals and objectives

- Consult with managers, supervisors, and employees on interpretation of personnel policies, career development, compensation, and benefit programs

- Supervise a HR Generalist along with indirect supervision of Payroll Specialist and HR Assistant

- Ensure compliance with all applicable laws and regulations

- Manage the recruitment process, consisting of screening and interviewing exempt and nonexempt personnel; make recommendations on hiring decisions and starting salaries; conduct employee orientation and manage the onboarding process

- Manage disciplinary and termination activities to reduce risks associated with employment decisions. Primary contact for TWC and EEOC charges.

- Administer salary ranges and job grades within the company to ensure internal and external equity

- Compile and analyze HR metrics to manage workforce data such as turnover, headcount, recruitment costs, and demographic profiles

- In conjunction with HR Director, administer retirement, executive compensation, and affirmative action plans

- Instrumental in opening and providing ongoing HR support to office in Nevada

- Actively participated in the implementation of an applicant tracking and time and attendance system

HR Generalist   1997–2005

- Effectively interacted with department managers and supervisors to ensure consistent HR delivery to the organization (i.e., staffing, performance management, compensation, employee relations, benefits, FMLA administration)

- Primary recruiter for nonexempt and exempt positions; conducted employment verifications, background searches, drug screens

- Conducted new employee orientation and managed the onboarding process

- Conducted or assisted with various training programs (i.e., Giving Recognition, Performance Management, Effective Interviewing, Writing Job Descriptions, The Family & Medical Leave Act, Implementation of Time & Attendance and Applicant Tracking Systems)

- Member of HR project team that created and implemented a new employee orientation and employee recognition program.

- Promoted to Human Resources Manager/Sr. Vice President in 2005

Town North Bank

Loan Administration Manager   1989–1997

Supervised the loan and credit departments consisting of a 7-member staff providing support to the bank's lending team servicing installment, commercial, SBA, mortgage, and student loans.

- Managed all aspects of loan operations, which includes document preparation, loan servicing, account reconciliation, compliance, credit analysis, preparation of loan packets and various reports for Board of Directors meetings and primary contact for loan-related internal audits and OCC bank exams

- Implemented an automated loan closing system (LaserPro)

- Restructured loan closing procedures and provided training to lending staff

- Refined loan audit procedures and implemented online exception tracking system

- Promoted to Vice President within 18 months

Other employment: Career progressions at various independent banks in the lending, credit, and lobby operations.

EDUCATION & CERTIFICATION

B.A. in Psychology, Pan American University; SPHR certification

PROFESSIONAL ORGANIZATIONS

Society of Human Resource Professionals, Dallas HR

Dallas Banking Professionals Group

HUMAN RESOURCES MANAGER

This résumé is good because it is easy to skim in 15 to 20 seconds, and the reader immediately sees the candidate's positions, tenure at each job, and duties and responsibilities without having to read paragraphs, which generally take longer.

SHARON A. GOLDSTEIN, PHR
Address   Phone #   Cell #   E-mail

PROFESSIONAL PROFILE

Results-oriented Human Resource Generalist and Benefits Manager with over 20 years' experience. A dedicated professional and self-starter, with strong interpersonal skills, able to identify, develop, and implement strategies consistent with an organization's goals.

PROFESSIONAL EXPERIENCE

GeorgeCo, Inc. (Construction Materials Supplier)   2000–Present

Human Resources Manager

- ▪ Built the Human Resources Division for 5 corporate subsidiaries totaling 170 employees

- ▪ Direct all Human Resource functions including:
  - Training managers in labor laws such as Harassment, Discrimination, FMLA, Wage and Hour, Disciplinary and Counseling Actions
  - Welfare and Pension Benefit Administration for self-insured and fully-insured Medical/Dental Plans, Cafeteria Plan, and 401(k) Profit Sharing Plan
  - Weekly Payroll Processing for Hourly and Salaried Employees with ADP payroll
  - Overseeing Annual Performance Evaluations for all personnel
  - Recruiting for exempt and non-exempt positions and performing initial interviews
  - OSHA, Workers Compensation, and Safety Program compliance

- ▪ Advise management and staff on employee relations issues and provide guidance on resolutions

- ▪ Develop and implement policies and procedures ensuring compliance with federal and state labor regulations

Specific Skills/Achievements

- ▪ Managed one-person HR Department with multiple state locations
- ▪ Conducted Conflict Investigations and recommended Resolutions
- ▪ Established Paid Time Off (PTO) policy
- ▪ Initiated Performance Evaluation and Coaching Program
- ▪ Developed and conducted HR training for up to 20 managers
- ▪ Launched Employee Assistance Program (EAP) and supplemental benefits
- ▪ Negotiated with brokers, vendors, and third-party administrators
- ▪ Initiated Employee Satisfaction Surveys and Benefit Summaries

- Interpreted and monitored federal and state labor laws for 3 states (TX, CO, MI)
- Analyzed overtime costs and reduced payroll expenses
- Designed and updated job descriptions, organization charts, HR forms

Smith, Underwood & Perkins   1997–2000
  Legal Assistant
- Researched pension/welfare plan issues for ERISA/Estate Planning Attorney
- Drafted plan documents, including adoption agreements, amendments, and client correspondence
- Provided technical support in the interpretation of plan design issues

NationsBank N.A. (Currently Bank of America)   1992–1997
  ERISA Team Leader, Assistant Vice President
- Provided technical and support services for clients utilizing the NationsBank Master Plan Document
- Prepared adoption agreements, amendments, and summary plan descriptions, ensuring compliance with ERISA and IRS regulations, and maintaining tax qualified status with IRS submissions

  Trust Officer
- Transferred employee benefit trust accounts to successor trustees, ensuring smooth transitions of asset delivery
- Processed plan terminations, verified compliance with plan documents, coordinated and processed final distributions to participants

  401(k) Plan Supervisor
- Supervised administration of the 401(k) Plan for NationsBank associates, verified compliance with Plan document, ERISA, IRS, and Department of Labor

EDUCATION/AFFILIATIONS
Bachelor of Science, Communications, University of Texas at Austin
Professional in Human Resources (PHR) Certification
Legal Assistant Certification, Southern Methodist University
Member of Society for Human Resource Management (SHRM)

SALES: RETAIL MANAGER

All the necessary information appears here in bulleted format, making this a reader-friendly résumé.

JOHN FRANKLIN

Address   Phone #   Cell #

EXECUTIVE PROFILE

13 years of experience planning and directing retail functions to meet time-critical deadlines as a multi-unit manager. Combined dynamic organizational and communication skills with the ability to independently multitask, plan and direct demanding regional and district operations, and devise complex schedules. Trusted advisor, liaison, and leader.

CAREER ACHIEVEMENTS

- Managed as many as 24 stores with total sales of over $30 million.
- While at Wal-Mart, was placed in charge of the computer systems and found a glitch in the system, corrected it, and saved the store over $100,000.00 in shrink.
- Trained and promoted over 15 associates to managers, and 3 managers to district managers.
- In my last position, supervising a store of 140,000 sq. ft., improved store standards from a C level to an A level, with increased sales and outstanding customer service.

QUALIFICATION HIGHLIGHTS

- Strong leader and focus on hiring and training the right people with attention to sales and customer service.
- Experienced in all aspects of computers and was in charge of the entire store systems at Wal-Mart. Proficient at Excel and Word.
- Multitasking is one of my strong points while handling multiple locations in as many as 3 states.
- Hard worker, dedicated leader willing to do whatever is needed to complete the job.

PROFESSIONAL BACKGROUND

General Manager   2007 to Present
Uptown Garden Supply—Frisco, TX
Responsible for all aspects of day-to-day operations of a 140,000 sq. ft. store, including hiring, training, merchandise display, customer service, sales and payroll budgeting, P&L controls, employee counseling and evaluation.

- Improved the store from a C level to an A level in 3 months while also improving customer service and sales.
- Improved the freight to floor process from over 100 pallets of excess freight when I arrived to completing all trucks daily.
- Increased sales by 11% while improving store standards, in stock and customer service.

Regional Manager   2002 to 2007
Marketing Plus—Frisco, TX
Supervised 12 to 14 stores with sales in excess of $28 million with around 170 employees. Responsible for hiring, firing, training, store openings, P&L controls, merchandise plans, sales, shrink, and payroll control.

- Helped train 3 regional managers and opened 9 stores. Responsible for communication and implementation of all company programs and changes to those programs and policies.

- Developed many Excel spreadsheets to help in planning and monitoring payroll and scheduling of stores. Involved on a daily basis with helping schedule the stores for proper coverage within the payroll guidelines of the company, including budgeting sales and payroll to maximize profitability. Monitored Profit and Loss statements and monitored the properties to schedule maintenance as needed.

- Sales in region increased by 3% while company sales decreased by 9.5%; also controlled payroll and expenses to under company goals. Involved in marketing our merchandise to the local communities by identifying their needs and methods needed to promote our items directly to the customers.

- Strong focus on training to improve sales, merchandise presentation, and retention of employees.

District Manager   2000 to 2002
Dollar Plus Stores—Carlsbad, NM
Responsible for all daily operations of 14 stores with 150 employees, including hiring, training, terminations, sales, payroll, P&L and shrink controls, identifying new locations and store openings, inventories, store standards, and customer service.

- Opened new stores, hired and trained managers for their locations, monitored the properties' maintenance needs, and scheduled repairs as needed.

- Conducted inventories and controlled shrink to under company goals.

- Focused on training to improve sales, store standards, and customer service. Involved in budgeting each store's payroll and scheduling daily to control expenses. Monitored corporate programs and changes to those programs to ensure all stores were in line with company guidelines.

District Manager   1994 to 2000
Carollton Manufacturing—Carlsbad, NM
Responsible for all aspects of daily operations of a 24-store district employing about 230 associates, including hiring, training, evaluations, terminations, monitoring P&Ls, sales and shrink controls, opened stores, store standards, and customer service.

- Increased sales consistently while controlling expenses and payroll by monitoring schedules compared to sales.

- In charge of locating and opening many new stores from an empty building to grand opening. Monitored store maintenance and scheduled needed repairs.

- Hired and trained many managers, as well as 2 of them to district manager. Responsible for all aspects of hiring, training, and termination of employees as needed.

EDUCATION
Associate Degree, Business Management, University of Texas
Completed Management Development Seminars I, II, and III with Wal-Mart

SALES: IT SOFTWARE AND SERVICES SALESPERSON

This is a creative résumé, but not so far out of the box that it won't get read. The idea of graphic logos works only if the logos are for recognizable companies. The identification with the logos says to the reader, "I've been associated with some well-recognized and prestigious organizations; therefore I am a successful person." The people who read Ron's résumé will recognize these companies. Even before they read it, they will note he has been associated with excellent organizations. Ron always sent this in PDF format so the logos were certain to come across clearly.

Ron Pecunia
Address   Phone #   Cell #   E-mail

EXPERIENCE

2007–Present

    **Develo Software Oil & Gas, Senior Account Executive—
Las Colinas, TX**
Sponsored into **Develo's Oil & Gas** team by SVP, Michael Schulze. Penetrated net-new Develo O&G targets as well as led Develo's software and Develo services pursuits. Installed Develo O&G customers globally and across upstream, midstream, and downstream segments. Certified in Develo Oil & Gas Business Process & Organizations. **130%** of quota in **2007, 142%** of quota in **2008, 125%** of quota in **2009, 130%** of quota in **2010.**

2006–2007

    Dvelo.org Services, Regional Sales Director—Las Colinas, TX
Recruited into newly created, dedicated services sales role for SW region. Surfaced net-new Dvelo.org Services opportunities and closed a significant, global, highly competitive Oil & Gas engagement against IBM, Deloitte, Capgemini, and BearingPoint. Dvelo.org provides implementation services for Develo Software. **180%** of quota for the year.

2002–2005

    **Crowdtilt Social Fundraising Platform, Vice President,
National Alliances Sales/Marketing—Dallas, TX**
Achieved 126% of plan and highest utilization in company history within first 12 months. Drove attainment of PREFERRED partner status, achieved 300% revenue growth. National role covering 18 Directors of Business Development across the dominant industries.

1997–2002

**The Job Search Solution, Sales Director—
Dallas, TX**

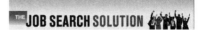

Top performer and sales director for America's only online job search program; five years straight, with 35 new deals, $7.5 million in software license revenue and $18 million in professional services revenue produced. Led regional sales team to record results. Averaged **140%** of quota all five years.

1996–1997

**Babich & Associates Placement and Recruitment Firm,
Recruiter—Dallas, TX**

Rookie of the Year. Booked and collected $350,000 in fees.

1994–1995

Austin Leather and Décor, Owner/Self-Employed—Austin, TX

Successful retail business startup—from business plan to startup to profitable, ongoing operation and ultimate sale.

1991–1993

George Group, Inc., Director of Regional Operations—Dallas, TX

Secured several business transformation engagements and over $3.5 million in professional services fees. Transition from services delivery/management to services sales.

1985–1991

Anderson Consulting, Manager—New Orleans, LA

Rapid career advancement. Managed, led, or participated in over 13 engagements ranging from IT systems to manufacturing productivity, reengineering, and continuous improvement projects.

EDUCATION

1980–1985 Louisiana State University, Baton Rouge, LA
Bachelor of Science in Mechanical Engineering, Senior Project Leader, Dean's list.

INSIDE SALES

This résumé of Steve Weiss is a good one for inside sales. It communicates the idea that he has done inside sales, account management, and business development. His summary is effective because he associates his successes with the companies he has worked for. He clearly explains what the companies do so that whoever reads the résumé will understand exactly what he sold. His accomplishments are highlighted in bold type.

STEVEN WEISS

Address   Phone #   Cell #

OBJECTIVE	Seeking a professional sales and/or management career position that will use my experience and talents in an organization offering commensurate opportunities.
SUMMARY	**Executive sales and account management professional,** offering an exemplary record of top sales within the enterprise software industry.

- Was **130% of quota** in 1999 and **197% of quota** in 2000 for i2 Technologies. Responsible for over $3 million in sales each of those years.
- Made **President's Club** every year while at Infor and i2.
- Achieved **#1 ranking** at Netopia for 2003 and 2004.
- Achieved **112% of quota** at Mindflow in 2005.
- Achieved **137% of quota** in 2006, **117% of quota** in 2007, and **119% of quota** in 2008 at Infor.
- Consultative Sales Pro, awarded the highest honors bestowed upon a select group of sales professionals by being invited to **President's Club** for two consecutive years at i2 Technologies.
- Extensive knowledge of selling high-end enterprise software such as Customer Relationship Management (CRM), Supply Chain Management (SCM), and Supplier Relationship Management (SRM), with deals in the range of **$500K to $300M.**
- **A to Z client project-management** experience. Recognized for abilities to cultivate profitable business relations, coordinate complex special projects, and manage diverse selling packages and contracts.

EXPERIENCE
2006 to 2009   **Infor, Dallas, TX—Strategic Account Executive**

- Identified areas of opportunity in Business Intelligence and valued ideas directly related to C-level and user audiences; also identified as well as built buying-and-decision-making contact chart.
- Served as Strategic Account Executive on a multi-member team for the West and Central regions, competing against companies such as SAP, Oracle, IBM.
- Created and delivered presentations and product demonstrations using Web-based remote demonstration technology for BI product sets; effectively built and executed a territory plan to maximize revenue; proactively called to identify prospects across a defined geography in order to achieve revenue targets.

2005 to 2006   **Mindflow, Dallas, TX—National Account Executive**

- Mindflow provides strategic sourcing software solutions to Fortune 1000 accounts.
- Served as lead salesperson for the North Central region, competing against companies such as Emptoris, SAP, Ariba, and Procuri.
- Accountable for cold-calling accounts with revenues of $500M to $100B, uncovering opportunities for strategic sourcing solutions.
- Used **state-of-the-art strategies** to get to the CEO 100% of the time.

2003 to 2005   **Netopia, Dallas, TX—National Account Executive**

- Netopia is the current leader in enterprise systems management for the government, hospitality, and discrete manufacturing industries.
- Managed South Central region consisting of many Fortune 500 companies.
- Served as lead salesperson, selling value-based solutions that help organizations maximize shareholder value.
- Was **126% of quota** in 2003 and **118% of quota** in 2004, achieving #1 ranking in both years.

1998 to 2002   **i2 Technologies, Dallas, TX—Software Sales Account Executive**

- i2 is the industry leader in Customer Relationship Management (CRM), Supply Chain Management (SCM), and Supplier Relationship Management.
- Served as lead salesperson on a multi-member team selling and marketing enterprise software. Company maintains position as #1 supply chain software manufacturer in the world, in direct competition with software companies such as Oracle, SAP, JD Edwards, PeopleSoft, and Manugistics. Served as outside field representative.
- Accountable for cold-calling within a 6-state area, opening doors to new business prospects. Researched company dollar earnings and applied a full range of resourceful techniques to secure a presentation to the top decision maker.
- Integral team player throughout the sales process, serving as key client representative from demonstration, client needs analysis, and software installation to sales close.
- Managed forecasting, advance team scheduling, and planning agenda. Tracked sales project throughout the life cycle of the account.
- Recipient of every award eligible for in this position. Selected as **Representative of the Quarter** (2nd quarter 1999 and 1st quarter, 2000). Member of **President's Club** for 1999 and 2000 (honor set aside for the top 200 sales representatives worldwide, in competition with 6,000 employees).
- Honored as Department's **#1 Sales Representative**. Recognized as 1 of the top 20 employees in the entire company for the year 2000. Selected for VIP sales trips and honors.

EDUCATION   **Bachelor of Arts in Finance,** 1994
University of Arizona at Tucson

REGIONAL SALES MANAGER

Very concise, detailed, and exudes success! Sales manager résumés *need* to have high impact. They need to reflect *performance*. The ability to lead is measured in *results*. John's results are obvious.

JOHN DAVENPORT
Address   Phone #   Cell #   E-mail

Relentless. Highly Intelligent. Charismatic. Energetic. Dynamic. Proven. A personality that radiates enthusiasm even under the most stressful situations. A senior sales executive with a twenty-year accomplished career spanning domestic and international experience.

EDUCATION

BS, Economics, United States Naval Academy, Annapolis, MD, 1987
MBA, Mendoza School of Business, University of Notre Dame, South Bend, IN, 2008

EXPERIENCE

BMC Software   **Oct 08–Present**
   Regional Sales Manager. Lead Regional Sales Team selling Business Services Management software to enterprise-size customers in NE, KS, MO, OK, AR.

   ▪ FY10 Q3 105% Year to Date (Oct–Dec 09) Projected to Exceed Annual Plan in Q3

   ▪ FY10 Q2   35% Year to Date (Jul–Sep 09)

   ▪ FY10 Q1   7% Year to Date (Apr–Jun 09)

   ▪ FY09 Q4 102% Special Quota (Jan–Mar 09)

Cognos, an IBM Company   **Aug 06–Jul 08**
   Regional Sales Manager. Led a Regional Sales Team selling Business Intelligence (BI) and Financial Performance Management (FPM) software. Key responsibilities included managing complex sales cycles, interacting with C-level executives, training and developing sales personnel. Identified as Cognos Top 10% personnel. Transfer of employment from Cognos to IBM on April 1, 2008. FY07 to FY08 Regional growth rate of 42%.

   ▪ FY09 Q2 (Apr–Jun 08)   93% of Quota (Region re-org and IBM Fiscal Q2)

   ▪ FY08 Q4 (Dec 07–Feb 08 plus Mar)   101% of Quota

   ▪ FY08 Q3 (Sept–Nov 07)   92% of Quota

   ▪ FY08 Q2 (Jun–Aug 07)   103% of Quota

   ▪ FY08 Q1 (Mar–May 07)   96% of Quota

   ▪ FY07 Q4 (Dec–Feb 07)   40% of Quota

   ▪ FY07 Q3 (Sept–Nov 06)   27% of Quota

   ▪ FY07 Q2 (Jun–Aug 06)   0% of Quota (Started last month of Q2, Aug 06)

Oracle **Sept 04–Aug 06**

Oracle Regional Sales Manager. Led a Regional Sales Team selling software applications consisting of Customer Relationship Management (CRM) and Business Analytics. Hired, trained, and fielded a team of 6 Senior CRM Application Sales Managers to start new Oracle CRM Region post Siebel Acquisition with Regional quota of $16 Million. FY06 at 186% of Quota, FY05 at 105% of Quota (partial year).

Siebel Systems Regional Sales Manager. Siebel Systems was acquired by Oracle. Hired, trained, and fielded a team of 8 Field Territory Managers responsible for selling full line of Oracle Siebel CRM Customer Facing Applications to the Small to Midsize Business (SMB) Market in the Region of the 16 Central US States, as well as the whole of Canada on a $12M Software License only quota. FY05 at 92% of Quota (from standing start as a newly created Region).

Clarify, a Division of Amdocs Inc **Sept 00–Sept 04**

General Manager, Asia Pacific. Sydney, Australia (Sept 02 to Sept 04). Directed Sales and Support Matrix Organization in Asia Pacific Region, selling Customer Relationship Management (CRM). FY04 at 126% of Quota. FY03 at 86% of Quota (compared to FY02 at 62% under previous General Manager).

Director of Sales. Dallas, Texas (Jan 02 to Sept 02). Responsible for selling Clarify software and services with significant focus on the Southwestern Bell Corporation (now AT&T). Selected to attend Amdocs Business School, Raanana, Israel, Feb-Mar 2002.

Strategic Account Manager. Dallas, Texas, (Sept 00 to Jan 02). Responsible for strategic accounts in Western half of US in mid-tier telecommunication account base. Identified as "Top Talent" retention and fast-track potential at Nortel. This time period encompassed Clarify's acquisition by Nortel and Amdocs Inc.

Vitria Technology Corporation **Oct 98–Sept 00**

Sales Representative. Sold Enterprise Application Integration (EAI) software technology in the Telecom sector. FY99 at 106% of Quota.

Parametric Technology Corporation **Apr 95–Oct 98**

District Sales Manager and Sales Representative. Led District Sales Team in selling high-technology mechanical engineering software. Primary duty as Sales Rep was to sell the Pro/Engineer product line and modules. Promoted to management after four quarters as a sales rep.

Zoll Medical **May 92–Apr 95**

Sales Representative. Responsibility for selling defibrillator and noninvasive pacemaker capital equipment into hospitals, fire departments, and medical flight services. Achieved and surpassed all sales objectives. Rookie of the Year, FY93.

MILITARY SERVICE

United States Marine Corps **May 87–May 92**

Officer Selection Officer, 8th Marine District, Oklahoma State University, Stillwater, OK
Field Artillery Officer, 5th Battalion, 11th Marines, 1st Marine Division, 29 Palms, CA

SALES MANAGER

The two résumés of Chris Malick that follow are of value because one could be used for a sales management position while the other could be for a sales position. First, the sales management résumé.

CHRISTOPHER D. MALICK
Address   Phone #   Cell #   E-mail

Vice President Sales Top-producing manager with over 20 years of experience in high-tech data communications and enterprise solutions.

EXPERIENCE

Vice President—Sales and Professional Services   1993–Present
General Datatech, LP, Houston, TX
A Gold-level Cisco data communications reseller

Personal production: 60% of performance was services contracts for consulting and outsourcing services:

Year	Quota	Performance	Percentage of Quota
2008	$ 6M	$ 8M	133%
2007	$ 6M	$ 8M	133%
2006	$ 6M	$ 7M	117%
2005	$ 6M	$ 8M	133%
2004	$ 6M	$ 9M	150%
2003	$ 6M	$ 8M	133%
2002	$ 8M	$ 10M	125%
2001	$ 8M	$ 13M	162%
2000	$ 7M	$ 14M	200%

- Key wins include Verizon, SBC, Archon/Goldman Sachs, JC Penney, and Pilgrims Pride Chicken

- Assembled and led 15-member team responsible for delivery services on contracts comprising $40M in service revenue since 1993

Extensive oil and gas experience with clients including Anadarko, Apache, Atwood, Baker Hughes, BHP, BJ Services, BP, Cameron, Caprock, Cheniere, Chevron Phillips, Chevron Texaco, Chicago Bridge, Conoco, Cooper, Devon, Diamond, Dril Quip, Dynegy, Eastham Enterprises, El Paso, Enbridge, Englobal, Enterprise Products, EOG, ExxonMobil, Global Santa Fe, Grant Prideco, Halliburton, Helmerich Payne, Horizon, Huntsman, Hydril Tenaris, Input Output, Kinder Morgan, Kirby, Koch, Lyondell Citgo, Marathon, Mariner, Nabors, Natco, National Oilwell, Newfield, Noble, Occidental, Oceaneering, Oil States, Parker, Plains, Powell, Pride, Quanex, Quanta, Reliant, Schlumberger, Shell, Smith, Spectra, Suez, Sungard, Sunoco, Swift, Transocean, Vetco Gray, and Weatherford.

- Hired to staff and manage fast-growing network and e-solution practice based on the ability to prospect, negotiate, and close service contracts; provide strategic vision; and execute broad-based marketing initiatives.

- Composed performance and action plan with 8 sales representatives and managed sales funnel for team. Utilized Miller Heiman account planning system.

- Demonstrated Cisco, HP, Micromuse, Netscout, Network Associates, Business Objects, and other offerings and led technical review meetings on architecture, security, and application hosting for large telecom and enterprise customers.

- Established reseller and business partner agreements with Cisco, HP, Micromuse, Netscout, Network Associates, Oracle, Sun, Compaq, AT&T, Qwest, NTT Verio, Siemens, and Agile Software and managed projects on joint engagements.

- Managed company tax reporting, finance, invoicing, purchasing, AP, AR, GL, and payroll with external CPA support.

- Have extensive experience partnering with channel managers and sales teams for Cisco TX sales offices.

Branch Manager—Sales and Marketing   1985–1993
   IBM Corp., Atlanta, GA

Year	Quota	Performance	Percentage of Quota
1993	$ 120M	$ 144M	120%
1992	$ 110M	$ 132M	120%
1991	$ 100M	$ 125M	125%
1990	$ 30M	$ 36M	120%
1989	$ 28M	$ 35M	125%

- Earned 100% Club from 1985 to 1989 as a marketing representative and Golden Circle (IBM's highest sales honors) in 1986 and 1988

- Participated in IBM marketing task forces and initiatives with IBM Marketing headquarters, which was also in Atlanta, GA

Contacted and contracted with resellers and business partners as local channel manager for Atlanta. Above group quotas are as Branch Manager from 1991 to 1993 and as a Marketing Manager from 1989 and 1990.

Engineer—Dynamics Group   1981–1983
   Boeing Corp., Ridley Park, PA
   Performed computer modeling of aircraft and spacecraft as member of dynamics group, conducted wind tunnel testing, programmed extensively in FORTRAN and BASIC.

EDUCATION / SKILLS

Master of Business Administration (MBA), 1985, University of North Carolina, Chapel Hill
   Major: Finance and Marketing; GPA: Not applicable, pass/fail grading

Bachelor of Science and Engineering (BSME), 1981, Princeton University, Princeton, NJ
   Major: Mechanical and Aerospace Engineering; GPA: 3.0

IBM Marketing Education (Base 1 to 4), 1985

Cisco Certified Design Associate, 1998

Proficient with Microsoft Office Suite (Excel, Word, PowerPoint, Access)

STRAIGHT SALES

This version of Chris's résumé is for regular sales positions.

Christopher D. Malick

Address   Phone #   Cell #   E-mail

Top-producing salesperson with over 20 years of experience in high-tech data communications and enterprise solutions.

EXPERIENCE

General Datatech, LP, a Gold-level Cisco data communications reseller   **1993–Present**

60% of performance was services contracts for consulting and outsourcing services

Year	Quota	Performance	Percentage of Quota
2008	$ 6M	$ 8M	133%
2007	$ 6M	$ 8M	133%
2006	$ 6M	$ 7M	117%
2005	$ 6M	$ 8M	133%
2004	$ 6M	$ 9M	150%
2003	$ 6M	$ 8M	133%
2002	$ 8M	$ 10M	125%
2001	$ 8M	$ 13M	162%
2000	$ 7M	$ 14M	200%

- Key wins include Verizon, SBC, Archon/Goldman Sachs, JC Penney, and Pilgrims Pride Chicken

- Assembled and led 15-member team responsible for delivery services on contracts comprising $40M in service revenue since 1993

Extensive oil and gas experience with clients including Anadarko, Apache, Atwood, Baker Hughes, BHP, BJ Services, BP, Cameron, Caprock, Cheniere, Chevron Phillips, Chevron Texaco, Chicago Bridge, Conoco, Cooper, Devon, Diamond, Dril Quip, Dynegy, Eastham Enterprises, El Paso, Enbridge, Englobal, Enterprise Products, EOG, ExxonMobil, Global Santa Fe, Grant Prideco, Halliburton, Helmerich Payne, Horizon, Huntsman, Hydril Tenaris, Input Output, Kinder Morgan, Kirby, Koch, Lyondell Citgo, Marathon, Mariner, Nabors, Natco, National Oilwell, Newfield, Noble, Occidental, Oceaneering, Oil States, Parker, Plains, Powell, Pride, Quanex, Quanta, Reliant, Schlumberger, Shell, Smith, Spectra, Suez, Sungard, Sunoco, Swift, Transocean, Vetco Gray, and Weatherford.

- Hired to staff and manage fast-growing network and e-solution practice based on the ability to prospect, negotiate, and close service contracts; provide strategic vision; and execute broad-based marketing initiatives.

- Demonstrated Cisco, HP, Micromuse, Netscout, Network Associates, Business Objects, and other offerings and led technical review meetings on architecture, security, and application hosting for large telecom and enterprise customers.

- Established reseller and business partner agreements with Cisco, HP, Micromuse, Netscout, Network Associates, Oracle, Sun, Compaq, AT&T, Qwest, NTT Verio, Siemens, and Agile Software and managed projects on joint engagements.

IBM Corp., Sales and Marketing, Atlanta, GA   1985–1993

Year	Quota	Performance	Percentage of Quota
1993	$ 120M	$ 144M	120%
1992	$ 110M	$ 132M	120%
1991	$ 100M	$ 125M	125%
1990	$ 30M	$ 36M	120%
1989	$ 28M	$ 35M	125%

- Earned 100% Club from 1985 to 1989 as a marketing representative and Golden Circle (IBM's highest sales honors) in 1986 and 1988

- Participated in IBM marketing task forces and initiatives with IBM Marketing headquarters, which was also in Atlanta, GA

Contacted and contracted with resellers and business partners as local channel manager for Atlanta. Above group quotas are as Branch Manager from 1991 to 1993 and as a Marketing Manager from 1989 and 1990.

Boeing Corp., Ridley Park, PA   1981–1983
Engineer, Dynamics Group
Performed computer modeling of aircraft and spacecraft as member of dynamics group, conducted wind tunnel testing, programmed extensively in FORTRAN and BASIC.

EDUCATION / SKILLS

Master of Business Administration (MBA), 1985, University of North Carolina, Chapel Hill
Major: Finance and Marketing; GPA: Not applicable, pass/fail grading

Bachelor of Science and Engineering (BSME), 1981, Princeton University, Princeton, NJ
Major: Mechanical and Aerospace Engineering; GPA: 3.0

IBM Marketing Education (Base 1 to 4), 1985

Cisco Certified Design Associate, 1998

Proficient with Microsoft Office Suite (Excel, Word, PowerPoint, Access)

MARKETING DIRECTOR

This résumé has a consistent format that makes it easy to read. The candidate includes a description of what each company does. Her job stability is great. She has an impressive list of professional recognitions.

KAREN CONWAY-GELFAND
Address   Phone #   Cell #   E-mail

MARKETING AND COMMUNICATIONS

Senior-level professional with demonstrated experience in integrated marketing, communications, and advertising campaign development designed to exceed P/L and traffic objectives. Skilled in managing and leveraging brand equity. Expert at creating and executing consumer programs that deliver a high ROI.

- Strategic Planning
- Marketing Communications
- Public Relations

PROFESSIONAL EXPERIENCE

Marketing Projects, Dallas, TX   2007–Present
Levenson & Hill Advertising (events/promotions plan); Utay Jewelry (marketing plan/sales analysis); Harvest Partners (Park Lane consumer launch); American Cancer Society (Communications Dept. internal marketing plan); RENG (e-collateral); Schulte Real Estate Services (sales collateral)

The Mills Corporation, Dallas, TX   1997–2007
A $4B shopping center developer, owner, and manager of a diversified portfolio of 40+ retail and entertainment destinations in the U.S. and internationally totaling 48 million+ square feet of gross leasable area.

Vice President of Marketing   2003–2007
(Asst. Vice President, 1999–2003)
Developed the strategies of internal/external marketing communications programs for all new brands. Guided development of affinity program consisting of 200,000+ members. Directed 10+ advertising agencies, PR firms, and other vendors. Created and directed marketing budgets of up to $6M and €4M, including $1.5M in advertising. Led 7 direct/12 temporary field and corporate staff reports.

- Produced an average of 350,000 consumers over a 4-day opening with the execution of large-scale launches for Mills's 1.1 to 1.5 million-square-foot landmark brand centers.
- Planned and orchestrated 150+ events and functions for up to 10,000 participants, including promotions and contests designed to create awareness, drive traffic, and generate sales.

Senior Marketing Director   1999–2002
Supervised marketing of Potomac Mills (Washington, DC) and The Block
at Orange (Orange, CA).

Director of Marketing, Grapevine Mills   1997–1999
Led the grand opening and on-site marketing activities of a 1.5 million-square-foot value retail and entertainment center, directing a marketing, tourism, customer service, and Mills TV staff of 17.

- Drew 130,000 shoppers on opening day (160% over goal) by developing and executing a consumer-oriented marketing, advertising, and events campaign that produced double-digit sales projection increases for a significant number of retailers.

- Increased marketing program support by retailers and improved overall customer service to shoppers with the creation of company's first-ever portfolio-wide Service Excellence program.

West End Marketplace (Market Street Developers, Ltd.), Dallas, TX   **1986–1997**

Festival marketplace noted as one of the most innovative retail venues and attractions in the Southwest.

Director of Marketing and Public Relations

Directed and performed full range of marketing, advertising, and communications initiatives for the center. Administered an annual marketing budget of up to $600K; led staff of 5. Produced $1M+ worth of media exposure by creating and hosting major events and promotions.

PROFESSIONAL RECOGNITION

Canadian International Council of Shopping Centers (ICSC), 2005 Maple Leaf Award for Public Relations Excellence (Vaughan Mills)

Spanish AECC 2004 Award for the Best Launching Campaign (Madrid Xanadu)

EDUCATION

B.A.A.S, Marketing, Sociology, Applied Economics, University of North Texas at Dallas, TX

A.A., El Centro College, Dallas, TX

SALES AND MARKETING ANALYST

An easy-to-read résumé, with all highlights bulleted and detailed.

MARILYN CAMP, MBA

Address   **Cell #**   **E-mail**

SALES AND MARKETING ANALYST

Sales Analysis & Reporting ▪ Sales Forecasting ▪ Product Deployment
Expertise in RETAIL LINK Database for Wal-Mart ▪ Strategic Planning
Program Development/Management ▪ Client Relations ▪ Team Building/Leadership
Training/Education ▪ Demographic Research

PROFESSIONAL HISTORY

GRAM Industries, Coppell, TX   **2003–Present**

    Sr. Sales and Marketing Analyst

    GRAM Industries is a leading supplier of seasonal décor, lighting, and animated novelty gift products.

- Developed sales analysis templates in Excel and Access for use on Wal-Mart, Kmart, and Target accounts utilizing data from Retail Link, Workbench, and Partners on Line, which in turn provided timely, up-to-date revenue and sell-thru reporting to senior management.

- Improved product mix and profitability of account programs by recommending future buy quantities, price points, and store distribution.

- Increased senior management's awareness of industry by researching and distributing fashion/designing trends, consumer behavior data, and economic indices.

- Made Gemmy Industries a "Go to Vendor" by being appointed by Wal-Mart buyer to write store orders for key product lines utilizing a linear regression template. Trained competitors on this template to achieve consistent results within Wal-Mart's seasonal department.

- Attended buyer's appointments in Hong Kong and Bentonville, AK, to support sales team with historical sales data as they presented new product lines. Prepared and presented sales presentations emphasizing Store of the Community (demographics) and Market Basket data.

Wholesale Cosmetics, Irving, TX   **2001–2003**

    Business Analyst

    Wholesale is a world leader in cosmetics, skin care, fragrance, and personal care.

- Retrieved data for and conducted various analyses such as sales trends by brand, effectiveness of FSI (coupons), and impact of television advertising on sales. Noted significant achievements as well as opportunities for improvements.

- Researched inventory and distribution levels, turns, profitability, and productivity to determine benchmarks by brand.

- Monitored new-product launches to ensure execution at store level with minimal stockouts.

Best Cookie Company, Ft. Worth, TX 1997–2001
    Regional Marketing Assistant Manager

Best is a brand under the Kellogg umbrella. With 2008 sales of nearly $13 billion, Kellogg Company is the world's leading producer of cereal and a leading producer of convenience foods, including cookies, crackers, toaster pastries, cereal bars, frozen waffles, and meat alternatives.

Promotional Planning (**Drive trial and increase awareness**)

- Developed and executed regional, local, goodwill, and profit-driven marketing programs. (Examples: Elves for Education, Feed the Children, Kid's Safari Tour, NASCAR, Big 12, free admission to State Fair of Texas, and $8 off Six Flags.) Worked with various marketing/media agencies to execute ideas. Wrote creative copy for media advertisements and commercials.

- Incorporated corporate-brand marketing guidelines (media advertising schedules, couponing, pricing floors, etc.) into promotional plans suitable for various markets within the region to most effectively utilize marketing funds.

- Utilized syndicated (IRI/Nielsen) and internal (SAP) data to identify successes and determine opportunities within markets and key accounts.

Promotional Negotiating (**Secured most profitable elements for marketing plans**)

- Contacted media, as well as merchandise and consulting vendors, to secure elements of promotional plans.

- Researched and secured promotional tie-in partners for events to drive trial and increase awareness.

Promotional Analysis

- Analyzed forecasted profitability of upcoming brand promotions/marketing events.

- Gave thorough attention to detail and rejected proposed marketing events erroneously submitted into SAP, thereby saving the company hundreds of thousands of dollars in marketing spend.

- Performed post-promotion analyses of marketing programs to determine profitability and share gains.

EDUCATION

University of Central Oklahoma, Edmond, Oklahoma
    Bachelor of Business Administration

Southern Nazarene University, Bethany, Oklahoma
    Masters in the Science of Management degree

Dale Carnegie Effective Communication and Human Relations course, September 2007

Toastmasters International Competent Communicator award, November 2007

ADMINISTRATIVE: CUSTOMER SERVICE REPRESENTATIVE

A customer service representative typically takes orders and follows through with the processing of those orders. The candidate's résumé below spells out everything she did to "manage" the accounts. Employers like to see details and follow-through skills.

PEGGY FULBRIGHT
Address   Phone #   Cell #   E-mail

PROFESSIONAL EXPERIENCE

Customer Support, National Accounts

TouchTunes Music, Dallas, TX   **August 2006 to November 2008**

- Managed National Accounts jukeboxes; placed orders, set up status and billing in Oracle and Navision.
- Provided customer support to major clients such as Hollister, TGI Friday's, Bennigan's, and Bose.
- Primary contact for all operators located in the US on installation of jukeboxes; provided support via phone or e-mail.
- Managed all jukebox pilots, moved pilot to sale in a timely manner. Handled new client paperwork and contracts.
- Set up billing procedures with accounting department for all National Accounts operators.
- Provided administrative support for Director, VP, Regional Salesman and IT Specialist; sent brochures, reviewed contracts, and created spreadsheets for location of jukeboxes.
- Interfaced with Credit & Collections, Billing, Customer Service, and Operations departments when problems arose.

Assistant Manager

Fashion Lady, Dallas, TX   **November 2004 to August 2006**

- Responsible for staff of 35–50. Coached and developed associate talents to maximize a flawless client experience.
- Managed visual standards and maximized real estate priorities to drive profitable growth.
- Analyzed key business metrics and results to identify store performance strengths and opportunities.

Customer Service Manager

Designers Plus, Dallas, TX   **April 2001 to November 2004**

- Responsible for staff of 26; scheduled interviews, reviews, and performance issues.
- Managed all point-of-sale functions; provided outstanding guest service in an efficient, friendly, and professional manner.
- Supervised returns, exchanges, special orders, and miscellaneous service and credit.

Training Manager/HR Administrator:
    - Provided administrative support to HR Manager, Store Manager, Operations Manager, and Project Mangers.

- Maintained communication with management team to determine store's training needs and provide feedback.

- Implemented training classes for all new hires as well as training needs for associates.

Operations Supervisor:
- Assisted Operations Manager in the overall operation of the store. Worked closely with vendors to manage facility and maintain standards.

- Managed operations office; coordinated store events, daily delivery, and in-store marketing.

- Managed A/P, supply orders, product flow activities, receiving, and merchandise pick-up.

Assistant Manager
Oriental Imports, St. Louis, MO   July 1999 to April 2001

▪ Ensured associate productivity by providing clear instructions, follow-up recognition, and accountability, as well as adhering to all sales and customer service standards, commitments, and goals.

▪ Managed closing procedures; conducted daily balancing and executed weekly payroll.

Administrative Assistant to CFO
Statler Construction, St. Louis, MO   October 1996 to November 1997

▪ Provided administrative support to CFO, IT, and Accounting department.

▪ Directed incoming calls, processed mail, and maintained calendars for CFO and Accounting department.

▪ Assisted in preparation and distribution of monthly quarterly reports.

Marketing Assistant
Morgan's Bakery, St. Louis, MO   November 1990 to November 1997

▪ Published and distributed pertinent marketing information; coordinated point-of-sales materials and marketing tools used in the outlet stores for merchandising and promotions.

▪ Identified process improvements within the department to increase efficiencies and/or service to the customer.

Human Resources Assistant:
- Provided support to HR Manager; maintained appointment schedule, travel arrangements, and meeting planning.

- Responsible for processing all confidential new hire paperwork, status changes, and drug screening for 50 outlet stores. Reviewed and maintained weekly and monthly period end reports for discrepancies.

- Planned company events, holiday parties, and employee recognition luncheons, as well as assisted with the yearly outlet store conference.

BUSINESS SKILLS
Microsoft Word, Excel, Outlook, Oracle, Navision 5.0, PowerPoint, QuickBooks, ADP

EDUCATION
Stephens Community College

ADMINISTRATIVE: EXECUTIVE ASSISTANT

The bulleted format makes this résumé easy to read and understand, showing at a glance the candidate's extensive responsibility and her job stability. Plus, she is a Certified Professional Secretary (CPS).

PATTY PEARSON, CPS
Address   Phone #   Cell #   E-mail Address

EXECUTIVE ASSISTANT

Skilled and effective Senior-Level Executive Assistant with strong organizational skills and years of experience in executive-level planning, coordinating, and supporting daily operational and administrative functions. Proven track record of successfully interacting with CEOs and developing streamlined systems for several organizations.

Executive Level: Demonstrated capacity to provide comprehensive support for executive-level staff; excellent at scheduling meetings, coordinating travel, taking minutes at staff meetings, and managing all essential tasks.

Takes Initiative: Established more efficient filing systems in two organizations after realizing the need.

Technically Proficient: Microsoft Office Suite (Word, including mail merges, Outlook, Excel, PowerPoint), QuickBooks Pro, and Gregg Shorthand.

PROFESSIONAL EXPERIENCE

Leggette Actuaries, Inc., Dallas, Texas   2004–Current and 1981–1991

Recordkeeping, benefit consulting, and actuarial services for businesses across the globe. Custom programs for 401(k) Retirement Accounts, Flexible Spending Accounts, Profit Sharing Accounts, Defined Benefit Pension, and Defined Contribution Plans, to name a few, before being acquired by DailyAccess Corporation in 2009.

Executive Assistant to the President/CEO

- Successfully managed a heavy schedule of meetings and travel arrangements.

- Prepared confidential items such as the President's personal financial statement and Human Resources issues. Screened job applicants and supervised two other employees.

- Maintained master database of approximately 500 clients and prepared mail-merged information for them.

- Provided administrative and secretarial support to the President, including correspondence, reports, financial data, taking minutes, and action items for weekly staff meetings.

- Implemented the word processing system and chaired the committee for standardized training of same, as well as served on the committee for selecting and implementing a new phone system.

- Prepared information for annual meetings of Actuarial Management Services, a subsidiary company for which I served as the Corporate Secretary.

Cern International Corporation, Dallas, Texas   1997–2003

Commercial property purchased by entrepreneur to refurbish and resell while at the same time marketing products in London and France, such as heavy-duty commercial batteries for use by telephone companies.

(Followed President of Integral Corp. to Cern International (at his request) after the company was sold.)

Office Manager / Executive Assistant to the President
- Established a highly effective filing system.
- Managed a heavy schedule of meetings and travel arrangements (domestic and international), as well as expense reports for same.
- Organized a spectacular Grand Opening.
- Provided administrative and secretarial support to the President, as well as maintained his personal finances on QuickBooks Pro.
- Served as Corporate Secretary for Zylec Corporation, a subsidiary company of Cern.

Integral Corporation, Dallas, Texas   1991–1997

North America's leading manufacturer of wire and cable used in the distribution transmission of electricity, before merging with Southwire Company in 1996.

Administrative Assistant to the President
- Managed a heavy schedule of travel arrangements (domestic and international), as well as expense reports for same.
- Kept minutes for staff meetings.
- Implemented Microsoft Word as the standard word processing system and trained others; provided administrative and secretarial support to the President.
- Established a more efficient filing system.
- Supervised two other employees.

SKILLS
Microsoft Word (including mail merges), Outlook, Excel, PowerPoint, QuickBooks Pro, Gregg Shorthand, 10-key by touch.

CERTIFICATIONS AND AFFILIATIONS
Certified Professional Secretary (CPS)
Certified Notary Public
Member of Career Connections

EDUCATION
CPS (Certified Professional Secretary) designation achieved (Business Law, Economics & Management, Computer Technology, Accounting, Decision Making, Behavioral Science in Business, and Office Procedures & Administration)

Brookhaven and Eastfield Colleges / Draughon's Business College, Dallas

ADMINISTRATIVE ASSISTANT

This is an impressive résumé for an administrative assistant. Sheryl's Summary of Qualifications lists some items that are appealing to an employer, especially "analytical, organized, detail-oriented." She explains her job responsibilities at Unity in detail. She also has her software listed and the information is easy to find.

SHERYL RUSSUM

Address   Phone #   Cell #   E-mail Address

SUMMARY OF QUALIFICATIONS

- Dedicated professional with 19 years of experience and a proven track record in Customer Service, Compliance, and Sales.
- Innovative, effective leader with the ability to train, supervise, and motivate team to perform to their peak potential.
- Develops and maintains an efficient team through proper training.
- Analytical, organized, detail-oriented, and self-motivated, with the ability to successfully manage multiple projects simultaneously.
- Highly developed interpersonal communications skills; able to successfully interface with a public of diverse backgrounds, as well as associates and management at all levels.

EMPLOYMENT HISTORY

Poker Training Network. Dallas, TX   **7/2009 to Present**
Independent Contractor for start-up direct sales company

- Assist with the development and design of Customer Service and Compliance procedures, form letters, and predefined chat responses.
- Assist with the development of company's Policies and Procedures for online marketing.
- Perform other customer service-related daily duties, including responding to incoming chats from Affiliates, replying to e-Tickets, and handling inbound and outbound calls.

Unity Microelectronics. Plano, TX   **5/2007 to 4/2009**
Office Sales Assistant

- Mentored, coached, and trained new team members.
- Worked directly with outside sales management, operations management, and all groups within the company to ensure smooth daily operations and customer focus.
- Helped ensure that new customer offerings are brought on with well-defined processes.
- Focused on business process analysis, development, documentation, and improvement
- Analyzed and refined processes for efficiency and quality.
- Managed team in establishing short- and long-term goals through Performance Workbench.
- Worked with management across the company worldwide to ensure process improvement and proactive, effective communication.

- Initiated and conducted interactive process with vendors and suppliers to ensure orders are taken care of within SLAs.
- Developed and maintained strong working relationships with vendors and internal partners, ensuring most current product information is proactively shared with team and customers.
- Responsible for order entry, tracking, monthly and quarterly sales forecasting.

Wellness International Network. Plano, TX   11/1998 to 3/2007
Senior Manager, Distributor Relations
Senior Manager, Compliance & Resolutions (Promotion in 2004)
Legal Administrative Assistant (Promotion in 1999)

- Managed a team of four customer service reps and one supervisor.
- Developed and maintained strong working relationships with vendors and internal partners by attending trade shows on a regular basis.
- Liaison, mentor, and trainer to the Compliance/Legal Department.
- Hired for, managed, motivated, and oversaw department and employee achievements.
- Oversaw operational policies and procedures to increase productivity, customer satisfaction, and sales revenue.
- Analyzed and refined processes for efficiency, quality, and proactive and effective communication.
- Managed, trained, and oversaw the Hospitality Desk for MLM Colleges and Gala Events.

TLPartnership. Dallas, TX   1998 to 1998
Administrative Assistant (9 months)

- Created presentation slides and "decks" for client meetings.
- Coordinated meetings.
- Performed other daily administrative duties.

EDUCATION AND SKILLS

Central Texas Commercial College; Graduate: Legal Secretary
Expert on all Microsoft Office applications. Type 70 wpm. Superior knowledge of Unix, Paperclip, TokOpen, Peachtree, Salesforce, Kayako, DataTrax.
Policy and procedure development, staff training, and professional letter writing and proofing skills.

ACHIEVEMENTS

November 2004   Employee of the Quarter, Wellness International Network.
December 2004   Top 5 Employee of the Year, Wellness International Network.
December 2005   Top 5 Employee of the Year, Wellness International Network.
December 2007   Rookie of the Year, Unity Microelectronics.

ADMINISTRATIVE: LEGAL ASSISTANT

Lauri's résumé is formatted well, has bullets, and is concise. She clearly describes the variety of law assignments she has worked on. In addition, she mentions that she is a Notary.

LAURI McKINNEY

Address   Cell #   E-mail Address

PROFESSIONAL EXPERIENCE

Sportexe—Irving, Texas   2008–2010
Contract Manager

- Managed over 85 projects from award phase through the closeout process
- Negotiated, reviewed, and revised Contracts, Subcontractor Agreements, and Change Orders
- Reviewed Letters of Intent (LOI) and Notice to Proceed
- Executed bonds and insurance requirements for Contracts
- Prepared and processed submittals and closeout documentation
- Prepared project budgets and sales orders

Texas Instruments, Inc.—Dallas, Texas   2007–2008
Legal Assistant (Contractor)

- Provided assistance to three attorneys in the Wireless Communications Division
- Prepared and revised License Agreements, Partnership Agreements, and Amendments
- Managed attorney calendars, scheduled meetings and conference calls
- Arranged domestic and international travel
- Managed time entries and expense reimbursements

Fisher Law Group, LLP—Dallas, Texas   2003–2007
Real Estate Legal Assistant

- Provided support to managing partner in all aspects of commercial real estate
- Prepared and revised Lease Agreements and Amendments
- Tracked deadlines, option notice dates, and lease expirations
- Calculated CAM charges, taxes, and insurance
- Managed time entry for attorneys
- Handled all firm billing

Silber Pearlman LLP—Dallas, Texas   2001–2003
Litigation Legal Assistant

- Scheduled depositions, meetings, and conference calls
- Interviewed clients to prepare for deposition
- Obtained discovery, product identification, and Social Security information

- Interfaced with medical professionals to obtain accurate diagnosis for clients
- Coordinated bulk copying, group distributions, and filings

Tricon Restaurants Intl—Addison, Texas   2000–2001
Trademark Legal Assistant
- Filed applications and extensions with the US Patent & Trademark Office
- Handled trademark work for Pizza Hut, Taco Bell, and Kentucky Fried Chicken
- Conducted Internet research regarding trademark infringements
- Worked with domestic and international agencies regarding same

General Airlines—Fort Worth, Texas   1997–2000
Corporate Finance Legal Assistant
- Provided support to three attorneys in the corporate finance division
- Prepared and revised Lease Purchase Agreements and Contracts related to commercial aircraft
- Managed time entries

EDUCATION
El Centro College
Berkner High School

SKILLS
Word, Word Perfect, Excel, Paradox, PowerPoint, Peachtree, Hummingbird, SAP, Timeslips, Outlook, and Lotus Notes
Typing 65 wpm
Notary Public for State of Texas; Commission expires 10/12/2011

ADMINISTRATIVE: SENIOR CORPORATE PARALEGAL

Donna's résumé is formatted with bullets, is easy to read, and flows well. She describes her experience with each firm and lists the different types of law she's worked with. She has good job stability and she is a Notary.

Donna K. Jarrell

Address   Phone #   Cell #   E-mail Address

EXPERIENCE

Tenet Healthcare Corporation, Houston, TX

Manager Corporate SEC Law / (f/k/a Senior Corporate Paralegal)   **Dec 2004–Present**

▪ Manage 800 subsidiaries of the Tenet Healthcare Corporation parent company.

▪ Assist in corporate real estate and corporation transactional work.

▪ Perform research related to corporate and litigation healthcare issues.

▪ Assist with Section 16 / SEC filings and requirements.

▪ Manage corporate secretary function and attend Board of Directors and Annual Shareholder Meeting. Assist with Proxy Statement, 10-K and 10-Q Filings.

Affiliated Computer Services, Inc., Houston, TX

Corporate International Paralegal   **Aug 2003–Dec 2004**

▪ Managed 25 international subsidiaries of the ACS parent company, including but not limited to formations, dissolutions, elections, resignations, annual returns, drafting transactional board consents.

▪ Maintained direct contact with international counsel in connection with compliance issues for international subsidiaries.

▪ Assisted with the negotiation and purchase of the Transcentive World Records Entity Management Database system; drafted Audit Report for each entity and performed Audit Scrub while working directly with each counsel to obtain current and correct entity information for inclusion in the Entity Management system.

Jones Day, El Paso, TX

Corporate & Real Estate Paralegal   **Mar 1999–Apr 2003**

▪ Managed over 700 United States and international real estate investment fund subsidiaries of Morgan Stanley Dean Witter, including but not limited to all formations and dissolutions; drafted all board consents authoring loan and acquisitions per transaction structure; draft all board consents regarding transaction, elections, resignations, formations. Maintained direct contact with international counsel regarding compliance issues involving international transactions.

▪ Assisted in all types of transactional work including real estate, healthcare, and mergers and acquisitions.

▪ Conducted due diligence, drafted documents; managed document distributions and assisted with closings.

▪ Implemented a database system to maintain current information on all domestic and international companies, including shareholders, officers, directors, and locations of registered agent.

- Trained legal assistants in connection with corporate secretarial issues, including the drafting of corporate minutes, the organization and maintenance of the corporate minute books, and the data entry for the Web-based client entity database system.
- Created library of over 900 original minute books, shadow binders, and corporate seals.
- Gave attention to Annual Meeting Minutes for all companies.

Physician Reliance Network, Inc., El Paso, TX
Paralegal   May 1997–Jan 1999

- Supervised information on 27 companies in 15 states, which included state filing schedules to keep current and in compliance with the particular state laws and filing of all licensing documents per state including company franchise taxes; maintained all state records for all companies, including each company's corporate records and minute books.
- Responsible for all officer and board of director's books, including résumés, offer letters, director and officer questionnaires, employment agreements, stock options, outside director stock options, Section 16 filing, forms 3, 4 & 5 filings with the SEC, and any severance package.
- In addition to all corporate records, maintained records for the Compensation Committee, Audit Committee, and Operations Committee, and Shareholders' Minute records.
- Maintained the company's 401(k) and profit-sharing records, including all amendments thereto. In addition to officer and director stock options, maintained all employee and physician stock option agreements for all locations. Maintained employees and physician offer letters and employment agreements and amendments and updates thereto. Maintained and updated all legal research reference materials.
- Nonprofit corporation / foundation: Solely implemented 501(c)(3). Operated and maintained all nonprofit cancer research foundation work, including initial setup of foundation, implementing checking account, election of officers, IRS requirements, all banking activity, reconciliation of bank account statements, and all acknowledgments letters to donors and family members.

SKILLS
Legal research and excellent organizational skills
Proficient with MS Office, Windows Office 2000, Microsoft Word 7.0, Windows 98, DOS, WordPerfect 5.1, Lotus 2, Displaywriter, Xerox 6020, and Wang
Notary Public in the State of Texas

EDUCATION
Blackstone Paralegal Institute
Richard College—Academic classes
Alvin Junior College—Academic classes
Attend continuing Legal Education Programs

ACCOUNTING: SENIOR STAFF ACCOUNTANT

The companies that this candidate has worked for are easily identified, along with the positions held, dates of employment, and responsibilities. This résumé answers the questions, *Where did he work? For how long?* and *What did he do?* Also, the résumé shows the candidate's progression in responsibilities over a reasonable period of time, gaining an understanding of the technology used for reporting to management.

Gary Arndt

Address   Phone #   Cell #

PROFESSIONAL EXPERIENCE

R F Monolithics Inc., Dallas, Texas   **2001–Present**

Public company manufacturing radio frequency chips, components, and modules with annual sales of $56M.

Senior Accountant
- Handled all accounting for payroll, fixed assets, 401(k), medical insurance, and SUI.
- Prepared month-end closing entries and reconciled bank and general ledger accounts.
- Prepared schedules for the auditors, tax filings, property tax renditions, 401(k) form 5500 audit, workers compensation audit, and other regulatory requirements.

Tube Forming Inc., Carrollton, Texas   **1996–2000**

$28M public company manufacturing copper components for air conditioners.

Accounting Manager
- Developed and analyzed monthly financial statements used by local management or reporting financial results to the corporate office.
- Calculated standard cost and analyzed material, labor, and overhead variances.
- Directed all accounting functions including general ledger, A/P, A/R, and payroll.

Inca Metal Products Corporation, Lewisville, Texas   **1992–1996**

$30M private company manufacturing pallet rack and metal shelving.

Accounting Manager
- Prepared monthly financial statements; performed bank covenant calculations and borrowing base computations.
- Calculated standard cost and analyzed material, labor, and overhead variances.
- Assisted with the annual physical inventory and reconciled to the general ledger.

The Brinkmann Corporation, Dallas, Texas   1990–1992

$60M private company manufacturing consumer products (smoker grills, flashlights).

Financial Reporting Manager

- Prepared monthly financial statements, including income statement, balance sheet, bank covenants, overhead, and variance analysis.

- Reduced the closing cycle from 15 days to 10 days by automating the journal entries.

Snyder General Corporation, Hutchins, Texas   1989–1990

$120M private company that manufactures residential heating and air conditioning equipment.

Financial Analyst

- Prepared monthly financial package, including income statement, balance sheet, departmental expense summaries, labor and overhead analysis.

- Performed general ledger review, account reconciliations, and reported monthly data to corporate headquarters.

Senior Cost Analyst

- Responsible for developing and maintaining the standard cost of inventory items and assured their proper application in all facets of the business.

- Prepared material and labor variance analysis and performed cost audits.

EDUCATION

University of Alabama, B.S.B.A. Accounting, with minor in Computer Science, 1986

COMPUTER SKILLS

Excel and Word. Ceridian and ADP payroll systems. Glovia & Cognos on an Oracle database. JD Edwards on an IBM AS/400. ManMan and Hyperion software. Several ERP and accounting software packages. Symix software on HP9000 in a Unix environment.

ACCOUNTING: BILLING ANALYST/ ACCOUNTS RECEIVABLE

Jim is an excellent candidate for a position in billing and accounts receivable—and specifically for a company that invoices based on time and projects. His experience in the architecture field is invaluable, and he has spelled it out nicely. He has detailed explanations of responsibilities, noting the number of projects and the dollar amount in collections.

Jim Brinker

Address   Phone #   Cell #   E-mail

CORE COMPETENCIES

Accounting & Finance	Collections	Cash Flow Management
Report Generation	Spreadsheet Development	Process Improvements
Administrative Management	Account Reconciliation	Business Analysis
Data Entry	General Ledger Activity	Customer Relations

PROFESSIONAL BACKGROUND

ACON, Inc.—Dallas, Texas (A computer service outsourcing firm)   2008–Present
Computer Services, Accounts Receivable Billing Analyst
Maintain full responsibility for 11 accounts, which included reviewing and monitoring account contracts, addendums, SOWs, CCCDs, and credit memos, as well as revising billing data in DP-Rams. Communicate with Account Managers / Account Analysts concerning billing issues associated with accounts.

- Provide high level of support in general ledger activity, billing summaries, and tax summaries.

- Research and resolve financial discrepancies utilizing exceptional business skills.

Wilberg & Associates—Dallas, Texas (An accounting firm)   2007–2008
Accounting Services, Senior Accountant
Participated in various aspects of accounting for multiple entities, which included reconciling bank accounts, reviewing expense reports, preparing journal entries, and making bank deposits. Assisted the Controller with special projects. Handled petty cash management functions involving 2 accounts. Led efforts to prepare taxes for Texas and New York.

- Managed financial functions for 6 companies located in Dallas (Corporate Headquarters), New York, Los Angeles, Singapore, Shanghai, and Johannesburg.

- Spearheaded the development of spreadsheets that detailed fixed assets for all 6 companies and applied payments on the Singapore accounts on a daily basis.

Community Home Loans—Plano, Texas (A mortgage company)   2006–2007
Human Resources Incentive Compensation Financial Analyst-II
Researched and resolved issues concerning Divisional Managers, Regional Managers, Branch Managers, and employee incentive bonuses on a monthly and quarterly basis. Aided the Employment Relations Department with termed employees. Provided high level of support concerning compensation inquiries.

- Developed variance reports and reviewed P&L ledgers for incentive compensation and quarterly bonuses pending payment.

- Played a key role in maintaining financial data integrity.

3 Partners Architects—Dallas, Texas (An architectural firm)　　　　1999–2006
Accounts Receivable Manager
Directed accounts receivable and collections efforts. Managed reimbursable invoicing for payments throughout the billing and collection process. Updated the system with current information. Ensured compliance with organizational policies and procedures concerning collections. Assisted Project Managers in setting up client files, shop drawings, client correspondence, meetings, and travel logistics.

- Maintained sole accountability for collections on invoices, which included up to $1.5 million.

- Led efforts to track 150+ project files with Owner/Architect agreements, additional service letters, and consultant agreements for each project.

Howells, Inc.—Dallas, Texas (An architectural firm)　　　　1998–1999
Billing Coordinator
Managed all areas of reimbursable and consultant invoicing for payment throughout the billing and collection process. Evaluated paid consultant invoices, expenditures, and reimbursable items as well as calculated the percentage fees for payment.

- Analyzed professional development fees, subscriptions, licenses, registrations, charitable contributions, and dues, which included presenting results to the Controller.

- Managed up to 100 project files with Owner/Architect agreements, additional service letters, and consultant agreements for each project.

ADDITIONAL EXPERIENCE
Assistant to the Accounting Manager /Assistant to the Landman Manager /MB Exploration LLC, Dallas, Texas (1997–1998)
Assistant to the Comptroller / Energy Arrow Exploration LLC, Dallas, Texas (1996–1997)
Accounting Clerk II / Triton Energy Limited, Dallas, Texas (1991–1996)

EDUCATION
University of Texas, Bachelor of Humanities in History/English, minor in Secondary Education (1996)

TECHNICAL SKILLS
Microsoft Office, ADP, AS/400, PeopleSoft, QuickBooks Pro, Windows 2000 Workstation, WordPerfect

ACCOUNTING: BOOKKEEPER

This résumé is appealing to an employer in need of a bookkeeper because, since the year 2000, the candidate's title has been "book-keeper." She is specific about her responsibilities, from accounts payable and receivables to payroll, audits, account reconciliations, and job costing, plus numerous reporting—all buzz words that most employers are looking for. In addition, she points out the software she has used and mentions her ability to train others on the software. Her résumé is organized and easy to read.

DEBBIE BRADBURY
E-mail   **Address**   **Phone #**

Extensive construction-experienced controller with a demonstrated track record of cost control and construction office management. Core competencies include:

Master Builder Certified	General Ledger	Technology Integration
Financial Statements	Budgeting	Regulatory Compliance
QuickBooks Certified	Cash Management	Job Costing

CAREER EXPERIENCE

AMES CONSTRUCTION, Plano, TX   **April 2009 to Present**
Bookkeeper
Complete all financial functions, including weekly cash flow projections, monthly financial statements, WIP (Work in Progress) Spreadsheet for bonding purposes, A/R, A/P, Job Costing, Payroll including quarterly reports and yearly audits, monthly/quarterly account reconciliations, progress billings including AIA billings, subcontractor billing workup, and lien releases. Use Intuit Master Builder 13.0 to Sage Master Builder 14.2.

- Corrected a bad conversion from QuickBooks Contractors Edition to Sage Master Builder.

- Completed account reconciliation for all accounts by August and was able to submit corrected books to accountant for a reviewed Financial Statement for bonding purposes.

O'MALLEY & ASSOCIATES ARCHITECTS, INC., Frisco, TX   **July 2007 to April 2009**
Bookkeeper
Implemented new computerized accounting system (Ajera); analyzed operations, trends, costs, revenues, financial commitments, and obligations incurred to project future revenues and expenses, using Excel. Prepared balance sheet, profit and loss statement, amortization and depreciation schedules, and other financial reports using Excel or Ajera. Reported finances of establishment to management and advised management about resource utilization, tax strategies, and assumptions underlying budget forecasts. Daily work included A/R, payroll, and all general ledger account reconciliations.

- Used advanced Excel functions including pivot tables, macros, charts, and formulas to complete company projections.

- Learned new accounting program, set up and entered all historical data in the program, and trained all personnel on the use of the program.

CENTRAL TEXAS CONSTRUCTION, INC., Minden, NV   March 2000 to June 2007
   Bookkeeper
   Completed financial functions including monthly/quarterly financial statements for the bonding
   company and bank, WIP (Work in Progress) Spreadsheet, A/R, A/P, Job Costing, payroll including quarterly reports, yearly audits and prevailing wage for both CA & NV, monthly/quarterly
   account reconciliations, progress billings including AIA billings, subcontractor billing workup,
   lien releases, and submittals. Used Intuit Master Builder 6.0 to Sage Master Builder 12.2.

   ▪ Managed the office single-handedly for a $6.5 million year to keep overhead down with
     minimal overtime.

   ▪ Restructured how the AutoCAD drawings were handled including setting up industry
     standard templates.

   ▪ Trained all subs on CA prevailing wage reports and requirements for all CA jobs, includ-
     ing apprenticeship contributions required by nonunion subcontractors and audited all
     prevailing wage reports before submitting them to the owner.

   ▪ Handled all IT issues for the company including troubleshooting networking issues.

   ▪ In 2005, researched and implemented Lord Abbott 401(k) with a 4% matching and profit
     sharing.

EDUCATION

Chemeketa Community College, Salem, OR—1986 to 1993: Classes Taken: Tax Preparation I&II,
   Financial Accounting, Business English, Business Math, Algebra I, World Civilization I&II,
   Psychology, Data Processing, Computers 101, Keyboarding and Word 6.0. Major coursework in
   Accounting.

Western Nevada Community College, Minden, NV—1997 to 2007: Classes Taken: Financial
   Accounting, Managerial Accounting, QuickBooks II&III, Intro to Computer Aided Drafting,
   Intermediate Algebra, Architectural CAD I.

Richland Community College, Dallas, TX—2008 to Present: Classes Taken: Advanced Excel, Micro
   Economics.

SOFTWARE USED FREQUENTLY

Microsoft Office Products: Windows 2000, Windows 2000 Server, XP, Vista, Office 2000, Office 2003
   & Office 2007 (Word, Excel, Outlook, PowerPoint)

QuickBooks: Pro, Accountants Edition, Contractors Edition, and Point-of-Sale (2000–2007)

Intuit Master Builder thru 11.0 and Sage Master Builder thru 14.2

AutoCAD/Architectural Desktop 2000, 2006, 2007, and 2008

Symantec Products: Winfax Pro 10, Act 2000, all Norton products

PURCHASING

This is a great résumé for someone looking for a job in purchasing—specifically in the residential construction industry. His bullet statements list specific responsibilities, including "produced take-offs," "created start packages," and "generated work orders," and also mention his communication with vendors.

ROGER WHITT

E-mail   Address   Phone #

EXPERIENCE

10/06–3/09   **Take-Offs Analyst**
MHI-McGuyer Homebuilders, Inc.—Dallas, TX

- Produced Take-Offs for new and existing house plans

- Incorporated and manipulated Take-Offs for house plans into new and existing communities

- Solicited bids from vendors for various materials for new and existing house plans

- Set up new communities including plan lineups, community features, and vendor lineups

9/03–9/06   **Purchasing Coordinator**
Kimball Hill Homes—Dallas, TX

- Created "Start Packages" for new home construction, which included all Purchase Orders and Work Orders for a given job

- Generated Variance Purchase Orders and Extra Work Orders

- Maintained purchasing database on AS/400

- Provided internal customer service to employees in the field

- Worked with vendors to expedite orders and resolve problems

2/02–6/03   **Level II Collections Agent**
Chrysler Financial—Roanoke, TX

- Collected delinquent retail auto loans

- Provided customer service

11/00–11/01   **Construction Accounting Specialist**
Remington Hotel Corporation—Dallas, TX

- Managed (6) multi-million-dollar construction budgets

- Implemented and managed general contractor agreements

- Processed payment applications from general contractors

- Generated and presented analysis of weekly and monthly budget status reports

- Purchased goods and materials related to construction projects

6/98–11/00 **Order Analyst**
Computer Associates—Plano, TX

- Generated and placed sales orders

- Assisted customers with problem resolution

- Assisted account managers with pricing, product information, and interpretation of customer contracts

- Maintained computer database

EDUCATION
University of North Texas, Bachelor of Business Administration in Marketing, 1998

COMPUTER SKILLS
Microsoft Office (Work, Excel, etc.)
IBM AS/400 Mainframe
Typing 70 wpm

TECHNICAL: DRAFTING

Dates and employers in this résumé are all in bold type and spaced for easy reading.

TONY MULLIGAN
Address   Phone #   Cell #   E-mail Address

EMPLOYMENT HISTORY

Berkley Engineering   **02/2007–Present**

CAD Technician

- Civil designer/drafter using AutoCAD Civil 3D 2009.
- Develop drawings from sketches or verbal directions.
- Develop Cover Sheets, Vicinity Location Plans, General Notes, Erosion Control Plans, Demolition Plans, Site Plans, Drainage Plans, Grading Plans, Utility Plans, and Details.
- Work with Utility Providers and Infrastructure Review Processes.

Ricks Engineering   **11/2004–03/2007**

CAD Technician

- Substation designer/drafter using AutoCAD 2005.
- Used my drafting skills in scaling, plotting, drawing layouts, and showed a high degree of accuracy in copying existing drawings.
- Used knowledge of Substation, Electrical Utilities Mapping, substation terminology, symbols, and Rural Substation Design requirements.

Fargo Piping Systems   **01/2000–09/2004**

Assistant Project Engineer

- **Detailer:** Used AutoCAD and manual drafting techniques.
- **Material takeoff:** Generated bills of material used for material requisitioning.
- **Unit price billing estimator:** Estimated and priced manufacturing labor costs.
- **Assistant project engineer:** Managed the engineering aspect of a job through that job's completion.

EDUCATION

Associate in Applied Science, Paris Junior College, TX; major, Drafting; GPA, 3.90

TECHNICAL: AERONAUTICS ENGINEER

This résumé is good because Marcus mentions every possible acronym that has to do with this industry, which helps me when an employer says the company needs to have this or that. He also doesn't include "filler" words and phrases.

MARCUS PETERSON
Address   Phone #   Cell #   E-mail

Special Training: Private Pilot, ITAR, Code Blue, Handgun, Boxing, & Executive Business
Languages (Speaking): English, French, Lao, Thai, Vietnamese, & some Chinese

- Stress Analysis & Design Software Packages: ITAR, MSC-PATRAN / NASTRAN, ABAQUS, ANSYS, CosmosWorks, SolidWorks, Material Properties, Hyper Mesh, CSW, IAS, SA, Stress Works, TubeCal, Swingz, FEADMS, Mathlab, MathCad, AutoCad-Inventor, CATIA V4-V5, DMU, ProEngineer, UG, Electronics-Workbench, & MS-Office: MS-Project Manager, Word, Excel, and PowerPoint; successfully completed Aviation Wichita State University Training Courses.

- Additional Packages: ITAR, ISO 9000 / 9001, ISO 14000 / 14001, ANSI Y14.5, ASME Y14.1, MIL-HDBK, Blueprint Reading, RF, Schematics Reading, Circuit Board Component Reading, Boeing PDM, CAPPS/SFM, APLG, File Net, ENOVIA, IVT, Photoshop, SAPlus, FEA, PLM, EMI, ECN, Matrix, EAR, ECCN, ELRE, BDS, ITAR, BCA, DWG, per procedure & FAA Requirement; successfully completed Boeing Standard Scale Training Courses from Aerospace.

EXPERIENCE

08/08–05/09 **Aviation Inc., Birmingham, AL**
Title: Structural Stress Analysis for Boeing Huntsville Design Center Integrated Defense Systems (IDS) Mission Division Composites Boeing 787-9 Fuselage STA1605 Sec. 46-47 Used: ITAR, CATIA V5, ABAQUS, PATRAN / NASTRAN, IAS, SA, ENOVIA, IVT, FEMAP, BCA, BDS & FAA Requirement, MS-Office: Word, Excel, PowerPoint, etc.

04/07–05/08 **Mid-Cities Aerosystems, Inc., Kansas City, KS**
Title: Structural Stress Analysis & Design Boeing: IDS P-8A MMA & Commercial Aircraft 787-8, 747-8 & 737-800 Fuselage Sec. 41. Used: ITAR, CATIA V5, ABAQUS, PATRAN / NASTRAN, PDM, File Net, CAPPS/SFM, ENOVIA, PLM, IVT, Win Beam, IAS, SA, ShrBeam, Feadms, MS-Office: Project Manager, Word, Excel, PowerPoint, etc.

02/05–4/07 **Wright Aircraft Industries, Everett, WA**
Title: Structural Stress Analysis for Boeing Military P-8A MMA & Commercial 747-8 Sec. 48, 787-8-9 Fuselage Section 41, 46, 47 & 48 Used: CATIA V5, FEMAP, ABAQUS, PATRAN / NASTRAN, ENOVIA, IVT, EMI, IAS, SA, FREADMS, per ITAR, BDS & FAA Requirement, MS-Office Project Manager, Word, Excel, PowerPoint, etc.

02/04–02/05 **White Clouds Industries, Inc., Grand Prairie, TX**
Title: Stress Analysis / Systems Design Engineer of Boeing 787-8, Composite Fuselage Sec. 47 / 48, Bell V-22 Used: ITAR, CATIA V5, PATRAN /

NASTRAN, ABAQUS, MathCAD, ENOVIA, IVT, PLM, EMI, EMC, MS-Office Project Manager, Word, Excel, PowerPoint, etc.

09/02–04/04   **Farmington Aerospace, Frisco, TX**
Title: Solid Model Design Engineer: for Military & Commercials Aircraft, Hydraulic-Fuel & Flight Control Systems Design of Boeing J-UCAS, 747, 777 MW4000 GE90, Trent 800, Airbus A380 GP7200, Lockheed F-35 F119 Engine, Bell Helicopter V-22 Used: ITAR, MIL-HDBK, PDM, CATIAV4-V5, Inventor, UG, Tube-C, ALGOR, Word, Excel, PowerPoint, producing solid model & drawings.

08/01–09/02   **Jet Stream, Inc., Alvarado, TX**
Title: Manufacturing Tooling Design Engineer. Project on Down hole Tools of Oil-Gas Used: Solid Works, COSMOS Works, ANSYS, PDM, ECN, Matrix, MS-Office: Excel Access, PowerPoint and MS-Project Manager, producing solid model & drawings, Understand Drawing per Standard ANSI Y14.5, ASME Y14.1, ISO 9000/9001, ISO14000/14001.

EDUCATION

Techniques Germany University, Munich, Germany: Bachelor of Science (B.S) in Electronics Engineering, 1978; Bachelor of Science (B.S.) in Mechanical Engineering, 1981

Northwest Campus, Torrent County Junior College, Fort Worth, TX: C.S.C. Computer Science, Mathematics, Physics, & ESL, 1987–1990

American Traded Institute (ATI), Fort Worth, TX: CAE, Computer Aided Engineering AutoCad, 1991

Anadite Aerospace, Inc., Hurst, TX: Blueprint reading for industries of Boeing Standard, 1991

Engineering Stress Analysis Training School, Plano, TX: ANSYS, COSMOS Works-Solid Works, 1996

Aerobotics Engineering, Euless, TX: CATIA V4, ALGO Boeing Standard PDM, 1998

Parker Aerospace Co., Fort Worth, TX: INCAT-T: CATIA V5, Project Manager, Excel, & PowerPoint, 2002–2004

South Campus, Torrent County Junior College, Fort Worth, TX: CosmosWorks-SolidWorks, CATIA V5, Pro/Engineer, 2005

Vought Aircraft Industries, Boeing Company, Spirit Aero Systems, 2004-2008: MSC Institute Technology: ITAR, PATRAN / NASTRAN, ABAQUS, CATIA V5,E PDM, CAPPS/SFM, PRR, ENOVIA, IVT, SOW, DWG, MS-Office Project Manager

Wichita State University, Wichita, KS: Completed training courses, 2005-2008: Master of Science in Aerospace Engineering (MSAE), MSC-I T: ABAQUS, PATRAN / NASTRAN, CATIA V5 Design, Aerospace's Structural Stress Analysis, Wireframe / Surfaces, Kinematics - Simulation, DMU, GD&T, PDM, ENOVIA, IVT, etc.

Boeing Company, Huntsville Design Center (HDC), Huntsville, AL: Completed training courses, 2008–2009: ITAR, PATRAN / NASTRAN, FEMAP v9.3, SA, ISA, CATIA V5 r18 Composites: Workbench, Fiber SIM, Composites Materials Plies layup, Skins Ramp and Stringers, etc.

TECHNICAL: INDUSTRIAL AND MANUFACTURING ENGINEER

Here's a combo résumé for someone with multiple degrees. Jim manages to incorporate all three degrees and uses bullets to highlight areas of expertise.

Jim Parker

Address   Phone #   Cell #

Supply Chain/Sourcing . . . Manufacturing & Engineering . . . Strategic Planning . . . Process Redesign
Cost Reductions . . . Transformation . . . Operations Improvement

PROFESSIONAL EXPERIENCE

Unitron Corporation—Dallas, Texas

Senior Managing Consultant (Supply Chain Strategy)   **2006–Present**

Consulted on SCM/operational issues, primarily to leading Consumer Products & Retail companies. Focus was Supply Chain, including Procurement/Sourcing, S&OP, Logistics/Transportation, PLM & Inventory.

- Developed the top-level framework for the global sourcing for one of the world's largest retailers.
- Led the technology strategy development for the private-label food manufacturing for a $70B grocer.
- Developed supply-chain benefits and execution details for one of the world's largest steel companies, in conjunction with a major SAP engagement to support consolidation of over (100) acquisitions.
- Identified business intelligence/reporting needs in Western Europe at the world's largest beer company.
- Served as Food Manufacturing SME for major market-entry for one of the five largest global retailers.

Unitron Corp., Production Division

Section Manager, Production/Operation (Pilot & Testing Plant)   **2004–2006**

Led a team of approximately (50) salaried associates, including (5) managers, for a 3-shift facility, with (6) production areas: Potato Chips, Corn, Extrusion, Baked Products, Pretzels, and Packaging, as well as (4) of the support functions: Quality, Laboratory & Analytics, Safety, and Sanitation/Food Safety.

- Supported new product tests, test markets, intermediate scale production, and equipment development.
- Improved customer service metric by 8% over previous year, measured across hundreds of tests.
- Reduced overall facility downtime by 20% and achieved aggressive production downtime goal.

Consulting Engagements   **2001–2004**

- Consultant to more than 10 companies in diverse areas, including Turnaround Management, Intellectual Property, Strategic Planning, Retail, Credit Scoring, M&A, Promotional Products, and Telecom.

- Developed Sourcing Strategy for a major national energy company, reviewing all areas of manufactured products and services ($1.2 billion) to best determine opportunities for short- and long-term savings against the spend. Targeted savings from project expected to surpass $30 million annually.

REOR-Graphics Group, Inc.—Irving, Texas
Management Consulting
Design & Implementation of Operations Improvements 2000–2001

Restructured operations of an industrial products division for a $5 billion conglomerate.

- Created a Production Control/Shop Management & Reporting System in Excel as a stop-gap for client while they were evaluating ERP systems. Throughput reached record levels: 30% increase in 6 weeks.

- Executed improvements in Manufacturing, Lab, Purchasing, and Returned Materials. Results included a 10% improvement in labor utilization and an 85% reduction in cost of rework of customer returns.

Littleton, Inc.—Boston, Mass.; Seoul, Korea; São Paulo, Brazil
Management Consulting
Operations, SCM, Engineering/PLM & Strategy 1994–1999

Led or participated in over 25 engagements in BPR, Productivity, R&D/Product Development, and Strategic Planning in the United States, Latin America, Asia, and Europe.

- Co-led Strategic Management of Technology (R&D) engagement for a $5 billion+ Korean oil and chemical producer. Developed Technology Strategy for four divisions, redesigned technology processes, and identified activities required for new R&D center in central Korea.

- Assisted a major integrated steel producer in closing the purchasing function at its mill and reopening at headquarters, as well as identified immediate cost reductions. Savings estimated at $15 million per year from improvements.

Ford Motor Company—Dearborn, Michigan
Marketing Leadership Program (MBA Internship) Summer 1993

Co-developed corporate strategy in Affinity Marketing (partnering) North American management.

B.F. Goodrich Aerospace—Chula Vista, California
Aircraft Engine Equipment Engineer 1989–1992

Managed technical coordination of a $23 million subcontract and developed specifications for various aircraft engine components. Evaluated suppliers and participated in selection process with purchasing.

EDUCATION

University of Texas at Austin, Master of Business Administration, May 1994
San Diego State University, Master of Science, Manufacturing Engineering, December 1993
Lehigh University, Bachelor of Science, Industrial Engineering, June 1989
Languages: Portuguese (Fluent), Spanish (Basic)

TECHNICAL: JOURNEYMAN ELECTRICIAN

Concise and easy to read, yet explains all of Bob's qualifications.

BOB FINCH
Address   Phone #   Cell #   E-mail

SUMMARY

More than 15 years of progressive, professional electrical, general repair, and installation experience.

QUALIFICATIONS

- More than 15 years' commercial experience.
- Self-motivated; able to work independently and as team member to meet operational deadlines.
- Function well in high-pressure atmosphere.
- Adapt easily to new concepts and responsibilities.
- Strong interpersonal skills, having dealt with a diversity of professionals and clients.
- Excellent ability to read blueprints and apply NEC through the full range of commercial construction work.
- Can bend conduit and pull wire.
- Knowledge of making up transformers for installing panels.
- Ability to use hand and power tools applicable to trade.
- Can plan layout and installation of electrical wiring, equipment, and fixtures, based on job specifications and local codes.
- Can diagnose malfunctioning systems, apparatus, and components, using test equipment and hand tools, to locate the cause of a breakdown and correct the problem.

PROFESSIONAL EXPERIENCE

3/09–Present	**KBI Electric, Garland, TX** *Foreman*
10/07–03/09	**McKenna Electric, Dallas, TX** *Foreman/Journeyman*
10/06–10/07	**GSL Electric, Dallas, TX** *Journeyman*

EDUCATION

FTS Electric, Dallas, TX	Journeyman
System Electric, Garland, TX	Journeyman/Apprentice
Humphrey & Associates, Dallas, TX	Apprentice

TECHNICAL: CONSTRUCTION ENGINEER AND ESTIMATOR

Neat and easy to read. Explains all the candidate's skills in a bullet-point fashion so the reader doesn't have to plow through a paragraph to see what this person does.

JOHN MICHAELS

Address   Phone #   Cell #

Mechanical/Plumbing Designer · Construction Administrator · Estimator

PROFESSIONAL EXPERIENCE

Nichols Construction Company—Houston, TX

Project Manager/Estimator   2006 to Present

- Prepare estimates and assess cost effectiveness of workforce relative to bids as project develops.
- Coordinate with clients on changes and adjustments to cost estimates.
- Write, design, and produce plan drawings for value engineering processes with AutoCAD.
- Spearhead employee policy program and hiring procedures.
- Supervise employees, schedule work hours, resolve conflicts, determine salaries.

University of Texas—Dallas, TX

Undergraduate, Ira A. Fulton School of Engineering   2003 to 2006

- Completed advanced internship programs for vertical and horizontal construction while working for Perini Building Co. & Hunter Contracting Co. general contracting companies.

Stichler Design Group—Phoenix, AZ

Mechanical/Plumbing Designer   1999 to 2003

- Completed multiple large-scale projects with competing deadlines.
- Analyzed all technical drawings and identified inconsistencies among designs.
- Managed quality of product in design, analysis, and procedures throughout project.

Robertson Mechanical Corp—Phoenix, AZ

Foreman/Estimator   1991 to 1999

- HVAC, plumbing, and on/off site underground utilities.
- Public and private work: educational, healthcare, warehouse, retail, and infrastructure improvement.

EDUCATION

Arizona State University—Tempe, AZ

Bachelor of Science in Construction   2006

- Program focused on Business, Engineering, and Construction.
- Courses in Advanced Estimating, Project Management, Structural Design, Accounting, Project Scheduling, Contracts, Mechanical Systems, Materials Testing, Soil Mechanics, Heavy Equipment, Heavy Highway Estimating, Labor Management, Survey, General Physics, Calculus, Electrical, etc.

LICENSE	CERTIFICATION
Journeyman Plumber	OSHA 10 HR. Training
	CPR Training
	Medical Gas Design

TECHNICAL: ELECTRICAL ENGINEER

This résumé shows where the candidate started in both process and manufacturing. He translated that experience into an operations management role, in which he led all departments and increased company productivity.

Paul Sellers
Address   Phone #   Cell #   E-mail

PROFESSIONAL EXPERIENCE

Franklin Robotics   2004–Present

Worldwide emerging robotics and technology company that specializes in design, development, import, and distribution channels for consumer, educational, industrial, and military (DoD) market segments.

Operations Manager

- Assembled start-up team and subsequently redirected company from import only to product development company with an integrated product line exceeding 30 items in multiple families.
- Member of Board of Directors; authored company's 3- and 5-year business plans.
- Responsible for all manufacturing, shipping, and receiving.
- Designed and implemented production procedures using Six Sigma, Lean Manufacturing, and other methodologies. Changes and procedures resulted in an increase of $10 million in revenues.
- Implemented safety and waste improvement measures.
- Worked with engineering department to rewire and redesign current equipment.
- Implemented a new automation system utilizing Allen Bradley PLCs.
- Successfully raised initial seed-round funding.
- Strategized and created new industrial product division.
- Developed and implemented company's global sales and marketing programs.
- Negotiated two new OEM, six new distributor partnerships, and US Army partnership.
- Led design of three new products, which increased sales by $1.2 million.

Sanderson Electric Corporation   1995–2004

A $700 million developer and manufacturer of enterprise-wide electronic design automation (EDA) software tools.

Director of Product Marketing and Product Manager, IC Products

- Organized program for multiple tool product lines, yielding $65 million annual revenue.
- Developed and managed business, marketing, and product plans for new products.
- Developed global strategies that increased revenues from approximately $18 million to $65 million in 18 months.

- Streamlined two product lines and negotiated acquisition of four new technologies valued at more than $80 million.
- Evaluated outside technologies and companies for acquisition, both business and technical.

Program Manager, Engineering & Applications, IC Products
- Consistently exceeded quotas and goals by 10 to 40%.
- Implemented three TQM programs, reducing department operational costs by 16%.
- Scheduled applications engineers, developed customer and trade show presentations, and provided technical engineering support activities for installed base exceeding $30 million annually.

Washington Instruments & Robotics   1990–1995

International technology manufacturer of electronics systems valued at approximately $3.5 billion.

Project Engineer
- Established and managed an $18 million test equipment program.
- Pioneered use of microprocessors and integrated circuits for portable field-test equipment.
- Reduced normal test times by 36% and realized additional trickle-down cost savings.

Design Engineer
- Created new quality standards for hardware and software test programs for a $200 million program.
- Instituted cost and weight reduction programs that utilized integrated circuit systems: increased baseline profit by 13% and achieved a 26.5% improvement in program quality control.
- Awarded high-level DoD security clearance (Top Secret SSBI).

EDUCATION & PROFESSIONAL DEVELOPMENT

University of Texas, Dallas, B.S. in Electrical Engineering and MBA

Additional advanced coursework in Electrical Engineering, Operations Management, Marketing, Sales, Life Sciences management; completed General Electric management program, Six-Sigma, TQM, Miller-Herman, Deming, and Malcolm Baldridge.

State-wide licensed Master Electrician and Electrical Contractor (Texas)

Technical skills: Java, C, C++, UNIX, Windows, Perl, Fortran, system/semiconductor design {Custom, SoC, ASIC, GA Analog}, front/backend EDA and CAD software tools, simulation such as Cadence, Mentor, Synopsys, others.

Membership: Institute for Electronic and Electrical Engineers (IEEE), American Electronics Association (AEA), X's and O's, Fabless Semiconductor Association, MIT Enterprise Forum.

TECHNICAL: MECHANICAL ENGINEER

This candidate has been at one company since he graduated. He has been promoted frequently, demonstrating quantifiable success.

GERALD McPHERSON
Address   Phone #   Cell #

PROFESSIONAL EXPERIENCE

HBC Materials Corporation   2003 to Present
A manufacturer of plastic and building materials

Engineering and Operations Manager (November 2006–present)

- Manage start-up operations of Thermoplastic Polyolefin single-ply roofing membrane production.
- Interview, hire, and train production operators for plant start-up.
- Develop plant safety, production, and management operating systems.
- Manage key production launch milestones to keep start-up on time and on budget.
- Develop production job descriptions and job safety analysis (JSA), resulting in zero lost time accidents to date.
- Led five process-improvement teams to reduce overall plant waste below 3%.
- Reduced raw material inventory carrying costs by $2 million by decreasing supplier lead times, analyzing raw material usage, and improving production scheduling.
- Designed and developed manufacturing process using Six Sigma/lean techniques, resulting in 50% increase in yearly production.

Quality Engineering Manager (May 2005–November 2006)

- Managed 24/7 laboratory staff with four technicians.
- Led three cost-reduction projects using Kepner Tregoe and Qualpro methodology.
- Implemented automatic data-collection system and improved data accuracy and reduced variation in key process areas by 1 to 5%.
- Utilized Six Sigma methodologies with key process variables to minimize raw material usage by 1%.
- Developed plant quality and product training plan, reducing new material claims by 15%.
- Led quality audits of raw material suppliers and implemented processes to reduce variation from outside suppliers.
- Successfully adjusted testing frequencies to yield a more efficient and cost-saving operation.

Production Supervisor (April 2004–November 2006)

- Supervised team of 16 operators' daily operations of laminated and three-tab roofing line.
- Managed daily personnel scheduling and planning of operations.

- Led production team through successful transition from 24/7 three-shift operation to 24/7 four-shift operation.
- Coached and counseled employees to improve and maintain performance levels.

Process Engineer (2003)

- Performed lab testing of finished product in accordance with ASTM D3462 standards for asphalt-based shingles.
- Analyzed data to look for trends or process changes and report findings to management.
- Led successful design of experiments to determine top two variables causing excess moisture in bundles.

EDUCATION

MBA, 2010, Southern Methodist University, Cox School of Business; GPA 3.6, Dean's List

BS, 2003, in Mechanical Engineering, University of Michigan, Ann Arbor

TECHNICAL: CHEMICAL ENGINEER

This is an excellent résumé because Mark shows his stability at current and previous companies, as well as that he worked in different arenas: process, design, and manufacturing. Mark implemented specific procedures and designs, which saved money and increased profits for both of his companies.

MARK RAMSEY
Address   Phone #   Cell #   E-mail

PROFESSIONAL EXPERIENCE

PLASTHERM (Houston, TX) 2002–Present
A manufacturer of specialty plastic and latex products for medical and industrial uses

Engineering/Manufacturing Manager

- Responsible for all designs of equipment and plant/facility layouts.
- Responsible for manufacturing processes, process improvements, and equipment analyses.
- Coordinated the design and installation of extrusion equipment, which resulted in a 75% increase in productivity in the manufacturing area.
- In charge of a massive overhaul of older equipment that extended the usefulness of the equipment for another 10 years, which saved the company over $200,000.

ADDCHEM (San Antonio, TX) 1995–2002
A manufacturer of commercial and industrial coatings, adhesives, and surfactants

Process and Plant Engineer

- Responsible for equipment and facility designs and improvements.
- Coordinated with production manager for manufacturing and production processes and improvements.
- Responsible for QA/QC and ISO certification.
- Came up with a process to reduce waste in the batch-making area. Worked with operators to implement process, which resulted in reducing waste to 1%.
- Worked with production and lab to increase productivity in the facility by 50% over a four-year period; resulted in adding $4,000,000 to the company revenues.

EDUCATION

BS Chemical Engineering, Texas A&M University, with minor in Chemistry, 1995

Computer Skills: Microsoft Word, Excel, PowerPoint, AutoCAD, Solid Works, Basic knowledge of Labview and Visual Basic.

TECHNICAL: MECHANICAL ENGINEER/DESIGNER

Randy has lined up his job descriptions and accomplishments nicely in bullet list format.

RANDY McKEY
Address   Phone #   Cell #

PROFESSIONAL DEVELOPMENT
- Experienced in using AutoCAD 14, ProEngineer, and Unigraphics.
- Experienced with reading electrical wiring diagrams and electrical wiring.
- Knowledge of PLCs and Ladder Logic Programming.
- Real Estate License in the State of Texas, December 2005.

WORK EXPERIENCE
Conoco Drilling Solutions, Garland, Texas   October 2007 to Present
Design Engineer

- Efficiently resolved design-related current production issues with the Midrange Drill product.
- Processed customer special-equipment requests, delivering quality design solutions that could be easily integrated into the current product.

Bakers Truck and Engine Corporation, Garland, Texas   April 2001 to October 2007
Truck Group—Design Engineer / Line Support Engineer

- Interfaced with customers/dealers to assess the need for truck performance.
- Successfully led efforts from conception to implementation of new designs by coordinating with engineers in departmental design teams, vendors, manufacturing representatives, and internal material procurement personnel to meet the customer's truck performance needs.
- Gave presentations to manufacturing personnel concerning the implementation of new components and/or system designs to determine the impact to production.
- Resolved problems identified with truck assembly during production by providing either design solutions or process improvements.
- Interfaced with customers/dealers for production plant tours and customer reviews of completed vehicles.
- Involved in mentoring new employees.
- Promoted from Associate to Design Engineer, December 2004.
- Promoted to Lead Design Engineer responsible for design activity on the TranStar model, February 2007.

Sanders International USA, Frisco, Texas   March 1998 to March 2001
Production Engineering Department—Design Engineer

- Designed machines and tools to improve production efficiency by reducing manpower and/or cycle time required to perform manufacturing-related tasks.

▪ Developed tools and modified assembly processes to accommodate new product designs.

▪ Educated production staff on the use of machines and tools.

▪ Assisted with the assembly, computer programming, and installation of machines.

▪ Assessed the feasibility of manufacturing new product designs.

EDUCATION

B.S. Mechanical Engineering, 1997, Southern Methodist University

Engineering Research Assistant, recipient of Embrey Scholarship, which supported research in the design and assembly of robotic arm

TECHNICAL: GRAPHIC DESIGNER

Although this is a plain and to-the-point résumé, a graphic designer normally has a portfolio to bring to the interview.

RANDALL COLLINS / GRAPHIC DESIGNER
Address   Phone #   Cell #   E-mail

EMPLOYMENT

Arnell Group / New York, NY / Freelance Designer / 2004–2006
Conceived of and designed packages, ads, logos, P.O.P., & architectural graphics for Reebok, Masterfoods, Listerine, Pepsi, Frank Gehry, and others; worked in tandem with copywriters, retouchers, production managers, printers, & vendors; researched references & materials.

Sony Music / New York, NY / Art Director / 2000–2004
Managed projects from conception to production; initiated dialogues with artists & management; organized photo shoots for CD, LP, DVD, AD, P.O.P., LOGO; DVD menu & Web site design; oversaw press runs; worked in tandem with copywriters, retouchers, proofreaders, production managers, printers, & vendors.

Tommy Boy Music / New York, NY / Freelance Designer / 2000
Assisted Art Director with CD and related Web, AD, P.O.P., & logo design.

Hey! / New York, NY / Freelance Designer and Copywriter / 1999–2000
Designed style frames for TV commercials and show opener for The History Channel; wrote and designed promo postcards, submitted names for HBO Family rename project.

Pratt Institute, Office of Publications / Brooklyn, NY / Junior Designer / 1999–2000
Worked with Creative Director to produce school catalog, posters, brochures, & invitations. Client list included HBO, Reebok, Pepsi, Masterfoods, Muhammad Ali, Listerine, Gerry Partners, Anthology Film Archives, Special Olympics, One Foundation (Jet Li), The History Channel, Michael Jackson, Herbie Hancock, B2K, Branford Marsalis, Mario Frangoulis, Richard Bona, Our Lady Peace, Shabba Ranks, Lil' Flip, Dj Envy.

EDUCATION

Pratt Institute, Brooklyn, NY. Art Direction major, Graphic Design minor; BFA with honors, 2000

SKILLS AND AWARDS

Skills: Adobe Indesign, Illustrator, Photoshop & Streamline, QuarkXPress. Experienced with professional printing processes from pre-press to final print. Experienced with silkscreen, relief printing, and photo processing & printing.
Awards: Othermobius, 1st place Packaging Design, 2003; work featured in *Print, How,* and *Medialine* magazines.

ARCHITECTURE: INTERIOR DESIGNER

For every job description, Sarah has added a description of her accomplishments.

SARAH GRIFFIN

Address   Phone #   Cell #   E-mail

WORK EXPERIENCE

Griffin and Co., Dallas, TX

Certified & Licensed Interior Designer/Founder　　　　　**October 2005–Present**

Provided complete interior services for $6.4 million, 52,000 square foot addition to Grace Community Church. Responsibilities included formulating and presenting of programming/schematics to four building committees; custom millwork and architectural detail design; design documentation (AutoCAD), ensuring interior code compliance; FF&E selection/specification; coordination with general contractor, architect, engineers, and other tradespersons.

- Managed residential renovations, working side-by-side with client to devise schematics through finished product, meeting both budget and timeline.

- Coordinated subcontractor bid/selection, reviewed submittals, and acted as owner's representative, ensuring completion and quality work.

- Consultant to residential clients for selection and placement of furniture, floor covering, custom window/wall coverings, and accessories.

- Designer for two retail showroom spaces. Included space planning, lighting design, millwork design, and finish selections.

United Fabricators, Inc., Fort Smith, AR

Manufacturing Design/Job & Benefits Coordinator　　　　　**October 2005–Present**

Produced shop drawings for custom stainless-steel food service equipment. Worked with customers, consultants, architects, and interior designers to develop designs for engineering and production.

- Consulted on space efficiency for kitchen fabrication on twelve Little Rock fire stations.

- Analyzed and coordinated 2007 employee benefits, reducing insurance overhead for company by 20% and cutting employee out-of-pocket expense 30% from previous year.

- Reviewed incoming architectural/consultant kitchen plans, gathered pertinent job information, devised production schedule for over 70 jobs.

The Hill Firm, Architects

Interior Designer　　　　　**May 2003–October 2005**

Interior Design Project Manager for high-end reurbanization project, the West End Lofts. Collaborated with lead architect to perform successful in-depth schematic presentation to multi-company investor group, space planning, design/detailing for custom millwork, architectural drafting, FF&E selection/specification, and construction document assembly.

- Gained knowledge in contract administration and construction supervision.

- Interior Designer for The Hill Firm's new office, designed to LEED standards. Extensively researched LEED system and applied to overall design, assisted lead architect in pre-project planning with MEP, civil and structural engineers; performed space planning, architectural drafting/detailing, and FF&E research and specification consistent with LEED standards.

- Assisted senior designer with two historical renovation projects. Duties included extensive site verification and documentation, space planning, architectural drafting, construction documents, implementation of building, city, and historical codes, procurement and custom designs for period-specific FF&E.

EDUCATION

Training & Honors

Texas Christian University, May 2003, Bachelor of Science, Interior Design with FIDER-accredited Program and Business minor. Coursework emphasized lighting design.

NCIDQ Certified, Number 021122, October 2005

Registered Interior Designer, Number 1062, Arkansas State Board of Registered Interior Designers, October 2006–Present

ASID, Professional Member, 2005–Present

Currently preparing for LEED Certification

ASID, IIDA Student Member, 1999–2003; **ASID Allied Member,** 2003–2005

Projects displayed in the Texas State Capitol in support of legislation for Interior Design Title Act, May 2003

OPERATIONS MANAGER

This résumé clearly shows both the candidate's job descriptions and his accomplishments.

DEAN MASTERS
Address   Phone #   Cell #   E-mail

WORK EXPERIENCE

2004–2009   **Cybron Laboratories, Inc., Fort Worth, Texas**
Facility/Equipment Manager
Manufacturer of cosmetics for spas and salons with over 200 skus.
Started out as a consultant, then was hired as Maintenance Manager. In 2005, was asked to become Production Manager. Was in charge of the planning, compounding, production, and printing departments, overseeing 15 people. In 2008, was asked to take the role of Facility/Equipment Manager after failure of previous manager in that position. Was responsible for acquisition of new or used equipment, installation of equipment, and preventive maintenance program for equipment.

1994–2003   **Carmichael Laboratories, Irving, Texas**
Operations Manager
Chemical processing laboratory.
Started out as an engineer technician in the maintenance department. Reduced machine downtime and reject rate. Rebuilt several pieces of filling equipment. Was promoted to Production Manager in 2000. Continued making improvements in manufacturing and production areas. Saved the company over $500,000.00 in three years. Champion for three PES teams, and a member of the Safety Team. Promoted to Operations Manager in October 2001. Responsible for the planning, manufacturing, packaging, and warehouse departments, managing over 25 people with 4 supervisors under me.

1989–1993   **Minor Packaging Machinery Corp., Dallas, Texas**
Production Coordinator/Mechanical Engineer
Manufacturer of packaging machinery.
Supervised the assembly department and purchasing department. Also responsible for testing finished packaging machines, production batching, scheduling of manufacturing, shipping/receiving, and inventory control. Also involved in servicing of machines in the field and spare parts sales and service. Helped design new equipment.

11/1987–11/1989   **Baxter Enterprises, Arlington, Texas**
Maintenance Manager/Mechanic
Manufacturer of mini-blinds.
Purchased and maintained parts and supplies. As manager of the maintenance department, developed and implemented a preventative maintenance schedule.

EDUCATION

Eastfield College, Mesquite, Texas; Certification in AutoCAD Release14 for the Professional 1, Professional 2, and Basic Electricity

SKILLS

AutoCAD 2000, Lotus 123, MFG/PRO, WordPerfect, Macola, Windows XP, MS Word, Excel, PowerPoint, and Outlook. Can read blueprints and electrical schematics. Experienced with Tube fillers, bottle fillers & cappers, Form, Fill and Seal Machines both vertical & horizontal, and Labelers.

Certificates & Achievements

1994 GMP Training

1994 Good Manufacturing Practices

1997 February Employee of the Month—Carrington Laboratories, Inc

1998 Lift Truck Operator Safety Training Course

1999 Certificate of Completion Performance Excellence Series

2000 Certificate of Perfect Attendance—Carrington Laboratories, Inc.

2001 Train the Trainer Qualification for GMP

2003 Excelling as First Time Manager

2005 May Employee of the Month—CBI Laboratories, Inc.

2005 CBI Champion for the Year

2007 October Employee of the Month—CBI Laboratories, Inc.

PRODUCTION MANAGER

Bob's résumé has a nice bulleted format with job descriptions.

BOB ROMERO

Address   Phone #   Cell #   E-mail

SUMMARY OF QUALIFICATIONS

- Eighteen years professional experience in food packaging industry as production manager
- Excellent working relations with the public, co-workers, and employees of all ethnic groups
- Proven record of reliability, responsibility, and leadership
- Skill in planning, coordinating, and supervising projects
- Bilingual: English/Spanish

PROFESSIONAL EXPERIENCE

12/2000–Present   American Food Processing—Allen, Texas

Production Manager

- Managed and scheduled 48 employees, meeting, exceeding, and setting production goals and records in dry beans and rice packaging
- Trained and evaluated the above employees, while maintaining safety, quality, and high score AIB certification
- Mediated major grievances onsite at the local plant and at the California plant
- Trained other production managers at other plants
- Traveled to customer sites as needed to resolve customer complaints and maintained customer satisfaction

6/1986–12/2000   Bowan Food Processing—Frisco, Texas

Production Manager

- Managed and scheduled 56 employees, meeting, exceeding, and setting production goals and records in food, lighter fluid, and seasoning packaging
- Relieved other plant managers at other company-owned plants in other states
- Implemented safety program, providing incentives to employees and eliminated lost-time accidents for 4 years
- One-year Metrocrest Leadership program

8/1980–1/1986   Mid-Cities Oil & Gas—Bryan, Texas

Maintenance Mechanic, Oil & Gas Services

- Maintained equipment for oil field services.
- Maintained a lubrication program for all equipment for daily, weekly, monthly services.

EDUCATION

8/78–5/79   2 semesters of undergraduate study at Richland College, Dallas, Texas

7

Nontraditional Résumés

FOR CERTAIN professions or positions, a nontraditional résumé is preferable. For example, you may need to use more than the standard two pages, as is the case in the academic world, or you may need to describe projects you have managed rather than give the particulars of a job. In these instances, hiring authorities know exactly what they are looking for, and they want to see it in your résumé.

For example, the people who look at architect Dwight Germer's résumé (page 164) know what HKS is—that is, they know exactly what Dwight's duties and responsibilities are. But they want to know what *kind* of projects he has worked on, so his résumé provides this information. Similarly, Professor Louis Gasper's résumé (page 174) is lengthy because it has to provide a lot more information. This is an academic résumé, listing Gasper's publications, the committees he serves on, and his association memberships—information that is especially important to academic hiring committees. In the same vein, positions in the healthcare field require résumés that mention certification, licensures, residencies, and specialty education programs.

Thus, these nontraditional résumés are longer and have more details. Nevertheless, the information has to be presented clearly so that the people reading them quickly find what they need to know. Following are over twenty-five résumés reflecting six major fields, plus information on résumé format best applicable to a position with the federal government. These all fall into the category we call "nontraditional."

ARCHITECTURE: SENIOR CONSTRUCTION ADMINISTRATOR

Dwight has one of those ambiguous positions whereby people know in general what he does, but they can't describe it specifically. Usually the résumé of a candidate such as this will concentrate on descriptions of projects completed rather than firms worked for. Dwight's résumé provides great detail on each project—descriptions phrased so as to invite questions from prospective employers. He has selected fairly well-known projects, thereby increasing his chances of meeting people who are familiar with his work or who have mutual experiences. This format helps potential employers envision Dwight's experiences as part of their future.

DWIGHT C. GERMER, AIA
Address   Cell #   E-mail

Registered Architect, 1990 State of Texas
NCARB File

REPRESENTATIVE EXPERIENCE

2004 to 2009   Associate   HKS, Inc., Ft. Worth, Texas

Dallas Cowboys Stadium, Arlington, Texas
Performed construction-administration duties for a new 80,000-seat enclosed football/multiuse stadium, including associated site work and infrastructure. Total construction amount, $793 million.

Fidelity Investments Phase II, Southlake, Texas
Assisted in performing construction-administration duties for a $183 million, 4-story, 650,000 s.f. office building. Also included is a new 5-tier parking structure.

JPS Patient Tower Addition, Ft. Worth, Texas
Performed construction-administration duties for a $62 million, 5-story, 220,000 s.f. 108-bed patient tower addition (ICU and Telemetry), including new surgery suites, emergency department, and trauma center. Also included is a new 7-tier parking structure.

Harris Methodist Southwest Patient Bed Tower Addition, Ft. Worth, Texas
Performed construction-administration duties for a $50 million, 5-story, 144-bed patient tower addition (ICU, Telemetry, and Women Services Rooms) and the update of existing medical facility, including an addition to the dietary area and relocation of the Cardio / Outpatient Services, Pharmacy, and Administration Office.

Harris Methodist Southwest Imaging Renovation, Ft. Worth, Texas
Performed construction-administration duties for a $3.6 million phased renovation of the existing imaging department.

Doctor's Surgery Center at Huguley, Ft. Worth, Texas
Performed construction-administration duties for a new $7 million, 3-story medical office building. First floor included tenant finish-out of a new day surgery center and a new imaging center.

2002 to 2004   Project Architect   JML Architects, Jacksonville, Texas

Cherokee County Teachers Federal Credit Union, Rusk, Texas
Developed program, coordinated the preparation of design and construction documents, and performed construction-administration duties for a new $750,000 addition and renovation of an existing building. The new addition includes new motor-banking lanes and drive-up ATM, larger lobby and teller area, loan offices, and work room.

Rusk Intermediate School, Rusk, Texas
Performed construction-administration duties for a new $5.4 million intermediate school for 350 students.

Autry Funeral Home, Jacksonville, Texas
Performed construction-administration duties for a new $1.4 million funeral home and cemetery grounds.

2002   Project Architect   Lopez / Salas, San Antonio, Texas

El Dorado Elementary School, San Antonio, Texas
Performed construction-administration duties for a 46,000 s.f. /$2.5 million renovation and code update of existing school facility, including an addition to the food service area.

1995 to 2002   Associate   Beaty & Partners, San Antonio, Texas

Northwest Vista College, San Antonio, Texas
Performed construction-administration duties for four buildings (31,000 s.f. Learning Center; 70,000 s.f. Academic Building; 40,000 s.f. College Commons; and Central Plant) and full site development/$19 million college campus for the Alamo Community College District.

Central Texas Medical Center, San Marcos, Texas
Prepared specifications and performed construction-administration duties for a 43,000 s.f. addition and the renovation of an existing 100,000 s.f. hospital, including a new ICU ward, endoscopy lab, heart catheterization lab, and physician's offices. Total construction amount $5.1 million.

San Pedro Springs Park, San Antonio, Texas
Prepared specifications and performed construction-administration duties for a $5 million comprehensive revitalization of a historic 46-acre municipal park.

Parkway Plaza, San Antonio, Texas
Performed construction-administration duties for a $6.5 million, 150,000 s.f. garden office complex of five buildings, plus site development.

Hope 6 Family Housing, San Antonio, Texas
Performed construction-administration duties for a $9 million, 76-unit multi-family housing complex with support facilities (Administration Building, Maintenance Building, and a Daycare Center).

San Marcos Activity Center, San Marcos, Texas
Prepared specifications, reviewed contract documents for quality assurance, and performed construction-administration duties for a 56,000 s.f., $5.4 million municipal sports, recreation, and conference center.

1989 to 1995   Project Architect   Jeter Cook & Jepson, Hartford, Connecticut

Wethersfield High School, Wethersfield, Connecticut
Prepared design and construction documents and performed construction-administration duties for a 256,000 s.f., $9 million code conformance and renovation project. Also provided contract drawings and specifications, and supervised a $1 million FF&E as part of the project.

Seabury Retirement Community, Bloomfield, Connecticut
Assisted in the preparation of design and construction documents for a $40 million continuing-care facility with 128 apartment units, convalescent housing, health commons, and ancillary spaces.

PGA's Tournament Players Club, Cromwell, Connecticut
Coordinated the preparation of design and construction documents for a new maintenance building. Also an addition and renovation to an existing clubhouse.

Plainville Middle School, Plainville, Connecticut
Provided contract drawings and specifications, and inventoried all existing furniture and equipment being reused for a $1 million FF&E project.

Alcorn Elementary School, Enfield, Connecticut
Assisted with preparation of design and construction documents for a $3.5 million code conformance and renovation project with a 2-story classroom addition.

Accelerated Prison Dormitory and Support Facilities, Niantic, Connecticut
Prepared design and construction documents for a $8.9 million new prison campus, including Dormitory, Gymnasium, Food Service/Medical Building, and Office/Prisoner Visitation Building.

Corrigan Correctional Institute, Montville, Connecticut
Supervised the procurement, inventorying, and invoicing of FF&E for an 800-bed medium/maximum security prison. Total budget amount $3.5 million.

Various Prison Additions and Alterations, Hartford, Bridgeport, and New Haven, Connecticut
Assisted with design and construction documents of new prison additions and alterations for various facilities throughout the state.

Foxwoods Resort and Casino, Ledyard, Connecticut
Assisted with the preparation of construction documents for new spa and exercise facility located in the Foxwoods Hotel complex at the 2 million s.f. resort/casino.

LEGO Corporate Headquarters, Enfield, Connecticut
Assisted with preparation of construction documents for new $14.4 million, 2-story office building.

1988 to 1989   Intern Architect   GBS&H Architects, Jupiter, Florida

Sergi Villas of Jupiter, Jupiter, Florida
Coordinated the preparation of design and construction documents for a 61-unit, 8-story oceanfront condominium.

Solid Waste Authority Administration Building, West Palm Beach, Florida
Assisted in performing construction-administration duties for a new 3-story office building.

1986 to 1988   Job Captain   Russell Gibson Von Dohlen, Hartford, Connecticut
(Now Stecker LaBau Arneill McManus Architects)

Cutter Financial Center, Hartford, Connecticut
Assisted in the design, production, and marketing efforts for a $250 million, 61-story mixed-use office high-rise project, including office, retail, residential, and 8 levels of parking for approximately 1,200 cars.

Aetna Realty Building, Hartford, Connecticut
Prepared and coordinated design and construction documents for 4-story vertical addition and renovation to existing downtown office building, including the use of several existing building facades for historical requirements.

Digital Equipment Office Building, Rocky Hill, Connecticut
Prepared and coordinated design and construction documents of a new 180,000 s.f. suburban office complex.

Hartford Whalers Locker and Athletic Facility, Hartford, Connecticut
Prepared and coordinated design and construction documents, and performed construction-administration duties for a renovation and expansion of an existing professional hockey locker room facility, including weight training rooms, equipment repair and storage, laundry facility, and offices.

Mercy Hospital Physicians Office, Springfield, Massachusetts
Assisted in producing construction documents for a 4-story office addition to existing hospital facility.

Otis Research and Development Office Expansion, Farmington, Connecticut
Assisted in producing specifications for a 2-story office expansion of United Technologies facility.

Otis Elevator Lobby Addition, Farmington, Connecticut
Assisted in producing specifications for Lobby Addition with an escalator display for United Technologies' world headquarters.

Connecticut National Bank, Bridgeport, Connecticut
Prepared interior design documents and specifications for a full-service downtown banking facility.

Woodbridge Corporate Park, Woodbridge, Connecticut
Coordinated the preparation of contract documents for a 3-story suburban office building.

175 Capital Boulevard, Rocky Hill, Connecticut
Coordinated the preparation of contract documents for a 4-story suburban office building.

Midpoint One, Middletown, Connecticut
Prepared design and contract documents for a 3-story suburban office addition.

1985 to 1986   Consultant   Crabtree Associates, Arlington, Massachusetts
(Food Service consultant to architectural firms as noted)

Museum of Science, Boston, Massachusetts
Prepared design and contract documents for a $400,000 full-service cafeteria and kitchen facility for a major addition and renovation project to Museum of Science (Stubbins Associates, Inc., Architects, Cambridge, Massachusetts).

United States Embassy, Department of the State, Amman, Jordan
Prepared design and contract documents for various kitchens and serving areas on embassy grounds. Project documents were prepared in metric (Perry, Dean, Rogers & Partners, Architects, Boston, Massachusetts).

Charley's Eating and Drinking Saloons, J.C. Hillary's, Danvers, Massachusetts; North Palm Beach, Florida; and Nashua, New Hampshire
Prepared design and contract documents for restaurant chain kitchens and serving areas (Westwood Restaurant Group, Inc., Boston, Massachusetts).

Dedham Country and Polo Club, Dedham, Massachusetts
Prepared design and contract documents for kitchen and serving area for renovation to a historical country club building (Ann Beha Associates Architects, Boston, Massachusetts).

Amherst College Student Center, Amherst, Massachusetts
Prepared design and contract documents for kitchen and serving area for a new campus student center building (Perry, Dean, Rogers & Partners, Architects, Boston, Massachusetts).

Epping Elementary School, Epping, New Hampshire
Prepared design and contract documents for kitchen and serving area for a new school building (Banwell, White, Arnold, & Hemberger Architects, Hanover, New Hampshire).

Kingswood Junior High School, Wolfeboro, New Hampshire
Prepared design and contract documents for kitchen and serving area for a new school building (Banwell, White, Arnold, & Hemberger Architects, Hanover, New Hampshire).

1982 to 1985   Interior Architect   Gee and Jensen, West Palm Beach, Florida
(Engineering firm, division of CH2M-Hill)

Boca Raton City Hall, Boca Raton, Florida
Prepared design and contract documents, and performed construction-administration duties for a new 4-story city hall, including renovation to the existing structure.

Palm Beach County Courthouse, West Palm Beach, Florida
Prepared programming, design, and contract documents for interior renovations to an existing courthouse facility.

Forest Hill High School, West Palm Beach, Florida
Coordinated design and contract documents, and performed construction-administration duties for a science department addition and renovations to an existing high school.

Plant City National Guard Armory, Plant City, Florida
Assisted in producing construction documents for new armory facility.

Ocala National Guard Armory, Ocala, Florida
Assisted in producing construction documents for a new armory facility.

Lajes Field Military Base, Lajes Field, Azores
Assisted in design and construction documents for various military projects, including Troop Bowling Alley, Department of Defense Elementary School, and Air Force Fire Station.

Immokalee High School, Immokalee, Florida
Assisted with design and construction documents, and performed construction-administration duties for a science department addition and renovations to existing high school.

1978 to 1982   Interior Architect   Quinn & Associates, Avon, Connecticut
(F. Jaworski & Interior Architect Associates; J & Q Partnership, Jaworski & Quinn)

Norwich Municipal Golf Course, Norwich, Connecticut
Assisted in producing construction documents of a kitchen facility for a new golf clubhouse.

Manchester High School, Manchester, Connecticut
Prepared design and construction documents for interior portion of a high school renovation, including industrial arts, science laboratories, and art classrooms.

Connecticut General C.I.S. Windsor, Windsor, Connecticut
Coordinated design and construction documents, and performed construction-administration duties for a fast-track cafeteria and kitchen for lease space of new insurance office building. Project was required to be designed and installed in 90 days.

Somers Correctional Institute, Somers, Connecticut
Coordinated design and construction documents for updating the equipment in the kitchen facility.

Rocky Hill High School, Rocky Hill, Connecticut
Prepared design and construction documents for interior portions of a new high school building, including industrial arts and a kitchen facility.

Cromwell School System, Cromwell, Connecticut
Prepared design and construction documents for interior portion of a new high school, renovation and additions to a junior high school, and renovation and additions to Edna C. Stevens elementary school. Performed all FF&E services for entire school system.

1976 to 1978   Designer/Drafter   Litchfield Builders, Simsbury, Connecticut
Designed and prepared construction documents for various upscale custom homes and additions.

AFFILIATIONS
American Institute of Architects
Texas Society of Architects

ARCHITECT

The graphics in Bob Brendle's résumé are done tastefully.

Haynes & Boone LLP
Richardson, Texas

Haynes & Boone LLP
Richardson, Texas

Bob Brendle, AIA, LEED AP

EDUCATION
University of Texas at Austin
    Bachelor of Architecture

PROFESSIONAL REGISTRATION
NCARB #309520
Commonwealth of Massachusetts #3698
Texas #20567

CERTIFICATION
LEED AP

PROFESSIONAL MEMBERSHIPS
American Institute of Architects, #3004 8525
TSA Interior Architecture Committee

SOFTWARE SKILLS
AutoCAD, Sketch Up, Revit training in progress, Word, Word Project, PowerPoint

VISION STATEMENT
Mr. Brendle's vision is to develop the highest possible level of design for architecture and interior architecture and through this help our clients exceed their expectations of how their projects can define and support their business and service goals.

PROFESSIONAL SUMMARY
Mr. Brendle has extensive experience in architecture and interior design. He has participated in all phases of the project including Programming, Building Analysis and Evaluation, Architectural Design, Space Planning, Interior Design, design and selection of furnishings, Construction Documents, and Construction Administration. Mr. Brendle's responsibilities have included leading the design teams for architectural projects including office buildings up to 125,000 SF and interior architecture projects of 2,000,000 SF. He has lead teams from Programming and Design through Construction Documents, as lead designer and project architect. He also participates in the Construction Administration phase to provide design follow through and design integrity. He has also designed furniture produced by national manufacturers.

Bob Brendle, AIA *continued*

First American Payment Services
Fort Worth, Texas

WORK EXPERIENCE

HOK Dallas	Feb 2007 – July 2009
Senior Designer Interiors	

HKS Dallas   June 2006 – Feb 2007
Senior Designer Interiors

Good Fulton & Farrell   July 2004 – June 2006
Senior Designer Interiors, Director of Interiors

Gensler Dallas   Feb 2001 – July 2004
Senior Designer

Leo A Daly Dallas   March 199 – Feb 2001
Senior Designer Architecture and Interiors

HOK St. Louis   March 1992 – March 1999
Senior Designer Architecture and Interiors

TESTIMONIALS

"Bob is the consummate professional. His quiet demeanor puts people at ease and allows him to be an objective listener. Having worked with Bob as an owner's representative on a hospital bedtower project, I can say he has the trust and respect of his clients. He demonstrates creativity coupled with practical application in his design"
Kathy Harper RN   214.695.0187

"As Studio Director, I counted on Bob to provide design solutions that fulfilled the clients business needs on schedule and in budget. He always delivered a well designed, well thought out project. I would embrace the opportunity to work with Bob again, he is truly a design talent that is an asset to every team. "
Brenda Buhr-Hancock, Director of Design and Special Projects
NorthPark Management Company
214.282.9824

"We worked with Bob as the lead designer for our offices on the fifth floor of the Chase Bank Building in Fort Worth. He listened to our goals for the design and our practice, and produced a unique design solution that reflects Cotten Schmidt,L.L.P.'s culture and vision. His design incorporated our need and captured our image in ways that exceeded our expectations."
Randall Schmidt, Partner - Cotten Schmidt LLP, Fort Worth, Texas
817.338.4500

Academic Résumés

According to Louis Gasper,* full contact information is critical for academic résumés. Listing an e-mail address for yourself is not enough; if you have a personal Web page or site, include the URL. If you maintain an academic Web site that describes the courses you teach, include that URL, too.

As for any other kind of résumé, list all present and past employment; exact dates of employment and academic rank are vital. List all courses you teach by their name and course number; if a course is unusual, include a brief description as well.

Your employment in the academic world almost universally includes teaching, research, and service, so devote a detailed section for each of these. In particular, list committees you have served on and cite all academic publications, whether published or in submission. For each publication, state the full title, any co-authors, and full publisher information so that the reader can obtain the text. For items accepted but not yet published, specify the journal or publisher and expected publication date. For items in submission, substitute the date of submission. Also state what research you are currently engaged in, publications you are preparing, and colleagues you are working with. Any grants you have received should be listed, including the dollar amount. If the grant will come with you, make that very clear.

Publications have effectively become the sole criterion for personal advancement at most schools. Search committees look for how many articles you have published in peer-reviewed journals. Being a co-author is just about as good as being a sole author. Candidly, it is the number of publications, not their quality, that is important. Self-published items are of no account, and in fact they arouse suspicion that you are out of touch with your field of work. Your current membership(s) in professional academic associations should likewise be listed.

As to including nonacademic employment, less detail is required. The most important thing a search committee is concerned with is any

---

* Our thanks to Louis Gasper, who contributed much of the information for this section.

outside connections you will be able to bring with you. Search committees judge whether such associations will help the school or not (or even be an embarrassment); they want to know how much time and attention you will devote to outside activities and whether you keep up with your field as it may be applied in nonacademic venues.

Many teachers include statements from student evaluations; these are of no importance because it is most likely that you are being hired principally to publish—teaching is a distant second. Every school will say it values excellent teaching, and of course it does, but its value is low relative to the value of publications that will enhance the school's reputation.

Personal references are usually included only if you are seeking a first full-time academic position. If you have a couple of peer-reviewed publications, personal references are superfluous.

COLLEGE PROFESSOR

Louis C. Gasper, Ph.D.

Address   Phone #   Cell #   E-mail

Curriculum vitæ—December 2010

POSITIONS HELD

August 1992–Present

Associate Professor and Director of the Center for Business Ethics,
   Graduate School of Management, University of Dallas

Graduate and undergraduate teaching, research, community service, administration.
Courses Taught:

Graduate division (Graduate School of Management)
  ‣ Financial Management (Finance 6301)
  ‣ Economics and Competitive Strategy (Economics 6305)
  ‣ Business Ethics (Business Administration 6390)

Undergraduate division (College of Business and Constantin College of Liberal Arts)
  ‣ Fundamentals of Finance (Business 3310/Economics 3322)
  ‣ Business and Society (Business 3341)
  ‣ Business Ethics (Philosophy 3334)

March 1994–December 1995

Partner in Global Derivatives, L.L.C., Somerset, New Jersey

Consultant in assessment of corporate risk exposure from investments in derivative financial
instruments; design and construction of systems for monitoring and managing such risks.

April 1992–January 1993

Chairman of the Board of Directors, Merrimack Mortgage Company,
   Tyngsboro, Massachusetts

Under consulting assignment from the Federal Deposit Insurance Corporation (as sole shareholder of Merrimack), had overall responsibility for interim operation of the company and for
sale of its capital stock.

July 1989–Present

Managing Director, Franklin Park Associates, Ltd., Bala Cynwyd, Pennsylvania

Business consultant, specializing in management and executive services, start-up and strategic
planning, and organizational ethics.

February 1985–July 1989

Executive Vice President, GNMA (Government National Mortgage Association),
   Washington, D.C.

As chief operating officer of GNMA, and chief executive and policy officer of GNMA during
vacancies of the president's office, had general responsibility for the overall operations of
GNMA, the largest guarantor of mortgage-backed securities in the world, with aggregate guar-
anties in force of over $500 billion. Received highest personal performance rating
("Outstanding") in every year of tenure. In 1988, received highest award of the Department of
Housing and Urban Development, "For Excellence."

August 1981–February 1985
Executive Assistant to President, Government National Mortage Assoc., Washington, D.C.
Assumed top-level managerial and policy responsibilities at the direction of the chief executive officer of GNMA.

March 1981–August 1981
Senior Economist, U.S. Senate Committee on Finance, Washington, D.C.
Provided economic, legislative, and budget analyses to the committee and to individual senators.

November 1980–January 1981
Member, Reagan Presidential Transition Team, Washington, D.C.
Responsible for the Department of the Treasury and the International Monetary Fund.

April 1975–March 1981
Economist, Minority Staff, U.S. House of Representatives, Washington, D.C.
For the Committee on Banking, Housing, and Urban Affairs. Also functioned as minority counsel for the Subcommittee on Domestic Finance. Provided economic and legislative analyses to the minority members of the committee and counsel to the ranking minority member of the subcommittee, with particular responsibility for oversight of the Federal Reserve System.

September 1973–March 1975
President, Criterion Analysis, Tucson, Arizona
Provided financial and economic analysis incident to portfolio management, investment, and tax planning for a private client.

September 1968–July 1973
Assistant Professor, Department of Economics, University of Arizona, Tucson, Arizona
Graduate and undergraduate teaching, research, and community service. Special sole responsibility for intermediate microeconomic theory courses in the university.

OTHER PROFESSIONAL ACTIVITIES
- Invited participant, Fides et Ratio Conference, Belmont Abbey, July 2009
- Member, Ethics Match Steering Committee, Texas Independent College Foundation, 2005
- Judge, Greater Dallas Business Ethics Awards, 1999
- Presentation to Catholic Schools conference on liberal arts and professional education, Benedictine College, 2003
- Participant in the Lilly Foundation Conference on Professional Education, 2002
- Consultant and coach, College of St. Thomas More team for the GE Ethics Bowl, 2002
- Presentations to conferences on professional ethics education, University of St Thomas, 2002 and 2003
- Active member of a group to establish an association to restore Catholic teaching in Catholic professional schools
- Co-anchor, Texas Cable News coverage of California State Legislature hearings on ethics violations in electric power trading, 2002
- Expert witness on valuations of lost earnings and on mortgage-backed securities

› Conference on Structured Trade Finance, Greater Dallas Chamber of Commerce, September 2000

› Member of the North Lake College (Irving, Texas) Management Advisory Committee, 1996–1998

› Judge, Regional GE Ethics Bowl

› Member of the Board of Advisors, Insurance Risk Management Service, 1998–2001

› Banking Seminar for College Faculty, Graduate School of Banking, University of Wisconsin at Madison, August 1993

› Member, United States delegation, Organization for Economic Cooperation and Development, 1987

› Member, U. S. Federal Government Credit and Guaranty Committee, 1981

University Service on Committees

› College of Business Economics Foundation Course Task Force

› College of Business Senior Comprehensive Examinations Board, May 2007

› College of Business Dean's Advisory Committee, 2009

› University Faculty Senate Ad Hoc Committee on Advancement and Alumni Initiatives, 2009

› College of Business Master of Science Continuous Improvement Committee, 2008

› University Distinguished Alumni Awards Selection Committee, 2007

› GSM Committee on Master of Leadership Studies program, 2006–2008

› University Council (ex officio), 2004–2008

› GSM Academic Review Board, 2006–2007

› ACBSP Accreditation Committee, 2004–2005

› Joint Committee on Business Education, 2002

› University Rank and Tenure, 2001–2005

› University Grievance Panel, 2000–2001, 2002–2003

› University Conflict of Interest Policy Committee, 2000–2001

› University Library Committee, 1992–1993

› GSM/Braniff Collaboration (Chairman), 2001

› GSM Lecture Series Improvement Committee, 2001

› GSM Academic Review, 1994–1995, 2000–2001

› GSM Core Course Coordinating Committee, 1998–1999

› GSM (AACSB) Professional Development Committee, 1997–1998

› GSM Dean Search Committee, 1995–1996

› GSM Domestic Recruitment of Students Task Force, 1994–1995

› GSM Admissions, 1992–1994

Other University Service

- Chair of the University Faculty Senate, 2007–2009
- Vice-chair of the University Faculty Senate and Chair of the University Faculty Assembly, 2005–2006
- Secretary of the University Faculty Senate, 2004–2005
- University Faculty Senate, 2003
- Faculty coach for the student team representing the University at the Texas Independent College Foundation annual ethics match, 2005
- Presenter to the University Faculty Seminar on Ex Corde Ecclesiæ, August 1995
- Conducted Business Ethics lectures twice each academic term. This series began in the spring 1994 trimester and continued through summer 2007

Service to the Catholic Diocese of Fort Worth

- Diocesan Pastoral Council member, 2007
- Diocesan Pastoral Council moderator, 2007–2009
- Diocesan Pastoral Council, Agenda Committee, 2007
- Diocesan Planning Committee, 2009

Publications and Other Scholarly Activities

"A View of Liturgical Changes in the Roman Communion." Paper read at a symposium conducted by the College of Saint Thomas More, Fort Worth, Texas, November 17, 1995.

"Architecture and the Academy." *Universitas,* vol. 2, no. 6 (February 1972).

"Business Ethics." On-line course, constructed in spring 2001; generally conducted in two trimesters each year.

"Case Study—Equity Bubbles and the Efficient Market Hypothesis," with Michael Cosgrove and Daniel Marsh. *ASBBS E-Journal* (American Society of Business and Behavior Sciences), vol. 3, no. 1 (2007).

Eucharistic Prayers II and III, and the proper prayers for the first ten Sundays in the liturgical year. Original English translation, from the Latin *Novus Ordo* of the Roman Catholic Mass. Submitted to the Wethersfield Institute, New York, January 27, 1996.

"Evaluating Your Bank" and "Evaluating Your Savings and Loan." In *The Bank Book,* chaps. 5 and 6 (pp. 71–92). Melrose, FL: Common Sense Press, 1982.

"Financial Management." On-line course, constructed in fall 2003; generally conducted in every trimester through spring 2007.

"Insurance Integrity: A Study in Competing Customer Focus," with Bruce D. Evans. *Insurers Guide to Enterprisewide Risk Management.* Arlington, VA: A. S. Pratt & Sons, 2000.

"Managing Derivative Financial Instruments." *Financial Derivatives Handbook,* February 1996.

"Managing Personnel Risk with a Virtue-oriented Ethics Program." *Insurers Guide to Enterprisewide Risk Management.* Arlington, VA: A. S. Pratt & Sons, 1998.

"New Lineup on the Hill." *NABW Journal,* vol. 5., no. 3 (January–February 1981), p. 5.

"Problems Encountered in Professing Catholic Social Thought in Business and Business Schools." Paper presented at conference on "Enhancing the Catholic Character of Business Schools," Loyola Marymount University, Los Angeles, California, July 27, 1996.

"Professing Catholic Social Thought in Business and Business Schools." *Review of Business* (St. John's University), vol. 19, no. 1 (Fall 1997).

"Reflections on Lumen Gentium." 1997 Lenten lecture series, Saint Mary the Virgin Church, Arlington, Texas.

"Risk, Uncertainty, and Interest Rates." *Derivatives Risk Management Service,* December 1997.

"Teaching Business Ethics as Virtue." Paper presented to meeting of the Academic Business World International Conference, Nashville, Tennessee, May 2007.

"The Development of Global Economic Policies." Paper read to the National Conference of the Cardinal Newman Association, August 1995.

"The 'Even Keel': Decisions of the Federal Open Market Committee," with W. P. Yohe. *Financial Analysts' Journal,* vol. 23, no. 3 (November–December 1970).

"The Moral Framework of the Free Economy." Taped lectures, Intercollegiate Studies Institute, September 1972.

"The Objectivity of Moral Judgements." Paper read to the Visitors and Fellows of the College of Saint Thomas More, Fort Worth, Texas, September 29, 1995.

The Principles of Criminal Economics. Monograph, National Technical Information Service, July 1972.

"Women in Poverty." In *Women's Handbook,* U. S. Department of Labor. Washington, D.C.: Department of Labor, 1991.

Presentations on Virtue-oriented Business Ethics

- Regular weekly commentator on Tony Beshara's *Faith & Work* program, broadcast on KATH (Guadalupe Radio), June 2009–
- American Business Women's Association, Dallas, Texas, October 5, 2006
- League of Women Voters, Irving, Texas, February 28, 2006
- Dallas Association of Petroleum Landsmen, November 15, 2004
- Dallas Society of Finance Professionals, 2002
- Irving Rotary Club, 1997 and 2002
- Our Redeemer Episcopal Church, February 15, 1998
- Fidelity Investments, Inc., June 20, 1997
- Spring Valley United Methodist Church, November 16 and 23, 1997
- Caltex, Inc., March 11 and 12, 1997
- Dallas Chapter of the National Association of Corporate Directors, February 11, 1997

Works in Progress or Circulating for Comment

A Manager's Introduction to Monetary and Fiscal Policy (book), under review

The Virtues of Business (textbook), in progress; current work is on East Asian business ethics

"Elementary Definitions, Concepts, and Rules in Algebra, Analytic Geometry, Differential Calculus, and Logarithms"

"Reading List for Managerial Ethics in Literature"

"An Annotated List of Suggested Readings in Business Ethics"

Other Public Presentations
- Notes, reviews, and comments in a variety of popular publications on various subjects
- Unpublished comments on papers, participations in seminars, and official speeches
- Interviews and appearances on news and talk shows

PROFESSIONAL MEMBERSHIPS

The Philadelphia Society

National Association of Scholars

Newman Association of America

Beta Gamma Sigma

Omicron Delta Epsilon

EDUCATION

B.S. (Business Administration), Duquesne University, 1965
  University competitive scholar, 1961–1965
  Major studies in economics
  Minor studies in English literature

Ph.D. (Economics), Duke University, 1969
  James B. Duke Fellow, 1965–1968
  Major studies in microeconomic theory
  Doctoral Dissertation: *Organized Crime: An Economic Analysis*
    Reader: Professor Joseph J. Spengler
  Minor studies: Money and banking; comparative economic systems

Graduate studies (toward Master of Arts in philosophy), University of Dallas, 1996–2000

Passed *viva voce* examination in theology administered by University of Dallas Theology
  Department, February 2006

Résumés in the Field of Information Technology

Our IT department at Babich & Associates, Inc. (which has more than twenty years' experience in placing IT professionals) provided these résumés because they:

▮ Can be scanned in about thirty seconds and allow the reader to come away with a big-picture understanding of the candidate

▮ Begin with a summary of the candidate's representative technical work

▮ List specific technical skills

▮ Provide a reverse chronological employment history, including company names, locations, and inclusive dates of employment, emphasizing what types of companies the applicant has worked for

▮ Identify both hands-on work experience and technologies used (i.e., tools, applications)

▮ List all educational institutions, with inclusive dates of attendance and degrees awarded

▮ List additional certifications and/or awards received

You will notice that most of these résumés are longer than two pages; this is not uncommon with IT résumés. They need additional space to communicate not only job function but also technical skills. Particularly, it is important to list technical skills at the beginning of the résumé so the reader can spot them right away. Especially if it is a third-party "screener" reading the résumé, he or she will be instructed to look for certain technical proficiencies and terms. Then, in the body of the résumé, you list where those technical proficiencies were applied.

SENIOR TECHNOLOGY MANAGER

This résumé works well because the candidate has a good summary of qualifications at the front, referencing his master's degree and Fortune 500 experience, as well as providing a thumbnail sketch of his experience. Additionally, his experience at each company is stated in a concise and understandable way, and his publications and certifications are detailed.

CHRISTOPHER WARD
Address   Cell #   E-mail

SUMMARY OF QUALIFICATIONS

Certified senior-level information security professional, combining a master's degree and solid experience with leading-edge information security systems and network design, analysis, and implementation. Proven track record in building and leading information security organizations, planning and analysis of security architecture, infrastructure and applications, policy, procedure and standards development and training for a wide range of Fortune 500 companies and government agencies. Solid background with front-line security implementations and regulation compliance, including encryption, firewalls, penetration testing, and applications.

EXPERIENCE

Accelerated Products, Dallas, TX

Senior Information Security Consultant   Aug. 2003–Present

- Managed project, designed, and deployed Symantec Control Compliance Suite (CCS aka Bindview) solution to audit all MS SQL, Oracle, Windows, and Unix servers for PCI, SOX, HIPAA, Gaming Control Board, and corporate policy compliance. Project resulted in significant ROI and reduced FTEs required.

- Managed project, designed, and deployed PGP PKI solution with data loss prevention (DLP) and content management servers and software across multi-national enterprise for PCI and privacy compliance. Servers scanned for inappropriate and proprietary data in motion and at rest on the corporate network, automatically encrypting sensitive data and notifying IT staff of potential data leaks.

- Managed and consulted on information security strategy, policy, and architecture providing compliance with ISO 17799/27001, Gramm-Leach-Bliley Act (GLBA), Sarbanes-Oxley Act, COBIT, DITSCAP, NIST, HIPAA, and state privacy regulations through matrixed staff at over 70 locations in the US and Mexico.

- Responsible for applications, systems, and database audit, vulnerability testing, and analysis (Oracle, DB2, MS SQL, LDAP) for SAS70, SOX, and other audit compliance.

- Performed extensive network security penetration testing, systems, and application vulnerability analysis and risk assessments for several national financial corporations, using a variety of tools, including Nessus, SAINT, COPS, nmap, SUS, TCPWrappers, Tripwire, L0phtcrak, Snort, ISS Scanner, and SUS. Architected and implemented enterprise-wide desktop security (VPN, PKI, identity management, anti-virus, anti-spyware, firewalls, centralized updates, patch management, and single sign-on).

Advance PCS, Dallas, TX   Mar. 2002–Jul. 2003

   Director, Information Security

- Managed information security strategy, policy, and architecture through a combination of direct and matrixed staff with over $1M budget.

- Developed Information Security Policies, Standards and Procedures in compliance with ISO 17799 Gramm-Leach-Bliley Act (GLBA), Sarbanes-Oxley Act (SOA), HIPAA, and state privacy regulations.

- Developed multimedia information security training program and ongoing security awareness campaign.

- Developed and implemented enterprise-wide information security architecture in conjunction with IT organization, resulting in a 24% ROI, regulation compliance, and significantly reduced development time for applications. Account registration turnaround time went from 5 days to 2 hours (Oblix/LDAP/RSA).

- Directed team of consultants to effectively implement, integrate, and automate information security throughout the enterprise. This included applications development in C, C++, JAVA, Perl, and other scripting languages, as well as integration of PIX and Checkpoint firewalls.

- Led forensic investigation teams for security incidents.

- Led team for penetration testing and security analysis, resulting in a major contract award.

- Represented AdvancePCS on industry standards committees.

PGP/Network Associates Inc., Dallas, TX   Apr. 2000–Dec. 2001

   Senior Security Consultant/Project Manager

- Managed NAI Global Services Center, providing managed firewall, anti-virus, and VPN security services for over 6,000 sites nationwide.

- Developed Best Practices Program and authored guides for anti-virus, firewall, VPN, PKI, encryption, penetration testing, and vulnerability analysis product delivery and configuration.

- Trained and mentored junior CISSP consultants and sales engineers to develop and deliver professional security services to Fortune 500 customers.

- Developed and presented security certification training on VPN, vulnerability analysis (CyberCop), intrusion detection, PKI, PGP encryption, and firewalls (Gauntlet and Raptor).

- Designed and developed custom security solutions for Fortune 500 corporate applications, Web-based e-Business, and B-to-B transactions.

WebLink Wireless, Inc., Dallas, TX   May 1998–Apr. 2000

   Director, Corporate Security

- Built corporate security organization and formalized security practices.

- Instituted corporate security policies, procedures, and standards in line with business best practices.

- Developed security training for new-employee orientation and ongoing awareness.

- Architected corporate firewalls, networks, DMZ, VPN, and secure interconnect with competitors.

- Led security investigations and advised CEO and board members on security issues.

- Proactively dealt with security threats through extensive use of security vulnerability scans and monitoring. This resulted in no downtime during Melissa virus attack or subsequent attacks.

- Represented company industry standards and compliance committees such as Common Access for Law Enforcement Agencies (CALEA) and other PCS standards bodies.

Texas Instruments, Dallas, TX   **Aug. 1995–Apr. 1998**
  Senor Information Security Architect

- Team leader and System Architect for TI Enterprise Security Team integration and development of Kerberos and x.509 certificate-based security and encryption utilities and API libraries.

- Developed security libraries for UNIX, Windows, and Web applications on C++ and JAVA.

- Developed security policy implementation procedures and led investigation of security incidents.

- Developed security-training classes for TI security managers.

EDUCATION
MS, Computer Science, University of Texas at Dallas, Dallas, TX
BS, Computer Science, Southern Methodist University, Dallas, TX

ASSOCIATIONS
ISSA, North Texas Chapter
(ISC)2, Certified Information Systems Security Professional (CISSP)

PATENTS AND PUBLICATIONS
ARMA magazine, "Preventing Identity Theft" (2003) · *PCIA Wireless Messaging Device Security Standard,* Author (2000) · *PCIA Standard for CALEA Compliance,* Contributing Author (1999) · *TI Technical Journal,* Information Security, Guest Editor 2Q98 Issue · *TI Technical Journal,* "Keeping Secrets—A Short Overview of Cryptography" (1998), "The Kerberos Security Infrastructure" (1998) · "Enterprise Security for the Web" (1997), paper on lights-out computer systems automation, Co-author · *Connections,* "Commercial Supercomputing" (1994).

SYSTEMS ENGINEER

FRANCIS THOMAS
Address   Cell #   E-mail

EXPERIENCE SUMMARY

- Motivated Engineer with proven technical experience and Data Center background.
- Formal Solution Sales and Presentation Training from leaders in the industry, such as Communispond.
- Ability to achieve Account Executive Sales Quotas year after year.
- Proven ability to establish company in competitive market.
- Effective resource management skills.
- Proven ability to develop relationships with Technical Teams, and consult as Trusted Technical Resource.
- Ability to effectively position product offering in regards to Prospects Architecture, Competitors, and Industry Standards.

WORK EXPERIENCE

Samuel Software, Ft. Worth, TX   **May 2005–Present**

Software Development Platform that offers Object to Relational Mapping capabilities, coupled with Data Services Access Object that offers Dynamic Distributed Caching for Distributed Applications.

Senior Pre-Sales Systems Engineer

Responsibilities: Include presales presentations and consultative sales role to identified customer base. Currently act as first primary technical contact for sales prospects in the U.S. Central region. Also responsible for evaluation of prospects' IT infrastructure and architecture to assure product compatibility and identify possible fit of DDC (dynamic distributed caching) within the J2EE, C++, or .net framework. Also responsible and act as primary project manager for all POC (proof of concept deployments) prior to sale, as well as manage and define staffing requirements for any defined POC. Also responsible for resolution of customer issues, as well as act as primary interface between customer base and software support.

Spartan Software, Dallas, TX   **March 2003–April 2004**

Business Process Management System that integrates business processes and automated-based processes to streamline and improve the efficiency and effectiveness of internal, customer, distributor, supplier, and partner interactions. Business Process Management to span the enterprise, from document management to workflow to systems automation and integration.

Manager, Pre-Sales Systems Engineering

Responsibilities: Included staff, design, and define roles and responsibilities of pre-sales engineering department. Position required relevant demonstration development (with the FUEGO business process management suite to include process designer & BPM integrator), in efforts to coordinate with marketing message as well as customer and prospects business requirements. Handled all presales management functions including equipment acquisition & configuration, expense management, training, and evaluations and acted as interface to other functional departments to include sales, post sales, and marketing. Also performed pre-sales functions in addition to managerial role.

Morgan Software, Arlington, TX   **April 2000–March 2002**

Concerning e-commerce and Content Management Platform in conjunction with OLAP e-Commerce Web Site User Interaction and Reporting.

Senior, Pre-Sales Systems Engineer

Responsibilities: Included pre-sales presentations and demonstrations to customer prospect base, as well as account qualification. Also responsible for customer and prospect onsite installations and training, for customer evaluations and proof of concept implementations. Supported vignettes Web development e-business platform (story-server and OLAP RMS relationship marketing server). Also held primary implementation support responsibilities across ported platforms to include HP/UX, AIX, and Solaris operating systems.

Blazetechnology Inc., Dallas, TX   **May 1995–April 2000**

Systems Engineer

Responsibilities: Application Lifecycle Development Suite, Network, Systems, and Database Management tools, Business Intelligence Suite, Systems Security Products and tools as well as CRM, Help Desk, and Knowledge Management Systems.

EDUCATION

University of Texas at Arlington, Arlington, Texas. B.S. in Information Systems, December 1996. Completed B.S. degree in Information Systems within the School of Business, with minor in Business Administration.

SENIOR DATABASE ARCHITECT/DEVELOPER

RALPH JONES

Address   Phone #   E-mail

Senior Database Architect / Analyst / Developer / DBA with areas of expertise including Infrastructure Planning, Data Modeling, Database Design, Database Programming, and Database Administration. Flexible, with strong organization skills and outstanding record of completing multiple enterprise projects simultaneously.

TECHNICAL SKILLS

Databases:	Microsoft SQL Server 7.0/2000/ 2005/2008, Oracle 10g
Langages:	T-SQL, PL/SQL, C#, VB 6, .Net, JAVA, Java Script, VB Script, Shell Script
Design Tools:	ERWIN, Microsoft Visio
Database Utilities:	SQL Server Integration Services (SSIS), SQL Server Reporting Server (SSRS), SQL Server Analysis Server (SSAS), DTS, Oracle Utilities, Squirrel-Sql.
Reporting Tools:	BIDS, Crystal Enterprise and Reports, ChartFX, Cognos
Development Tools:	Visual Basic, Visual Studio, Enterprise Manager, Eclipse
ERP:	SAP (FICO, MM, APO)
Web Servers:	IIS, Websphere
Application Server:	WebLogic, Biztalk Server, MSMQ Series, SharePoint
Source Control Tool:	Visual Source Safe, ClearCase
Operating Systems:	Windows, UNIX, Linux
Office Tools:	MS Office, MS Project, OpenOffice, Lotus Notes
Editors:	XML SPY, UltraEditor
Issue/IR Tracking Tools:	PVCS, CMIS Web Enterprise

TECHNICAL SUMMARY

- Senior Database Architect and SQL Server DBA, experienced in designing, implementing, and maintaining server infrastructure and database for several Enterprise data warehouse and OLTP applications in development and production environment with high availability.
- Capacity and Storage Planning on SAN.
- Deep experience with SQL Server 7.0/2000/2005.
- Design logical, physical data model for Enterprise application.
- Design Star Schema, Snow Flakes Schema.
- Designed and implemented Active/Active Clustering for SQL Server database.
- Formulated and implemented the Database Data Archive Process with Automation/Multi-server Jobs Administration of database maintenance processes.
- Upgraded application from SQL Server 7.0, 2000 to SQL Server 2005.

• Worked with programming team to provide tuning and optimization of Complex Scripts, Queries and Stored Procedures, Triggers, and User Defined Function.

• Maintained all scripts and jobs, resulting in the scripts monitor system process (O/S) and database objects maintaining 99.5% reliability.

EMPLOYMENT HISTORY

High-Caliber Designs, Dallas, Texas   **Mar 1998–Present**
System Engineer
Provide intensive high-caliber Systems Design & Development support for variety of applications, including:

A. *Ordering Flow*
Designed and developed DSL Ordering Flow for the business customer. Implemented the various back–end interfaces needed for the ordering, like telephone number reserve, credit validation, and address validation using Web-Service technology.

> • Designed and developed the architecture for DSL Order.

> • Designed and implemented the database required for the DSL Ordering using ASP 1.0.

> • Designed and developed the Web interface required for the Ordering Flow.

B. *CX Order*
Call Center Application for data gathering for Enterprise Telecom Products. User interface was designed and developed using Visual Basic 6.0 Form; COM+ components were designed in Visual Basic 6.0, and Oracle 7.3 was used as the database.

> • Users were given an ability to design their own reports and schedule them.

> • Designed and implemented data migration for a system being retired to Go-Live System. More than 500K business accounts migrated. Data transformation was performed from Informix database to Oracle database.

> • Developed data-gathering forms using Visual Basic 6.0.

> • Designed and implemented the interim Oracle database.

> • Wrote the scripts to load data from the source systems.

C. *Maslsr*
Assisted with the design, development, and implementation of applications for Complex Telecoms Products. Participated in all phases of the project, including business process evaluation, requirements gathering, unit testing, system testing, user acceptance testing, deployment, and production support. Components of the system were developed using a range of technologies including C++, VB6, and ASP. More than 2,000 CLEC representatives used the application.

> • Prepared the implementation documentation.

> • Designed and programmed ASP Web page.

> • Implemented client validations using JavaScript.

> • Interacted with the database using the command objects.

EDUCATION
MBA, University of Texas, MS in Computer Design, BS in Engineering

SOFTWARE DEVELOPER/ENGINEER

All skills and responsibilities are clearly stated in a bulleted format, making this résumé easy to read.

DUSTIN BAKER
Address   Cell #   E-mail

PROFESSIONAL SKILLS

- Operating Systems: Windows 7/Vista/XP/2000/NT, Linux, Unix

- Languages: C/C++, C#, ASP.Net, VB.NET, VB, SQL, Java, Assembly

- Win32: Win32 API, MFC, ATL, STL, COM/DCOM, ActiveX, COM+, WDM (Windows Driver Model), named pipe, completion port, shared memory, kernel objects, security, encryption, communication (serial port, USB), Internet programming

- Database: ADO.NET, ADO, OLEDB, DAO, ODBC, MS SQL server, MS Access, Sybase

- Networking: Windows Socket, TCP/IP Protocols (TCP, UDP, IP, ARP, ICMP, DHCP, DNS, SNMP, DNS, HTTP, SMTP), Router, Hub/Switch, Ethernet/Token Ring

- Web Application: Web Service, VBScript, JavaScript, ASP, DHTML, HTML, CSS, XML, XSLT, XPATH, SOAP, MS IIS

- Microsoft.NET: .NET Framework, .NET Class Library, Windows Form, ASP.NET, ADO.NET, Web Service, .NET Remoting, .NET security, C++ Managed Extension, Interop

- OOA/OOD/OOP: Object-oriented analysis, design and programming, Unified Process, UML

EXPERIENCE

Malcom Computing Solutions, Arbury, TX   2009–Present

Senior Software Engineer (Contractor)

- Plan, architect, and develop commercial real-time data acquisition and instrumentation analysis software for Windows 2000/XP platform using Visual C++ 7.0, MFC, ATL, C#, .NET Framework on Visual Studio .NET.

- Build and manage software development team to analyze, design, develop, and deliver software in time-satisfying production requirements or on time in a dynamic custom requirement-driven production environment.

- Maintain, debug, and update software on technology advancement and in response to production or customer requests.

- Manage software development process, software verification and validation, version /release control, defect tracking, and documentation.

- Handled E-commerce, Shopping Cart.

- Supervise the administration of company LAN/WAN and enterprise servers.

- Lead the development team, primary designer, and developer. Key technologies involve:

  - ASP.Net, VB.Net, C#, C++/C, MFC, ATL, .NET Framework, Windows 2000/XP

  - Multitasking (multiple applications), multithreading, true event-driven model

  - Multilayer program structure, real-time data sampling/control engine, built-in script engine, data logging engine, on-line data monitor/graph/control, script editor, hardware calibration, off-line data analysis, and management

- DCOM/COM, ActiveX

- High-performance, highly scalable server/client model, support protocols TCP/IP (WinSock) and Named Pipe, based on Completion Port

- Device communication: kernel device driver (parallel I/O, USB), RS232, TCP/IP

- Relational database: MS SQL,OLEDB, DAO, ADO.NET

- Advanced GUI (data grid, data graph, tabbed windows, tree, list, embedded Web control, real-time update with UI thread, etc.)

- Interlop between managed code and unmanaged code, mixed managed/unmanaged code with Visual C++ Managed Extension

- HTML help system, built-in diagnoses system, event log, InstallShield, VSS, etc.

Western Communications, Terrell, TX   2001–2009

Senior Systems Engineer II, 2008–2009

- Created test-case documents following CMMI level 5 processes and below.

- Responsibilities included forecasting, managing contractual budgets, and schedules.

- Directed communication with government personnel pertaining to project design, project schedule, and project budget.

- Managed and supported ROM, bid preparation, requirements generation, development support, and integration efforts.

- Developed hardware and software requirements allocations and performed traceability to design requirements specifications and software requirements' specifications from these requirement allocations.

- Responsible for taking requirements from the system level to the lower level design and develop software and hardware requirements.

- Responsible for generating ground test procedures and flight test procedures.

- Responsible for taking requirements from a system-level prime-item performance specification to a Critical Item Development Specification (CIDS) level and producing corresponding hardware and software requirements allocations from the CIDS level.

- Responsibilities required strong written and oral communication skills to prepare and present briefings for customer/executive management, and communications between engineering functional skills.

- Utilization of tools including DOORS, UML, EEST, EST, Interchange, PRET, AR Database to track requirements.

- Involved in establishment of an IPT plan for developing and implementing software.

- Familiarity with CMMI level 5 and below organizations.

- Delegated modules to the team members and tracked status of the project life cycle.

- Developed software to communicate on the ARINC 429 data bus.

- Led work-study groups to learn new innovative concepts.

Senior Software Engineer II, 2001–2008

- Developed reusable components for C#/VB. Net applications and reusable Web user controls.

- Designed system architecture, supervised network deployment and construction, developed and implemented Internet/intranet/e-commerce applications.

- Built and managed software development team to analyze, design, develop, and deliver software in time-satisfying production requirements or on time in a dynamic custom requirement-driven production environment.

- Designed, developed, and integrated Windows applications that communicate with Aircraft COMMS, navigational systems, and in-flight self protect systems.

- Managed software development process, software verification and validation, version/release control, defect tracking, and documentation.

- Supervised the administration of company LAN/WAN and enterprise servers.

- Led the development team; was primary designer and developer.

New Alliance, Tomball, TX   1998–2001
Simulation Engineer

- Responsibilities included managing projects from conception to completion.

- Duties included complete interaction with astronauts and trainers to determine user requirements.

- Translated user requirements to system level requirements.

- Duties included system designs, identification of and ordering of parts, and fabrication of panels.

- Duties included installation of equipment, system integration and design of circuit boards for shuttle simulators.

- Designed Programmable Logic Controllers systems.

- Designed Avionic systems utilizing the 1553 interface.

EDUCATION
Master of Science, Technical Management, Louisiana Aeronautical University, 2000
Bachelor of Science, Electronics Engineering, Texas University, 1998

INFRASTRUCTURE ARCHITECT

JANICE MCDONALD
Address   Cell #   E-mail

Results-driven, hands-on Infrastructure Architect with expertise in development and operations environments, leading teams, implementing and driving technology programs, and managing multimillion-dollar projects. In-depth knowledge of emerging technologies. Track record of successful planning and implementations.

EXPERIENCE

- 18+ years Systems Architecture, Engineering, and Support experience of IBM midrange systems with a variety of hardware (RS6000, pSeries LPAR/MPAR/WPAR-APV) running different versions of AIX (3.2.3–6.1) for various databases and real-time applications.

- 10+ years Sun OS/Solaris experience on various Sun and Sun clones platforms.

- 10+ years of UNIX Identity and Access Management with 4 years of integrating UNIX environment with Windows AD2003/R2 in multi-domain and multi-forest environment.

- 10+ years of Data Center technologies deployment and consolidation experience, including provisioning, management, and performance monitoring; capacity planning; and forecast using NetCool, Tivoli TEC, HP OpenView, DSView, Concord's eHealth, OS Native Tools.

- 7+ years of network (LAN/WAN) implementation with three years of network design experience using Marconi (Fore Systems), Cisco, Nortel, DEC, and Equinox.

- 7+ years of RedHat Linux (AS 2.1, 3.0, 4.0 & 5) serving various applications.

- 6+ years of designing and deploying virtual computing environment using VMWare Infrastructure 3, ESX 2.x, 3.x, VM Server, VM Workstation, etc.

- 5+ years in HP-UX and Digital UNIX.

- 5+ years of database development and administration of different versions of MUMPS with MUMPS programming in healthcare industry.

- 5+ years of designing and implementing enterprise backup solution using Veritas Netbackup and ADSM (Tivoli Storage Manager). Storage solution design and implementation (SAN / NAS), NetApp filers, HDS, EMC.

- 4+ years of design and managing deployment of Out of Band Infrastructure (OOBI) for different devices using different OOB protocols.

- 4+ years of deploying different monitoring solutions (Tivoli monitoring, eHealth, SiteScope, HP OpenView) to monitor midrange environment.

- 2+ years of hands-on experience in deploying and managing Symantec's ESM on more than 10,000 UNIX servers corporate-wide (US and international), using different provisioning methods.

- PMP certified with 10 years of operational experience with all aspects of project and program management, including defining policies, methodologies, business objectives, and strategies and in ensuring that projects are aligned with business objectives.

- CISSP & CISA certified with in-depth hands-on work experience in various Information Security domains and IS auditing.

- Certified AIX 5L Administrator, Certified RedHat (RHCT 4.0), Certified VMWare Technical Sales Professional (VTSP). Trainer for RedHat Linux, Solaris, and AIX.

TECHNICAL SKILLS

Languages: Shell scripting, C, FORTRAN, MUMPS, Visual Basic, Power Builder, PL/SQL, Assembly.

Operating Systems/NOS: AIX (3.2.3 to 6.1), HP-UX 10 & 11, Digital UNIX 4.0, LINUX (AS 2.1, 3.0, 4.0), Sun OS/Solaris (2.5, 2.6, 2.8, 10), Windows NT 3.51/4, Windows 95, Windows 2K, MS DOS, VAX/VMS and Open VMS, Netware 3.11/4.01, Lantastic 5.0.

Computer / Network Hardware: PC, IBM xSeries (Blades), IBM RS6000 / pSeries (various PowerPC, P4, P4+, P5, P5+, P6), Sun Sparc 5/10/20, Ultra 2/5 E 4000/6500, E-450/420/220, SunFire V210/280/480/880/1280, 4800/F12k/15k, Niagara T1000/2000 & Fujitsu Sprac systems, MV10000, DEC Alpha (various models), HP 9000 series, Macintosh etc. ASX-1000/200BX, LE 155, Catalyst 5000/8510, ESX4800, PowerHub 5000/7000, ASN 9000, ES3810, Nortel's Annex III/Micro Annex, DEC's 200/700/90TL/900TM, Equinox ELS 8/16/48, Lightwave, Cyclades, Nokia Firewall IP330/IP650, Cisco 6509/5500/2900/2600, Cisco/ArrowPoint CSS11050/CSS11150/CSS11800, etc.

EMPLOYMENT

Central Bank & Trust   2007–2011

Senior Infrastructure Architect

- Designed and deployed a solution for UNIX users' identity and access management with Single & Simplified Sign On (SSO) using multi-domain / multi-forest Microsoft AD 2003/R2 infrastructure as primary directory source. Used VAS (Vintela Authentication Service) version 3.0.x & 3.3.x for LDAP client configured with PAM and Kerberos on different UNIX (Solaris, AIX, Linux, HP-Ux) platforms, NetApp filers, VMware Infrastructure and other appliances used for UNIX environment support. Used Microsoft Group Policy for configuration and user access management on UNIX clients. Used MIIS (Microsoft Identity Integration Server) with MS-SQL 2003 server to keep different repositories in sync; this included design deployment and integration of MIIS, MS-SQL server, and various identity repositories.

- Senior UNIX systems architect on wide variety of UNIX initiatives and support. Supported day to day server operations including IBM AIX, Sun Solaris and RedHat RHEL 4 & 5.

- Developed and standardized Midrange Technology Security Baselines including UNIX users' access and privilege baseline in accordance with Corporate Security policies. Architected flexible and scalable solutions to comply with these Security baselines following both domestic (USA) and international regulations.

- Developed and executed migration strategies for identity and access related information from standalone UNIX systems, NIS, NIS+, and LDAP to Microsoft AD 2003/R2. Migrated 15000+ UNIX servers with 30,000+ users from 32+ NIS/NIS+ and standalone multi-site environments.

- Deployed Concord's (CA) eHealth agents on more than 3000+ UNIX (AIX, Linux, Solaris) systems for performance monitoring, capacity planning, and forecast.

- Deployed security monitoring tool (Symantec's ESM) on more than 10,000 UNIX servers using different provisioning methods. Established security baselines based on environments and regulations in ESM to automatically perform system security audit, send alerts, and create status reports. Performed POC testing of SNORT for Intrusion detection / prevention.

- Worked on multiple projects using different UNIX/Linux platforms (IBM pSeries, xSeries / Sun / HP) for critical trading environment with contingency environment in compliance with SOX guidelines.

- New installs, upgrades, patch management for all kinds of UNIX / Linux platforms using NIM, Jump Start, and Kick Start.

- Tested and supported RedHat Linux (AS 2.1, 3.0, 4.0) with all information security baselines on HP and IBM Blade hardware (HS20, HS40, LS20, JS20 & JS21).

- Designed and deployed VMWare products (VMWare Infrastructure, vCenter, VIClient, ESX, GSX, VMWare server, etc.) for Windows, Solaris x86, and Linux guest operating systems.

- Participated in Technology Architect group to review, test, certify, and approve new IBM RISC Hardware and AIX operating system in bank. Designed and deployed AIX NIM infrastructure for rapid and automated deployment of Bank's customized image of AIX (5.1, 5.2 & 5.3, 6.1). Led AIX 5.3 and 6.1 certification for standalone, LPAR and micro-partitioned (APV) environment. Designed and deployed several HACMP 5.1/5.2, VCS multiple node clusters for critical applications/databases. Participated in Solaris 10 certification on Sparc and X86 with zones.

- Architected Tivoli infrastructure on IBM platform running AIX and RedHat Linux.

- Designed and implemented enterprise wide out-of-band management solution using Cyclades ACS, CISCO, MergePoint and Avocent KVM switches with DSView software for different devices using different OOB access protocols (e.g., iLo, iPMI, iLOM, HMC, Serial, KVM, etc.).

- Tested and implemented SnapMirror data synchronization over WAN for NetApp filers.

- Participated in testing, Beta testing, and benchmarking different hardware and software.

- Provided end to end engineering solution for operational issues and several critical projects related with trading floor on hardware running UNIX (AIX & Solaris) / RedHat Linux.

Peterson-Sloane Credit Union   2004–2007

Senior Systems /Network Engineer

- Managed UNIX operations / support group for critical business units.

- Network design, integration, and management (LAN / WAN).

- Systems design, administration, and integration using AIX and Sun OS/Solaris.

- Managed production and development support team for critical trading-floor business; was responsible for day-to-day production support and expansion of midrange infrastructure (UNIX and Wintel); supported MS-SQL (Windows), Sybase (AIX), and Oracle (Solaris) databases.

• Designed and deployed backup solution with NetBackup, using shared media servers with multiple tape libraries and vaulting for offsite storage.

• Replaced ATM network infrastructure (Fore Switches) by Cisco Ethernet in core and access.

• Network design, integration, and management (LAN / WAN).

• ATM infrastructure design and deployment using Fore switches in LAN and WAN at multiple cities. Implemented ATM using LANE 1.0/2.0 with server fail over and DLE (Dynamic Lane Emulation), UNI, ILMI, NNI, PNNI (Fore PNNI & ATM PNNI), MPOA (MPS/MPC), RFC 1483 PVC, and QoS, etc. Used Fore (ASX 1000, ASX200BX, LE155, ESX4800, ES3810, ASN9000, and PowerHub5000/7000) and Cisco 4500 and 8510 to implement network. Analyzed, troubleshot, and monitored network using various tools and utilities (e.g., TDM meter, Sniffer, and ForeView software, etc.).

• Member of Y2K committee for midrange systems and network. Tested and resolved Y2K issues by patching OS, firmware.

• Designed and implemented enterprise network printing solution including application printing running on Windows NT 4.0, AIX 3.2.5 / 4.1.4 / 4.2.1/4.3.3 and Sun OS/Solaris.

EDUCATION & PROFESSIONAL CERTIFICATIONS

M.S., Electrical Engineering, University of Texas at Arlington, Arlington, TX (May 1996)

B.S., Electrical Engineering, University of Tennessee, Knoxville, TN (May 1992)

Certified Information Security Auditor (CISA)

Certified Information Systems Security Professional (CISSP)

Project Management Professional (PMP)

VTSP (VMWare Technical Sales Professional)

RedHat Certified Technician (RHCT) Enterprise Linux 4

IBM AIX 5L Certified System Administrator

PROJECT MANAGEMENT PROFESSIONAL

Interesting breakdown of areas of expertise, which definitely catches the eye of the reader.

MICHAEL JOHNSON, PMP
Address　　　Cell #　　　E-mail

AREAS OF EXPERTISE

.NET Development	Gap Analysis	SDLC
Business Analysis	MS Office Suite 2000, 2003, 2007	SEI-CMMi Methodology (level 4 cert.)
Business Process Reengineering	MS Project 2000, 2003, 2007	SharePoint Portal
Business/Use Case Development	Process/Data Modeling	SQL
Change Management	Project Management	Technical Writing
Critical Path Analysis	Quality Management	Troubleshooting/Problem Solving
Enterprise Planning	Rational Suite of Tools	Visio
Executive-Level Presentations	RFP Management	Work Breakdown Structure (WBS)

PROFESSIONAL EXPERIENCE

Michaelson Mortgage, Plano, TX　　　　　　　　　　　　　　**2002 to Present**
　　Senior Project Manager

- Responsible for critical path analysis, budget oversight, and reporting and risk management.

- Use Agile-based methodology while managing up to 36 concurrent projects in various phases.

- Manage a team of 30+ project members consisting of legacy developers, network engineers, database technical and nontechnical personnel, and off-shore teams.

- Manage project schedules, scope, budget, task assignments, status reporting, risk management, project documentation, resource management, and project communications for moderate to highly complex projects under demanding time constraints.

- Oversee various corporate IT initiatives and loan production activity.

- Manage work product of legacy, Enterprise planning, .NET and Web developers, requirements managers, quality assurance analysts, and other project team members as assigned.

- Use MS Project 2007 to manage, update, and age project timeline commitments to monitor critical path and resource centime conflicts.

- Use various advanced technologies to include .NET, Active Directory, Project Server, etc.

- Oversee team development and architecture of major initiatives.

Melon Markets, Frisco, TX　　　　　　　　　　　　　　**1999 to 2002**
　　Senior Project Manager

- Oversaw various multimillion-dollar IT and infrastructure projects.

- Interfaced with business units and executives to ensure total satisfaction.

- Managed work product of mainframe distributed and Web developers, requirements managers, quality assurance analysts, and other project team members as assigned.

- Used internal development methodology based on "Waterfall" to manage up to 10 concurrent projects in various phases.

- Responsible for critical path analysis, budget oversight, and reporting and risk management.

- Assisted business units with needs definition as it related to overall corporate goals and mission.

- Oversaw all activities in an 18-week SDLC requiring requirement negotiations, code reviews, and schedule modifications.

- Managed a team of 10 project members consisting of mainframe developers, network engineers, desktop specialist, telephony engineers, and database technical and nontechnical personnel.

- Managed project schedules, scope, budget, task assignments, status reporting, risk management, project documentation, resource management, vendor relationship, and project communications for moderate to highly complex projects under demanding time constraints. Managed implementation to include new development, third-party vendor solutions, and maintenance projects.

- Oversaw and facilitated revision management of project plans, project artifacts, deliverables, and other project-related documentation.

Roberts Corporation, Richardson, TX   1995 to 1999
  Project Manager

- Oversaw $30M program consisting of three concurrent projects to design and upgrade safety technology and network applications using .NET development.

- Managed a team of 20 project members consisting of network, desktop, telephony, network security, database technical and nontechnical personnel, and vendor teams.

- Collected and reported system /staff performance metrics, and suggested improvements to ensure customer service goals were realized and federal, state, and municipal regulations were adhered to.

- Performed the following duties in gap analysis: review, analyze, and evaluate business process systems needs; formulate systems to parallel overall business strategies; write detailed description of business needs to develop, modify, or implement technology solutions.

EDUCATION

B.S., Computer Science, University of Texas at Arlington, Arlington, Texas (May 1994)
MBA, Business Administration, with concentration in Information Technology, University of Maryland at Baltimore, Baltimore, MD (1998)

CERTIFICATIONS

Project Management Professional (PMP), PMI (2004)

SOFTWARE DEVELOPER

John's résumé is clear, concise, and easy to understand. He explains his duties well in this bulleted format.

John Edwards
Address   Cell #   E-mail

PROFESSIONAL EXPERIENCE

Grandson Corporation, IS Civilian Systems—Plano, TX

Software Developer   04/07–12/10

Technologies Used: J2EE, ATG 2006.3 - 9.0 Portal & Adaptive Scenario Engine, JBOSS 4, DAS, Perl, Oracle 10g, Rational Clearcase, BIRT 2.x, (X)HTML, CSS, JavaScript

- Developed and enhanced the NAS Adaptation Services Environment, an ATG-Portal-based system used by 4000+ users within the FAA and DoD organizations
  - Developed and designed at least 30% of enhancements, features, and bug fixes in releases
  - Integrated and introduced the Mootools and jQuery JavaScript frameworks to securely add AJAX capabilities to improve application responsiveness
  - Redesigned the ATG Portal template to a more modern (X)HTML compliant template
- Led the development effort to port an ATG 2006.3 system on DAS to ATG 2007.1 on JBOSS 4.0.5
- Developed an adhoc-reporting infrastructure portlet, which communicated with the ITAM data warehouse, for the ITAM-RS portal
- Integrated the BIRT reporting framework into the portal using a custom AJAX portlet

Wallis Bros Property and Casualty, Claims Field Development—Waco, TX

IT Programmer/Analyst   06/06–04/07

Technologies Used: AIX, Perl, X12 EDI, MVS, Java, JMS

- Led project transition of automated claim auditing system from DEV to O&M
  - Ensured remaining defects and enhancements from DEV team were closed out
  - Centralized the JMS error queues in order for O&M team to quickly diagnose and reprocess messages
- Provided 3rd-level support and enhancements for Unix and MVS applications used for processing auto and property claims
- Managed packaging and deployment schedules for laptop applications used by claims field appraisers

Hallis Web Creations—Houston, TX

Web Site Producer (Contract)   2/05–05/06

- Converted a Photoshop-generated Web site (30 HTML files) to an XHTML, CSS, and JS design (2 HTML files), thereby reducing page download size by roughly 90%

University of Texas—Dallas, TX

Research Fellowship   06/04–01/05

- Quantitative and Physical Sciences Summer Undergraduate Research Fellowship (QP-SURF) Program

› Improved the processing and statistical analysis of images using an extended version of ImageJ

Western Intl, Unmanned Systems—Los Angeles, CA

IT Intern 06/02–06/04

› Assisted in managing the installation of the Rancho Bernardo branch CWIN (Cyber Warfare Integration Network) node

› Researched the latest collaboration technologies in the areas of VTC, Blackberry, and data mining, which led to the installment of the Google Search Appliance

COMPUTER SKILLS

Languages, Software & Methodologies: Java, J2EE, JSP, JMS, JSTL, PHP, Zend Framework, ANSI C++ & STL, OpenGL, RUP, XML, XSD, XSL(T), Mootools, Prototype, jQuery, Perl, BIOPerl, Subversion, shell scripting, MySQL, design patterns
Operating Systems: RHEL, Solaris, AIX, Windows, TSO/MVS

EDUCATION

Bachelor of Science in Informatics, University of Texas; concentration in Bioinformatics, minor in Chemistry; GPA: 3.3

TECHNICAL SUPPORT

All certifications listed here and responsibilities given are presented in an easy-to-read format.

LEWIS ANDERSON

Address   Cell #   E-mail

Microsoft Certified professional with over 14 years Information Technology & Systems experience supporting large national and multinational financial, telecommunications, and publishing corporations.

CERTIFICATES OF ACHIEVEMENT

- **Microsoft Certified Professional**
  70-290 Managing and Maintaining a Microsoft Windows Server 2003 Environment
- **Microsoft Certificate of Achievement**
  5105 Deploying Windows Vista Business Desktops
- **AST Certified**
  PC Architecture, S.T.E.E.R. Troubleshooting, Electrostatic Discharge

PROFESSIONAL EXPERIENCE

Malcom | Plano, TX | May 2007–May 2010
  Desktop Engineer / Level 3 Support

- Managed user and workstation OUs within Active Directory
- Patched internal systems within 90 days of patch release
- Reverse-engineered MSI installs in order to resolve common installation errors
- Provided Tier 3 support for custom in-house and industry standard applications
- Provided technical guidance and training to the Service Desk and Desktop Support
- Acted as technical liaison between clients, customers, and vendors as required to implement new technologies or bring issues to resolution
- Collaborated across departments to resolve ongoing issues and address root-cause analysis
- Performed basic application packaging and testing
- Ensured all audit controls were adhered to when making changes in the production environment
- Wrote technical procedures and documentation for applications, operations, and policies and procedures

Falcom Enterprises | Carrollton, TX | Aug 2001–May 2007
  Systems Administration & Support

- Maintained Windows 2003 & Apple OSX Servers in a production environment
- Managed domain user accounts, computers, and security groups via Active Directory
- Installed, maintained, and repaired IT hardware, such as servers, workstations

- Maintained daily system backups, software updates, and current anti-virus software definitions

- Resolved firewall and connectivity issues for field offices

- Designed and implemented a company-wide mass-deployment solution

- Planned and implemented a rollout of over 500 laptops

- Entered as a Production Systems Analyst, where I analyzed production needs and designed and implemented new procedures and software, resulting in the direct reduction of cost per page in the production of magazines

Walker Group | Irving, TX | **June 2000–July 2001**
  Information Analyst / Problem Management

- Managed problems impacting enterprise-level systems, resources, and services

- Ensured the proper execution of issue resolutions and avoidance

- Investigated system and branch outages/impairments to ensure the awareness of the impact to the environment and business units

- Gathered information pertaining to outages, service-level reporting, and problem trend analysis

- Tracked outage reports and assignment of postmortem reports

- Maintained and distributed documents to aid business units in identifying and correcting issues affecting environmental stability

- Point of contact for all business lines for historical information and status of current issues

AT&T | Irving, TX | **Oct 1997–Apr 2000**
  Desktop Support Technician

- Proactively deployed and maintained IT assets within a Novell enterprise environment

- Responsible for purchasing decisions within the Supply division

Mega Computer Systems | Frisco, TX | **July 1996–Oct 1997**
  Product Support Representative Level II

- Functioned as a level 2 SD specialist in a department consisting of over two hundred people providing in-depth support spanning multiple operating systems, applications, and hardware configurations

- Researched and evaluated new software and hardware prior to global distribution

SKILLS SUMMARY
  Systems
    Microsoft Windows Server 2003, Windows XP, Windows 7
    Apple OS 9, OS X, & OS X Server
    Active Directory, Open Directory, Past Novell Experience

  Software
    Altiris Deployment Solution, Marimba / BMC Configuration Management, Shavlik Patch Management

Altiris SVS, VMware, MS Virtual Server & PC

Retrospect, ArcServe, & Veritas

WISE Packager, PC Transplant, Ghost, & ImageX, Script Logic, Desktop Authority

Remedy, Support Magic, DynaComm/Elite, WRQreflection

MS Office Suites, MS Project, MS Visio

Lotus Smart Suite, Lotus Notes, ccMAIL, & Word Perfect

Hardware

Servers, SAN, NAS, Switches, Routers, PC & MAC Workstations / Laptops, Printers, Peripherals, Mobile Devices, Wireless Cards, & various Backup Devices

Languages

Batch Script, Java Script, Action Script, HTML, Some PHP

Networking

TCP/IP, DNS, DHCP, WINS, Ethernet

Additional Skills

Freelance infrastructure support for small / mid-sized law firms

Familiar with MySQL, Wordpress, Joomla & Drupal Content Management Systems

7yr+ freelance design for both web and print utilizing such applications as Adobe CS & Quark

EDUCATION

Currently pursuing completion of B.S. in Computer Science Engineering

SQL SERVER DEVELOPER

Ed shows his roles and responsibilities in a clear and concise manner by using bullet points.

ED JONES
Address   Phone #   E-mail

PROFESSIONAL EXPERIENCE

Data Aps, Inc., Carrollton, Texas   08/2008–Current
  SQL Server Developer

The company's core skills in database administration, systems integration, and application design are delivered in a variety of business solutions. The project involves creating store procedure to produce the reports for company clients, daily administration/maintenance of development databases, troubleshooting blocking issues, and rewriting existing store procedure.

Roles & Responsibilities:

‣ Create different SSIS packages to satisfy users' different reporting needs.

‣ Monitor and schedule daily, weekly, monthly SQL jobs to run different reporting SSIS packages.

‣ Debug any issues related to failed job or data discrepancy by exploring the SQL Server agent job history and data pattern.

‣ Perform data migration (using tools like DTS, SSIS, BULK, INSERT, BCP, and Replication) between SQL Server (heterogeneous/homogenous) using .net through different GUI.

‣ Develop stored procedures, views, required functions, and indexes and indexed views.

‣ Create and maintain various databases required for developing report and backups.

‣ Design and provide access to different users to databases and respective tables and determine the level of access required by them and maintain the security to protect the data and environment.

‣ Create and maintain automated jobs for database backup based on the percentage used to ensure that the backup is up to date, should it be necessary to restore the database.

‣ Monitor performance of queries on SQL Server using SQL Profiler and optimize it by creating appropriate indexes using Index Tuning Wizard and Windows Performance Monitor and address any issues forwarded by data warehouse group regarding the performance of our queries.

‣ Monitor SQL Server performance using SQL Profiler, Query Analyzer, Index Tuning Wizard, and Windows Performance Monitor.

‣ Check and monitor the health of tables and databases, using the proper method of normalization and necessary indexes.

Global Data Services, Plano, Texas   05/2006–07/2008
  SQL Server Developer

Global Data Services is a diversified global financial services company offering a broad array of credit, savings, and loan products. Worked on a project to maintain and enhance databases for the Credit Card and Merchant Resolutions departments. Worked on various performance-related issues including database tuning to achieve faster response times and better throughput. Worked to automate extracting third-party flat file to and from SQL Server via DTS, SSIS, and BCP as per the business requirements.

Roles & Responsibilities:

- Developed stored procedures and views to meet the business and reporting project requirements.
- Provided automated, scalable, and robust data importing and exporting from multiple heterogeneous data sources to SQL Server by using DTS and SSIS packages.
- Created a scheduling process to extract and import data from text files using DTS packages and BCP utility.
- Suggested best practices for SSIS implementation.

Goodwin Information Systems, Dallas, Texas   04/2005–04/2006

SQL Server Developer

Company rents a variety of products, including home electronics, appliances, computers, furniture, and accessories. The project was designed to implement and manage the Customer Information System. Was involved in Customer Focus project that looked through the company's entire customer database for every region and separated them based on customer details and their business profiles. The work also involved extracting old data from Oracle database into SQL Server.

Roles & Responsibilities:

- Interacted with clients to assess the system and gathered user requirements for the inventory database and handled client requested enhancements.
- Built DTS packages for data transfer from heterogeneous data sources like MS Access, MS Excel, and text files to SQL Server using VBScript, Stored Procedures, and T-SQL Scripts.
- Created views to reduce apparent database complexity for end users.
- Developed stored procedures and optimized SQL queries for efficiency and helped the front-end developer with queries and procedures.
- Used efficient transactions and appropriate error handling steps.
- Modified existing database by adding tables and altering referential integrity to avoid relationship-sensitive columns from being selected.

Mid-Cities Hospital, Topeka, Kansas   02/2004–03/2005

SQL Server Developer

Mid-Cities Hospital is a nationally recognized and award-winning hospital dedicated to the prevention, diagnosis, and treatment of cardiovascular disease. The project involved designing the databases of patients' registrations, their appointments with various doctors/physicians, and patients' visits, as well as their related procedures, medications, and inventory of pharmaceutical stocks.

Roles & Responsibilities:

- Involved in all stages of Project Life Cycle Development.

- Participated in gathering user requirements and system specifications.

- Designed and developed database infrastructure. Developed the databases for the individual departments and the central database, which contains information about all the departments.

- Developed ER diagrams (physical and logical using Erwin and Visio) and mapped the data into database objects.

- Wrote SQL queries to generate reports based on the business requirements.

- Created stored procedures, views, triggers, constraints, and indexes.

Veteren Flight, Topeka, Kansas   **11/2002–01/2004**
SQL Server Developer
Veteran Flight is a world leader in commercial and military aviation repair, maintenance, and engineering. Developed the Helpdesk application database and worked with application developer to complete portions of the Chat application's database design and create objects.

Roles & Responsibilities:
- Installed and configured MS SQL 2000 for Helpdesk and Chat application.

- Installed service packs and security patches for MS-SQL Server.

- Assisted in design, development, and implementation of various applications.

- Migrated schema and data from development to production server.

- Managed the use of disk space, memory, and connections. Ran DBCC consistency checks and fixed data corruption in application databases.

- Experienced on backing up databases on HP Tru64 UNIX 4.0g.

A. Helpdesk Application:
- Designed and implemented database for a Helpdesk application.

- Created tables and column-level check constraints (primary & foreign keys).

- Created stored procedures.

- Created normalized tables.

- Created separate tables for customers, customer details, tickets, ticket details, ticket history, customer category, and ticket category.

- Created stored procedures to insert new tickets, update tickets, update ticket history, and issue reports.

B. Chat Application:
- Created the table structures for Chat application. One of the tables stored all the messages that were communicated between all the senders and receivers. There was a bit field to notify whether the message was received or not.

- Created stored procedures to write and receive messages and update the bit column as necessary.

EDUCATION
Bachelor's Degree (B.B.A), concentration in Management Information Systems,
  University of Kansas

NETWORK/SYSTEMS ADMINISTRATOR

This résumé states all of Robert's qualifications, job history, and responsibilities. It is short and to the point.

ROBERT FOSTER
Address   Cell #   E-mail

SKILLS

Servers: HP, Dell, and proficient in Windows platform including Windows 2003/2008 Server, Microsoft Exchange Server 2003/2007, Microsoft Office SharePoint 2007 Server, Network Infrastructure Administration, Directory Services Administration, Designing Windows 2003/2008 Directory Services, Designing Windows 2003/2008 Network Security, SQL Server 2005 System Administration, and System Management Server 2003.

Circuits: SONET (OC-12 to OC192), SONET DS3 (T3), DS1 (T1), Frame Relay, DSL, and IDSN (PRI and BRI), circuit-switched, cell-switched, packet-switched, dedicated connections.

Networking: BGP, FDDI, FTP, HDLC, EIGRP, IGGP, OSFP, IEEE 802.16(e), IS-IS, MPLS, OSPF, PPP, RIPv1, RIPv2, RSTP, SMTP, STP, SNTP, VTP, ATM, HDLC, IP, TCP, MPLS, VLANs, VLSM, VPN, Local Area Network (LAN), Wide Area Network (WAN), Metropolitan Area Network (MAN).

Hardware: Cisco 7200 and 7600 Series Routers, Catalyst 2950, 3560, 3750, 4500, and 6500 Series Switches, PIX/ASA Firewall, CSU/DSU, T1/T3.

Software: Cisco IOS, Cisco Works, Checkpoint Firewall, Norton Anti-Virus, MacAfee, HP Systems Insight Manager, WhatsUp, Veritas Backup Exec, Retina, Nessus, WebInspect, Enterprise Security Analyze, LogLogic.

CERTIFICATIONS

CCSA (Check Point Certified Security Administrator), 2004
CCSE (Check Point Certification Security Expert), 2004
MCITP (Microsoft Certified IT Professional), 2005
MCSE (Microsoft Certified Systems Engineer) 2005
MCDBA (Microsoft Certified Database Administrator), 2005
CCNA (Cisco Certified Network Associate), 2006
CCSP (Cisco Certified Security Professional), 2006
CCNP (Cisco Certified Network Professional), 2006

EXPERIENCE

Mainline Trucking, Inc. Pine Bluff, AK   04/2008–Present
    Network Administrator

- Support Microsoft Exchange 2007 and Office SharePoint 2007 server.
- Install, maintain, and administer all 2003/2008 servers.
- Manage User Account, Group Policy, DNS/WINS/DHCP/WSUS in Windows 2003/2008 Active Directory.
- Monitor all production systems and ensure uninterrupted processing.
- Manage system backups (Veritas Backup Exec) to ensure disaster recovery preparedness.
- Support Citrix System (Servers and Clients).

- Support ACT 2009/21010 application.

- Manage security log files, Internet access (Barracuda Webfilter), and Anti-Virus (SEP).

- Manage Cisco Routers, Switches, PIX/ASA firewalls, and VPN Concentrators.

- Maintain and troubleshoot LAN and WAN communications networks.

- Support 12 USA offices remotely including network connectivity, servers, and end users.

- Support laptops, PCs, and phone system and provide phone Helpdesk support to users.

Brighten Securities, North Little Rock, AK   06/2003–04/2008

Systems/Network Administrator

- Supported PCI compliance and SAS70 project.

- Performed Vulnerability Threat Assessments, including Network, Host, and Application scans.

- Analyzed all security Penetration testing, Vulnerability Threat assessments.

- Supported application security scan (HP WebInspect), Network security Assessment (Retina), Nessus, nCircle.

- Performed Network Monitor as Intrusion Prevention System (IPS) and Intrusion Detection System (IDS).

- Managed Cisco Routers, Switches, Mars, and PIX/ASA firewalls, and VPN Concentrators.

- Maintained and troubleshot LAN and WAN communications networks.

- Monitored security log file, Internet access, virus attacks, VPN, and Internet security facilities and tools.

- Supported Lotus Notes at the end users.

- Server systems administration (2000/2003/2008: installing, maintaining, and administering).

- Managed User account, Group Policy, DNS/WINS/DHCP in Windows 2003/2008 Active Directory.

- Planned, developed, and supported SMS 2003 (Systems Management Server 2003).

- Supported hardware and software inventory, remote control, and software package & distribution components.

- Deployed critical security patches, systems management, active agent monitoring, and reporting tools.

EDUCATION

B.S., Computer Science, Arkansas University, 2003

SYSTEMS ENGINEER/ANALYST

Easy to read and good description of skills, experience, and responsibilities.

SAM FULLER

Address   Cell #   E-mail

SUMMARY OF QUALIFICATIONS

Networking specialist with 10+ years of experience in the computer industry.

Diverse training in Cisco, Alcatel, Microsoft, and UNIX networking products.

Outstanding productivity as a networking specialist.

CERTIFICATIONS

CCIE Service Provider

Cisco Certified Internetwork Professional (CCIP)

Cisco Certified Voice Professional (CCVP)

Cisco Certified Network Associate (CCNA)

Microsoft Certified System Engineer (MCSE)

Microsoft Certified Database Administrator (MCDBA)

Microsoft Certified Professional (Internet)

EXPERIENCE

SALEM CABLE, Plano, TX   **May 2006–Present**

Sr. Network Engineer

› Design and implement network element configurations, develop and execute test plans for validation, and write MOPs for the deployment into the production network of the initial implementations of each network architecture phase.

› Design, plan, and implement high-speed backbone (OC3, OC12) to provide connectivity among the Core Data Center. Deploy MPLS to separate production, staging, and lab traffic through the high-speed backbone. Deploy MPLS traffic engineering to provide fast converge using fast reroute to minimize the downtime.

› Design, deploy, and maintain router network to support remote locations.

› Design solutions that include redundancy of hardware and software.

› Have excellent understanding of MPLS traffic engineering and RSVP signaling.

› Manage 7x50 routers and switches, including installations, upgrades, configurations, and management.

› Design configuration of IPTV networking architecture.

› Assist in performing network analysis, monitoring, and troubleshooting tools.

› Assist and advise network architecture engineers and work as part of network architecture implementation team.

› Provide expert knowledge of VLAN, VPLS, OSPF, BGP/MPLS, RSVP, SSM, and other routing protocols.

• Responsible for all routing and MPLS issues in the IPTV project.

• Provided expertise in VHO to VHO live migration in IPTV project.

CITYWIDE INTERNET SYSTEMS, Dallas, TX   August 2003–May 2006
Network Engineer

• Configured Cisco routers with protocols, such as OSPF, EIGRP, and BGP4.

• Provided high-level technical support, including identifying and resolving problems on Cisco supported products, for external routing and internal/intranet routing for DMZ servers.

• Managed Cisco routers and switches, including performing installations, upgrades, configurations, and management.

• Implemented route-maps, prefix-lists, and AS-path filters.

• Responsible for configuring frame relay networks.

• Assisted in performing network analysis, monitoring, and troubleshooting.

• Worked on WAN technologies, including ATM, frame relay, and point-to-point circuits.

• Provided in-depth knowledge of routing and switching protocols.

• Provided expert knowledge in the development of DMZs and other security tools and processes.

EMERSON SYSTEMS, Irving, TX   June 2002–July 2003
Network Engineer

• Managed Cisco routers and switches, including performing installations, upgrades, configurations, and management.

• Configured Cisco 2500, 2600, and 3000 routers to provide Ethernet, serial, Bri Interface access.

• Designed, configured, and deployed VPNs.

• Configured static NAT and dynamic NAT.

• Implemented traffic filters on Cisco routes using Standard and Extended access list.

• Provided expert knowledge of development of DMZs and other security tools and processes.

• Designed and implemented Exchange 2003. Exchange server was outsourced to a hosting company. Used Exmerge to export/import user mailboxes from the hosting company Exchange 2000 server to the in-house Exchange 2003 server.

• Designed and implemented Blackberry Solution for Microsoft Exchange 2003.

• Designed the solution based on customer requirements, such as Sun, Microsoft, EMC, and Oracle, as well as recommendations for third-party host hardware and software tools.

• Provided expertise in WAN technologies with ATM, frame relay, and point-to-point circuits.

- Designed and implemented LAN/WAN network, equipment, connectivity, and service delivery.

- Managed Cisco routers and switches, including installations, upgrades, and configurations.

SEGAL INTERNATIONAL, Frisco, TX   June 2000–June 2002

Network Engineer

- Evaluated and tested Netware 5 and NT 5 Operating Systems.

- Designed, implemented, deployed, and supported NT and Novell Netware Servers.

- Managed and supported internal and external DNS servers.

- Monitored, managed, and filtered Internet traffic on LANs and the WAN.

- Performed installations and configurations with SQL and SMS servers.

- Administered Windows NT domain relationships and centralized management of mixed NT and NetWare Network with Novell NDS.

EDUCATION

B.S., Computer Science, University of Houston (May 2000)

Résumés for the Healthcare Field

Healthcare résumés are also an exception to the two-page rule. People reading these résumés expect specific details.

PHYSICAL THERAPIST

This résumé flows in the right direction. A reader can see immediately that this candidate meets the requirements educationally, while the current work experience covers hands-on clinical experience. The mention of continuing education shows that he is on top of the latest treatments in the field.

BILL SAUNDERS
Address   Cell #   E-mail

CAREER OBJECTIVE: Physical Therapist

PROFESSIONAL EDUCATION

2000–2002: Master's in Physical Therapy. Northwestern University of Health Sciences

1995–1999: B.S. in Exercise and Sport Science. University of Wisconsin

CONTINUING EDUCATION

2009: Bioness H200 Certification, Bioness

2008: Spinal Cord Injury, Contemporary Forums

2008: Bioness L300 Certification, Bioness

2007: CSCS Certification Course

2004: NDTO Certification, Adult Hemiplegia and Brain Injury; NDTO

2004: Prosthetic Advancement; Hanger Prosthetic and Orthotic

2003: Total Joint Replacement, Advances in Total Hip, Knee, and Shoulder

2002: Sunrise Symposium, Wheelchair Seating Evaluation and Assessment

PROFESSIONAL EXPERIENCE

Physical Therapist: January 2009–Present
  Plainview Hospital, Wells, CO
  Inpatient/Outpatient Rehabilitation

  ‣ Inpatient neuro and ortho

  ‣ Outpatient neuro

  ‣ Stroke Support Group Leader: Pioneer Valley Hospital

  ‣ MS Support Group Leader: Jordan Valley Medical Center

Clinical Specialist: April 2009–December 2009
  Hamilton Hospital, Hamilton, CO
  Clinical Specialist, per diem

  ‣ Use electrical stimulation devices for neurologically impaired individuals

       • Provide clinical support to the Utah facilities personnel trained in the technology

       • Assist with education and training at the Utah facilities

Physical Therapist: May 2002–January 2009
   Mid-City Rehabilitation Hospital, Desoto, CA
   Inpatient/Outpatient Rehabilitation, May 02–January 09
   Inpatient Therapy Manager, January 08–January 09
      • Management of PT, OT, ST, and aides in a 60-bed inpatient rehabilitation hospital

      • Monthly scheduling and monitoring of FTEs

      • Monthly therapy intensity report

      • Monthly staff meeting, competency training, and quality improvement

   Clinical Site Coordinator, March 05–May 06
      • Management of an off-site outpatient orthopedic/neuro clinic

      • Management of 2 clinicians and 2 front office staff

      • Review and reporting of daily visits

      • Marketing to local physicians and clinics

      • Clinical instructor for 6 physical therapy students

Physical Therapist: June 2006–December 2006
   Wells Point Physical Therapy, Desoto, CA
      • Outpatient Orthopedics

      • Outpatient Pediatrics

      • Supervision of physical therapist assistant

Physical Therapy Student Intern: April 2001–July 2001
   Franklin Rehabilitation Hospital, Desoto, CA
      • Inpatient Rehabilitation

Physical Therapy Student Intern: December 2000
   Main Point Physical Therapy, Desoto, CA
      • Outpatient Orthopedics

Physical Therapy Student Intern: July 2000
   Manfield Children's Services, Desoto, CA
      • Outpatient Pediatrics

OTHER EXPERIENCE
Student Athletic Training Internship, Arizona University, Phoenix, AZ
Physical Therapy Aide: March 1998–July 1998
   Outpatient Orthopedics, Sportsmed Physical Therapy Clinic, Phoenix, AZ
Physical Therapy Aide: September 1995–July 1997
   Inpatient Rehabilitation, University Hospital, Orem, UT

REGISTERED NURSE AND DIRECTOR OF SURGICAL SERVICES

The candidate has laid out the productivity of her directorship experience and responsibilities, showing that she is well organized and pays attention to detail. Her résumé also includes her first assistant experience, from which a knowledgeable reader will recognize that she knows firsthand how the OR runs and what it takes for a nurse to be successful in that arena. (For clarification, an RNFA is a registered nurse who can cut skin, suture, and be left unsupervised to close cases. This position is the right-hand surgical assistant to the surgeon.)

PATRICIA GILMORE, RN, RNFA
Address   Cell #   E-mail

Goal: *To apply my 27 years of proven knowledge and leadership skills to make your hospital the best!*

PROFESSIONAL EXPERIENCE

Hanson Medical Center, Birmingham, AL **Apr/09–Present**
   Director of Surgical Services

   370 Acute Bed Facility
   20+ OR Suites
   Managed 100+ FTEs
   15,000+ Cases/Year

   ‣ Increased 0730 Starts from 34% to 90%

   ‣ Increased Surgical Revenue by 20%

   ‣ Decreased Nonproductive Overtime to .05%

   ‣ Implemented First Endoscopic Vein Harvest for Open Heart Program

   ‣ Increased Compliance of National Patient Safety Goals

   ‣ Decreased Hand Supplies by <1% over Previous Year

   ‣ Implemented Bariatric Program

Mid-Cities, Nederland, TX **Sept/07–Feb/09**
   Director of Surgical Services

   140 Acute Bed Facility
   14 OR Suites
   Managed 60+ FTEs
   7,000+ Cases/Year

   ‣ Increased 0730 Starts from 23% to over 85%

   ‣ Increased Surgical Productivity to 108%

   ‣ Increased Revenue by $27M over Previous Year

   ‣ Increased Volume by 40%

ᐧ Increased Staff and Physician Satisfaction by 32%

ᐧ Decreased Hand Supplies by $300K

ᐧ Implemented Bariatric Program

Mary Margaret Catholic Hospital, Port Neches, TX **Feb/07–Aug/07**
Interim Director of Surgical Services

350 Acute Bed Facility
12+ OR Suites
Managed 60 FTEs
8,000+ Cases/Year

ᐧ Increased Surgical Productivity to 114%

ᐧ Increased Surgical Compliance to AORN Standards

ᐧ Increased Overall Compliance to National Patient Goals to 2nd in Corporation

ᐧ Increased Total Volume of Cases from 362/mo. to 473/mo. for Month of April

ᐧ Increased Patient /Staff and Surgeon Satisfaction by 20%

Angel of Mercy Medical Center, Beaumont, TX **Sept/05–Feb/07**
Director of Surgical Services and Chief Nursing Officer

114 Acute Bed Facility
6 OR Suites
Managed 20+ FTEs
2,500+ Cases/Year

ᐧ Increased Surgical Productivity from 52% to 136%

ᐧ Increased Overall Hospital Productivity from 76% to 114%

ᐧ Decreased Staffing Agency in the Hospital to 0%

ᐧ Decreased "Left without being seen" in ER to below 3%

ᐧ Increased Nurse Retention to 85%

ᐧ Decreased Hospital Length of Stay by an Average of 1 day

ᐧ Increased JACHO Compliance from 13 Deficiencies (conditional) to 1 Deficiency

ᐧ Hospital Made Budget for the 1st Time in 3 Years

ᐧ Hired 35 Nurses within 4 mos.

Broken Arrow Hospital, Broken Arrow, OK **Aug/01–Sept/05**
Independent Director of Surgery Contractor

ᐧ Served as independent Director of Surgical Services for Various Hospitals in US

ᐧ Increased Surgical Productivity

ᐧ Increased Surgical Compliance to AORN Standards

ᐧ Taught and Trained New Directors

ᐧ Directed Hospital-Based Surgical Technician School

ᐧ Set up Standardization of Procedural Equipment

ᐧ Increased Flow of OR Procedures

› Decreased Lost Revenue

› Decreased Turnover Time to under 15 min.

U.S. Army **Aug/86–Aug/01**
   Sgt. US Army, Special Forces, Operating Room Specialist

EDUCATION
ADN, Carl Albert State College, Poteau, OK
RNFA, Front Range College, Denver, CO
CNOR, ACLS, PALS (expired)
BCLS
OR Technician
Combat MedicBSN, Ashwood University (online)
Plan to further my education to a BSN level (accredited organization)

PHYSICIAN

This résumé lists everything in the order he had studied—plus, he was board-certified in each specialty. Note: Any physician's CV is going to be terribly long. This doctor posted only the necessary information.

ROBERT McBRIDE M.D., F.A.C.S.
Thoracic and Cardiovascular Surgery
Address   Phone #   Cell #   E-mail

CURRICULUM VITAE

Pre-medical education: Bethany College, Bethany, WV; B.S., 1961
Professional Degree: University of Maine; M.D., June 1965

Specialty: Thoracic and Cardiovascular Surgery

Internship: St. Louis Medical Center, St. Louis, MO, 7/1/65–6/30/66
Residency: University Medical Center, St. Louis, MO
   Assistant Resident Surgery, 7/1/66–6/30/69
   Senior Resident Surgery, 7/1/69–6/30/70
   Chief Resident—General Surgery, 7/1/70–6/30/71
   Senior Residency, Cardiothoracic Surgery, 7/1/71–6/30/72
   Chief Resident, Cardiothoracic Surgery, 7/1/72–6/30/73

Research:
Senior Vascular Research Fellow, Downstate Medical Center, Brooklyn, NY, 1968-69
Senior Research Consultant, Brakeman Inc., 2001 (First laser-powered Photonic Implantable
   Pacemaker, in concert with Mr. Wilson Greatbatch, the inventor of the lithium battery and
   the permanent heart pacemaker)

Board Certification:
American Board of Surgery, 10/13/72; Certificate #17989
American Board of Thoracic Surgery, 1/26/74; Certificate #4807

Licensures:
New York State, #05804715
California, #G080452125

Academic Appointments:
Associate Professor Surgery, **North Carolina College of Osteopathic Medicine,**
   March 1966–Present
Assistant Clinical Instructor Surgery, **Uptown Medical Center,** Dallas, July 1966–June 1974
Assistant Instructor Thoracic Surgery, **Galveston College of Medicine,** Galveston,
   July 1966–June 1974
Instructor in Clinical Surgery, **State University of Texas,** San Marcas, July 1966–June 1974
Instructor in Gross Anatomy, **Yale University School of Medicine,** New Haven, 2005
   academic year

SOCIETY AFFILIATIONS
   Fellow, American College of Surgeons
   Fellow, American College of Chest Surgeons

Fellow, American College of Cardiology
American Medical Association
Nassau County Medical Society
New York State Medical Society
Nassau Surgical Society
American Heart Association
Lt. Commander, U.S. Navy Reserve 1966–73
Fellow, New York Cardiological Society
North American Society of Pacing & Electrophysiology

PUBLICATIONS

Rohl, D., Summers, D., Nacht, R., Saul, B., Wechsler, B., McBride, R., Rubin, R., Keates, J., OMalley, G., Stuckey, J., Dennis, C. "Combined pharmacologic, pump support and surgical attempts to salvage patients in cardiogenic shock." *Thoraxchirurgie Vaskulare Chirurgie* 21, no. 4 (1973): 332–36

McBride, R., Rubin, R., Stanczewski, B., Parmeggiani, A., Costello, M., Lucas, R.R., Srinivasan, S. "Electrochemical modification of hyper acute immune rejection." *European Surgical Research* 5, no. 2 (1973): 901–4.

Summers, D.N., Kaplitt, M., Norris, J., Rubin, R., Nacht, R., Arieff, A., Lee, M., Wechsler, McBride, R. "Salvage of patients in cardiogenic shock." *Archives of Surgery* 99, no. 6 (1971): 389–401.

Summers, D.N., Nact, R., Rohl, D., Saul, B., Wechsler, B., McBride, R., Rubin, R., Keates, J., OMalley, G., Stuckey, J., Dennis. C. "Intra-aortic balloon pumping: hemodynamic and metabolic effects during cardiogenic shock in patients with triple coronary artery obstructive disease." *Journal of Cardiovascular Surgery* 13, no. 4 (1972): 313–23.

OTHER

Interests:
Occupational/Environmental Medicine
Toxicology/Public Health
Preparedness Training & Emergency Response
Member, U.S. Department of Defense, Ad Hoc Advisory for Pulmonary Medicine

In Service Education:
Biodetection/Biomedical Consultant, U.S. Environmental Protection Agency, October 2001.
"Environmental Security; A New Technology; A New Frontier; A Multidisciplinary Approach to Environmental Problem Solving," R&D Proposal, U.S. EPA, Research Triangle Park, North Carolina.

The Legal/Political Response to Bioterrorism: A Joint Agency Community Forum, in concert with Duke Law School, U.S. State Department, November 2001.

Public Health Response to Bioterrorism/Biodetection Control Technologies, CDC-sponsored research, April 2002, R&D Technological Advancement Forum with U.S. Department of Defense, Centers for Disease Control, U.S. Environmental Protection Agency, Agency for Toxic Substances & Disease Registry.

John Hopkins School of Civilian Biodefense/School of Public Health, Lecture Series Attendance, Maryland campus, 2001.

"Medical Effects of Ionizing Radiation," Uniformed Services, University of Health Sciences, Bethesda, Maryland, May 2002.

SPEECH THERAPIST

This is an easy read, with all the qualifications summarized in a clear outline—nothing left out. The educational and clinical experience is detailed, and the reader can see Denise is an achiever in her field.

Denise Sawyer MA, CCC-SLP
Cell #   Address   E-mail

SUMMARY

Over 25 years as a Speech-Language Pathologist providing assessment, diagnosis, and therapy for neonate, pediatric, and adult populations with communicative disabilities within multiple settings (clinical, home health, residential, schools)

Autism Treatment Approaches	Literacy Based Strategies
Due Process and Compliance	Integrated Treatment with Other Disciplines
Effective Team and Independent Worker	Strong SLP Knowledge Base

SELECTED ACCOMPLISHMENTS AND DEMONSTRATED SKILLS

- Built and maintained successful relationships and communicated effectively with co-workers, administrators, parents, patients, and individuals with disabilities across various socioeconomic, educational, and ethnic backgrounds.

- Applied comprehensive range of screening and assessment tools while correlating with other appropriate data to best benefit the individual and support best practice.

- Enhanced the regular educational experience of children by providing strategies and materials while assisting student support teams in implementing response to intervention.

- Provided techniques and materials to parents enabling them to supplement treatments, resulting in exit from speech services prior to child's entry into kindergarten.

- Determined most effective treatments through application of research-based practices to establish a reliable baseline and comparative records of progress.

- Accelerated communication improvement in individuals by identifying and helping them to obtain appropriate assistive/augmentative technology devices.

- Teamed with teachers to integrate current classroom course of studies and activities into speech/language treatments, increasing overall effectiveness of remediation.

PROFESSIONAL EXPERIENCE

Dallas County Board of Education, Dallas, TX   1998–Present
  Speech Language Pathologist
  Pre-K through Twelve (up to age Twenty-one). One of the first providers to identify students potentially on the autism spectrum and provided teachers strategies for successful education.

Brigham Young University of Idaho County Board of Education, Ricksburg, ID   1994–1998
  Speech Language Pathologist
  K through Eight. Provided therapy for most of the hearing-impaired students with "Total Communication."

Pittsburgh County Board of Education, Pittsburgh, PA   1984–1994
    Speech Language Pathologist
    Pre-K (Headstart) through Eight. In addition to SLP assessment and treatment, in charge of
    compiling all documentation on developmental assessment and re-assessments for EC psycho-
    logical evaluations at my home-base elementary school.

Oakford County Board of Education, Oakford, IL   1983–1984
    Speech Language Pathologist
    K through Eight. Serving three elementary schools in a rural setting.

OTHER EXPERIENCE
  - Ramsey Rehab (Home Health). Assessment and treatment; PRN as needed for pediatric
    clients with severe communication challenges.

  - NovaCare. Provided treatment and assessments for adults with developmental disabilities
    in a residential setting.

  - Granger Speech and Hearing Center (Clinic). Provided assessment and treatment for pedi-
    atric population.

EDUCATION—PROFESSIONAL DEVELOPMENT
Master of Arts in Communication Disorders, Pittsburgh University—1992
Bachelor of Arts in Speech-Language Pathology, Orange, CO—1983
Bi-Annual Audiometric Hearing Screening Training, Dr. Mary Mundy
All Class Modules for Auditory/Verbal Therapy Certification

CERTIFICATIONS AND LICENSES
Certificate of Clinical Competency – American Speech and Hearing Association—Cert #01084332
Orange County Board of Examiners—License for Speech Pathology and Audiology #4625
Texas Department of Public Instruction License
Paraprofessional Speech Training Certification—KY Educational Development Corporation

PROFESSIONAL ASSOCIATIONS
Orange County Speech Hearing Language Association (OCSHLA)
OCSHLA—Education Committee Chairperson 2005–2009
OCSHLA—Spring Convention Committee member for 2009, 2010
OCSHLA—Fall Conference Chair for 2004
American Speech Language Hearing Association
Special Interest Division Sixteen Orange County Liaison—ASHA

AWARDS
Award for Continuing Education—ASHA

REGISTERED NURSE (RN)/OPERATING ROOM ASSISTANT DIRECTOR

This candidate is an RN certified operating-room nurse and certified RN first assistant, employed in an assistant director of perioperative services role. The résumé shows her obvious commitment to her field and the time spent perfecting her résumé. The profile and summary include detailed responsibilities for each position, as well as her certifications and CEUs. It's obvious to see she carefully planned her career and has climbed the educational ladder, as well as "paid her dues" as a staff operating-room RN. Her résumé indicates she is motivated, strives for success, and has the experience, drive, and educational background for an upper management–level position.

MARY E. BAKER, RN, BSN, CNOR, CRNFA

| Address | Phone # | E-mail |

QUALIFICATIONS PROFILE

- Dedicated and patient-focused Registered Nurse with proven strengths in perioperative nursing, staff development, and leadership.
- Exceptional capacity to multitask: manage numerous, often competing priorities with ease and foster the provision of superior patient care.
- Widely recognized as an excellent care provider and patient advocate.
- Demonstrated ability to forge, lead, and motivate outstanding healthcare teams that provide top-quality patient care.
- Facilitated high-quality healthcare to diverse groups of patients entering the perioperative environment.
- Outstanding interpersonal and communication skills: superior accuracy in patient history, charting, and other documentation.
- Ability to troubleshoot many types of surgical equipment with knowledge of surgical instruments and procedures.

EDUCATION & CERTIFICATIONS

Currently Enrolled in Graduate Program—MSN/MHA
University of Colorado, Denver, CO; Current, to graduate in 2011

Higher Education
University of Texas at Dallas, 2008; MSN courses

Bachelor of Science, Nursing
University of Colorado, Denver, 2007

Gayleside College of Nursing
Perioperative Plus Associates, Denver, CO, 2003
Certified RN First Assist Program

Associates Degree RN, Nursing
Nederland College, Nederland, TX, 1998
Nursing Honors Society, Phi Theta Kappa
IVN program
University of Dallas, Dallas, TX, 1991

PROFESSIONAL EXPERIENCE
Wakefield Hospital, Wakefield, NC

Assistant Director of Perioperative Services   2008–Present

› Report directly to Director of Perioperative Services and governing body on quality issues

› Support the vision of the Director of Perioperative Services

› Support and develop programs and mission that further develop the hospital

› Support the professional and technical needs of employees

› Provide strong contribution to the North Hills Hospital Heart Program by providing support and guidance for the 100+/yr heart surgeries, as well as general/vascular procedures yearly. Very active in the clinical role with staff

› Able to perform multiple roles in the OR, including secretary, circulating nurse, scrub nurse, certified first assistant, holding area nurse, board runner, and charge nurse

› Exhibit motivation and dedication by providing the highest quality of care to each patient

› Always maintain a positive attitude and strong work ethic despite negativity and heavy workloads

› Work well with other departments to promote cohesiveness and open communication

› Ensure high level of external and internal customer satisfaction

› Recommend and revise departmental policies

› Ran the board for both main OR and CVOR 10 rooms daily

› Eager to learn administrative duties

› Eager to help other services

› Maintain accurate preference cards for cost-effective cases

Mid-Cities Surgical, Orange, TX

Self-Employed   2005–Present
Certified Registered Nurse First Assistant, CRNFA

› Provide first-assistant services during the operative procedure, general/vascular/GYN

› Support the professionalism and technical needs of the surgeon

› Take calls with surgeons

CHIEF NURSING OFFICER

The best thing about this résumé is the format, with a summary of experience that provides at-a-glance information. Résumés of hospital executives tend to be very long.

MICHAEL HASKET, RN, BSN, MSHA, FACHE
Address   Cell #   E-mail

SUMMARY

Senior Management Experience as the Chief Nursing Officer in a 300-bed hospital partnered with Rockford Clinic.

Cardiovascular professional with 20 years of clinical and management experience.

Strong commitment to Care of Excellence and Quality Care for every patient every day.

Very goal oriented, focusing on exceeding targets through strong cohesive teamwork.

Committed to hard work that will better position the organization to accommodate ambitious market share and maintain excellent quality care.

EXPERIENCE

January 2006 to Present   **Richardson Clinic Partnership Hospital, Richardson, Tex.**

Chief Nursing Officer, International Medical Center (IMC)

IMC is a state-of-the-art 300-bed for-profit hospital established in partnership with Rockford Clinic. It is considered one of the chief referral centers providing multidisciplinary health services. IMC has 5 centers of excellence that offer very specialized high quality care.

- Oversee 660 FTEs in the nursing manpower. Responsible for all nursing operational activities at IMC. These responsibilities range from complete drafting of the budget to complete commissioning of the hospital in terms of manpower, supplies, equipment, and policy and procedures.

- Member of the hospital executive committee, which meets at least weekly to address a wide range of hospital issues.

- Heavily involved in the strategic direction of the hospital, service line management, and marketing.

Accomplishments at IMC

1. Culture: Nursing department comprised 100 nurses in June 2006. This department had no cohesive plan or well-defined culture that gave direction to the nursing department. In the last 6 months we were able to wrap nursing around the IMC culture, motivating staff about the direction and prospective plans for IMC. The deep sense of IMC mission is very palpable anywhere in the nursing department.

2. Recruitment: Manpower of the nursing department grew from 100 nurses in June 2006 to 400 nurses at present. Nursing was put in charge of the full process of recruiting, which gave us the driver-seat view of the process. Nursing recruitment has been very selective, whereby we picked 100 nurses out of 3,000 candidates. The work continues to reach about 600 nurses for the hospital-wide manpower.

3. Nurse Managers: We have hired all 12 nurse managers. All nurse managers are high caliber, with a collective clinical experience adding up to more than 100 years.

4. Organizational Chart: The nursing organizational chart was completed whereby it could be adjusted to fit IMC organizational chart. The organizational chart was designed to offer the best clinical support to the patient population. Every nursing division has a clinical nurse specialist focused on advancing the clinical practice.

5. Nursing Budget: The 2006 and 2007 manpower distribution and budget have been completed and submitted to the CEO.

6. Patient Satisfaction: Nursing department initiated the patient satisfaction surveys in IMC. Nursing scored over 95% patient satisfaction continually.

7. Home Health Department: In October, Home Health came under Nursing and did 200 visits the first month and 300 visits the next. The plan is to have 1,400 visits per month yielding gross revenue of 3,300,000 SR annually. Home Health department now has a plan to have 32 staff in total. We have 6 staff now doing over 350 visits a month. We have focused on comprehensive home healthcare that includes not only nursing but also physical therapy, occupational therapy, and social work. Presently, Home Health is a good revenue generator, and should have a dominant role at IMC and the community.

8. Educational Department: Since June 2006, we have started education seminars of 200 in-services per month. In addition, we have conducted the following courses:

Preceptorship

Pain Management

Conscious Sedation

IV Therapy

Computer packages (how to use Outlook and Basic computer skills)

Telemetry package developed and placed on unit

Complete midwifery for L & D and OB staff

9. ACLS, PALS, BLS: The following employees have been certified as follows:

ACLS: 102

PALS: 43

NRP: 35

BLS: 865

10. Nursing Department Involvement: Nursing has participated in several projects, such as inventory, billing, diabetic day, pediatric day. Nursing continues to play a positive role, cooperating with all departments in the hospital to achieve the common goal of IMC—to offer the best holistic care and increase our patient volume.

11. Nursing Policy and Procedure: Nursing department established its own policy and procedure review committee, which was able to draft 320 hospital-wide policies.

12. Aramco Survey: Nursing department has successfully passed Aramco Survey, which is similar to Joint Commission survey, with all units scoring greater than 90%.

January 2005 to January 2006   St. Mary's Hospital, New York, N.Y.

Health Administration Consultant

The General Authority for Health Services is responsible for running 8 hospitals, 2 of which are trauma hospitals, and 1 is a 500-bed teaching hospital. All 5 other hospitals are secondary-care hospitals.

- Responsible for planning hospital's medical consumables, and allocate resources to special care programs.

- Established contracts for the cardiac services for both medical and surgical services. This involved Cardiology department, both adult and pediatric, Cath. Lab, Cardiac Surgery department, CVICU, Perfusion, and Anesthesia department.

- Responsible for drafting the 2006 consumable budget for all hospitals and clinics under the General Authority for Health Services. Planning work involved extensive consulting on my part to the hospitals, with delegated tasks to the team at the particular hospital. In addition, was also responsible for the standardization project at GAHS to standardize all contracts for medical consumables across GAHS facilities.

- Designed and implemented quality improvement and quality assurance protocols in relation to medical consumables. Established an access database system that encompasses all contract items for GAHS facilities.

March 2003 to January 2005   McDaniel Medical Center (BMMC), White Plains, N.Y.

Nurse Manager of Cardiovascular Services

BMMC is a licensed 590-bed hospital. This position reported to the Chief Nursing Officer, and was responsible for 58 FTE in Cardiovascular Intensive Care Unit and Cardiovascular Surgical Unit (CVICU/CVSU).

- Responsible for the daily management duties of the post cardiothoracic units, which included payroll, staffing, quality management, monitor care, as well as exceeded or met targets in financial, quality, and patient satisfaction.

- Was awarded Nurse Manager of the Year for service of excellence.

During this employment manpower distribution and labor cost budget was restructured. Kept patient satisfaction above 95% for a full year in the cardiovascular department. Was team member of the Joint Commission that prepared the hospital for Joint Commission inspection.

March 2001 to March 2003   McDaniel Medical & Heart (HCA), New York, N.Y.

Director of Cardiovascular Services

HCA is a 300-bed for-profit facility, and it focuses on cardiac services. Responsible for 96 FTEs in CVICU, CVSU, CCU, and MICU and running the daily operations of Cardiovascular Services, which included staff management, quality assurance, JCAHO ready preparation, financial, and patient-care monitoring. The heart program did over 4,600 Cardiac Cath, and 400 open heart procedures.

Significant Accomplishments at McDaniel Hospital:

1. Involved in JCAHO preparation that led to a 98% score and no type.

2. Restructured staffing and eliminated contract-labor travelers nurses and agency-contract nurses, which led to a major financial savings and resulted in a strong core staff focused on high accountability and professionalism.

3. Fostered teamwork approach and staff engagement. Patient satisfaction as a result increased (Gallop) from 2.9 to 4.0 and later plateaued to 3.8 (4.0 is a perfect score).

4. Headed a committee that established cardiothoracic protocols, post-op cardiac surgery orders.

5. Conducted and arranged for clinical critical care seminars that the staff attended to improve clinical experience.

September 1993 to March 2001   **Twin Falls Hospital, Rockford, Idaho**
Staff Nurse in CVICU
Responsible for the total care of patients undergoing cardiothoracic and vascular surgery. Took care of patients ranging from cardiac bypass and valve replacement to thoracic surgery. Operated a wide range of machines in the CVICU, ventilators, L-VAD, and Integrated Cardiac Monitoring System.

August 1989 to May 1993   **Twin Falls Medical Research, Twin Falls, Idaho**
Staff RN and Charge Nurse
A very busy Emergency Department. Took care of a variety of trauma and emergency patients, ranging from gun shots to traumatic injuries, to cardiac and medical problems. Member of local emergency response team.

COMMITTEE MEMBERSHIPS

Hospital Executive Committee: Worked along with CEO and other department chiefs to ensure the strategic direction of the hospital. HEC oversaw and approved dept. budgets, and approved capital budget. In addition, discussed quality reports, financial reports, and others.

JC Leadership Committee: Responsible for making sure the hospital is prepared for Joint Commission visit. Established a system where the hospital is ready for visit at any time of the year.

Pharmacy Nursing Liaison: Evaluates medication accuracy, recommends ways to improve pharmacy/nursing communication to improve medication safety.

CPI CABG: Meets with cardiac surgeons and cardiologists monthly to discuss cardiac surgery and cardiology statistics that includes number of cases, complications, deaths. This committee approves changes that would take place in cardiac division.

Critical Care Counsel: Made up of directors of divisions, all nurse managers, charge nurses, and 2 staff members of all units. The counsel meets monthly to discuss quality issues, improvement initiative, and information sharing for all units.

Patient Satisfaction Committee: Focused on evaluating patient surveys and suggesting ways to improve care and patient satisfaction.

LICENSURE AND CERTIFICATIONS
Registered Nurse, State of Florida # RN 91675060
RN Licensed, Kansas #1- 054568,
RN Licensed, New York #1-985524
Advance Cardiac Support Instructor, ACLS Instructor

EDUCATION
Master of Science in Health Administration, University of Alabama
Bachelor of Science in Nursing, University of New York
Diploma in Nursing, School of Allied Health and Sciences

PROFESSIONAL AFFILIATION
FACHE (Fellow of American College of Healthcare Executives)

COMPUTER SKILLS
Microsoft Word, Microsoft Excel, Kronos Payroll System, Ansos Staffing System, and Financial
Hospital Software (Budgeting, Cost Analysis, and General Ledger Analysis)

CERTIFIED REGISTERED NURSE FIRST ASSISTANT

An excellent résumé that describes all the duties in an easy-to-read format.

Mary Jones
Address   Phone   Cell #

EXPERIENCE

SURGICAL ASSOCIATES OF EAST TEXAS, Tyler, TX

Office Manager, CRNFA   **May 2008–Present**

- Responsible for ordering surgical office supplies and maintaining all sterile supplies, as well as instrumentation for busy surgical office

- Provide support for surgeon and patients during pre- and post-operative office visits

- Ensure all medical paperwork, labwork pre- and post-op completed

- Schedule all surgical cases with a variety of hospitals and outpatient facilities

- Schedule consult appointments for patients and follow-up with consults

- Provide cosmetic services

- Provide first-assistant services during the operative procedure, general/vascular/GYN

- Support the professionalism and technical needs of the surgeon

- Take calls with surgeon

HUGO BROWN MEMORIAL MEDICAL CENTER, Fort Worth, TX

Staff Nurse, Operating Room, Open Heart Team

CRNFA, Charge Nurse   **2000–2007**

- Performed multiple roles in the OR, including secretary, circulating nurse, scrub nurse, certified first assistant holding care nurse, and evening charge nurse in a busy OR

- Took full load of calls, both main OR and heart team; very active in the clinical role

- Assisted during off hours or nights when called

- Exhibited motivation and dedication to providing the highest quality of care to each patient

PLAINVIEW HOSPITAL, Hillsboro, TX

Infection Control Officer   **1998–2000**

Staff Nurse—Emergency Room and Operating Room

- Reported directly to the CNO for Infection Control issues

- Performed Infection Control duties

- Educated staff with Infection Control issues

- Worked mainly in the ER, providing quality patient care

- Supported the professional and technical needs of ER physicians and staff

- Worked in OR as needed

- Took calls as needed in the OR

MID-COUNTY REGIONAL HOSPITAL CLINIC, Forney, TX
  Clinical Charge Nurse   1996–1998
  - Reported to regulatory agency and ensured compliance
  - Supervised every aspect of the clinic Quality Improvement program
  - Monitored environment of care
  - Reported directly to the CNO of Hill Regional Hospital and governing body quality issues
  - Supported and developed programs and mission that further developed the clinic
  - Ensured a high level of internal and external customer satisfaction
  - Supported the professional and technical needs of the clinic physicians

WELBOURN HOSPITAL, Plano, TX
  Scrub Nurse, Operating Room   1995–1996
  - Performed scrub nurse duties in an extremely busy OR
  - Supported the professional and technical needs of the surgeon, main OR, and vascular OR
  - Scrubbed on general, vascular, GYN, ortho, and urology cases
  - Managed preference cards

WACO REGIONAL HOSPITAL, Waco, TX
  Staff Nurse—Med/Surg Floor   1993–1995
  - Worked on the medical surgical floor routinely
  - Floated to nursery when needed
  - Committed to facility—worked extra shift and double shift when needed
  - Exhibited motivation and dedication by providing the highest quality of care to each patient

WILBURN KIDNEY DISEASE CENTER, Wilburn, TX
  Kidney Transplant Coordinator   1991–1993
  Dialysis Charge Nurse
  - Facility coordinator for dialysis patient to be put on list for transplant
  - Charge nurse
  - Reported to CNO of facility
  - Monitored environment of care
  - Provided professional and technical services for dialysis patient
  - Adjusted dialysis machines to ensure adequate treatments for patients

ASSOCIATION MEMBERSHIP
2001–Present, AORN (Association of Operating Room Nurses)
2003–Present, RNFA of Texas Association

CERTIFICATIONS

2003–Present, CRNFA (no expiration date)

2013, CNOR

2011, BCLS

2007, ACLS, December 2009

CONTINUING EDUCATION

Previously enrolled in University of Phoenix for MSN/MHA degree

25 Hours of CEU credits every 2 years for RN license renewal

125 Hours of CEU for renewal of CNOR/CRNFA Certification

QUALITY CONTROL/RISK MANAGEMENT REGISTERED NURSE

This is a polished, extremely detailed résumé. This candidate has meticulously outlined her experience and educational background, as well as included a slight biography/profile to sum up her proven abilities. This is one of those rare situations when a functional résumé can be effective. All of the work experience is in nursing so the functions are more important than where they occurred. The reader is more interested in the accomplishments themselves rather than where they were performed. But nursing is an exception to the general rule.

AGNES ROGERS

E-mail   **Address**   **Phone #**

OBJECTIVE

Quality Improvement/Risk Management position that provides an opportunity for promotion in an organization dedicated to providing efficient, effective, and safe healthcare to the community served.

PROFILE

Motivated, enthusiastic Registered Nurse with a Master's degree in Nursing, Business, and Healthcare Administration and a successful history in project leadership and implementation. Management experience in both the inpatient and outpatient healthcare settings with director supervision of up to 14 staff members. Professional and compassionate with the ability to maintain confidentiality and tact in handling sensitive matters. Dedicated to patient safety and customer service while focusing on state and federal regulatory requirements. Ability to function independently and in team settings to meet organizational goals. Enjoys working with others and maintains a positive attitude and sense of humor while under pressure. Prioritization and multitasking ability to ensure project goals are achieved at the highest level.

PROFESSIONAL EXPERIENCE

Risk Management

- Failure, Mode, Effects Analysis and Root Cause Analysis experience.
- Development of Physician Peer Review, Focused Physician Performance Evaluation, and Ongoing Physician Performance Evaluation program.
- Data collection, analysis, and prompting of process improvement projects in response to incidents, patient complaints, and medication errors.
- Response to potential legal issues with focus on service recovery and organizational transparency.
- Integral role in periodic chart reviews for inpatient and outpatient services.
- Assistance in development of organizational contracts and policies and procedures for clinical, administrative, and ancillary departments.
- Participation in quarterly risk management meetings.

Quality Improvement/Patient Safety/Customer Service

- Committee Chair of the Quality Council.
- Designed and implemented Interdepartmental Hand-Off Checklist to improve communication.
- Developed and implemented Hourly Rounding Program.
- Had integral role in design and implementation of Rapid Response Team.
- Developed and monitored Surgical Safety Checklist and "Time-Out" Checklist.
- Designed and implemented Medication Reconciliation Program Project.
- Had integral role in implementation of ICARE program focused on Customer Service and Service Recovery.
- Managed organization-wide Quality Improvement goals for each department.
- Oversaw state and federal required reporting of hospital data and core measure results.
- Managed customer satisfaction survey process and disseminated monthly and quarterly reports.
- Developed process to decrease readmissions related to congestive heart failure.

Compliance

- Committee Chair of the Corporate Compliance Committee.
- Monitored updates by state and federal regulatory agencies to ensure corporate compliance.
- Participated in new employee orientation and competency related to compliance issues.
- Communicated revisions of requirements to all levels of the organization.

Accreditation

- Directed facility through accreditation process.
- Maintained communication with accrediting body and organization throughout survey process and follow-up.

Communication/Presentations

- Provided daily communication between departments and administration.
- Reported monthly to Quality Council, Credentialing Committee, and Medical Staff.
- Oversaw bi-monthly presentations to new employees.
- Periodically attended all staff meetings to provide updates on new processes, issues, regulations.
- Developed annual patient safety initiative presentations for all staff.
- Provided quarterly presentation to the Governing Board.
- Developed annual Quality Improvement/Risk Management report for the Governing Board.
- Made periodic presentations to Leadership Team.

EMPLOYMENT HISTORY

Kingston Heart Hospital, White Plains, NY
Director of Quality Improvement, Risk Management,
  Compliance, and Accreditation   January 2008 to Present

Wild Valley Teaching Medical Center, White Plains, NY
Associate Degree in Nursing Instruction   August 2005 to July 2008

Southside Hospital, Seattle, WA
Staff Nurse   March 2002 to January 2006

Lakeside Hospital, Tacoma, WA
Emergency Department Staff Nurse   January 1996 to July 2002

EDUCATION

University of Kansas (online), **Masters in the Science of Nursing, Masters in Business Administration/Masters in Healthcare Administration,** August 2003 to July 2006

Challenger College, Seattle, WA, **Bachelors in the Science of Nursing,** August 1997 to December 1999

Seattle College, Seattle, WA, **Associate Degree in the Science of Nursing,** August 1995 to May 1997

PROFESSIONAL MEMBERSHIPS

American Society for Healthcare Risk Management

Health Care Compliance Association

The Honor Society of Nursing, Sigma Theta Tau International

PHARMACIST

Typically, résumés for pharmacists are lengthy; however, this one provides the details and accomplishments in a way that eliminates having to "search out" pertinent information. All of his clinical experience (meaning nonpaid) and publications are omitted because those have no bearing on his experience.

ROB RICHARDSON R.PH., M.B.A.
Address   Phone #   Cell #

PROFESSIONAL PROFILE

Results-oriented MBA-level professional with experience boosting productivity, cutting costs, and increasing efficiencies in a 137-bed hospital.

- Problem solver and decision maker with experience in both financial and clinical areas.
- Strong leader and manager of personnel with good interpersonal skills and experience managing a hospital pharmacy department.
- Good communicator with analytical skills. Able to develop detailed reports.
- Competent multitasker who adheres to regulatory and accreditation agency requirements.
- Computer-literate performer with technical proficiencies covering a wide range of applications and platforms, including McKesson HBOC, Meditech, Pyxis, Omnicell, MS Office: Excel, Access, Word, PowerPoint, First DataBank, MicroMedex, and MediSpan, as well as Process Improvement, Performance Measurement, Quality Improvement, LEAN.

Areas of Expertise

Inpatient Hospital Pharmacy	Pharmacy Policy and Procedure
Oncology Pharmacy	Hospital Drug Formulary Management
Database Management	Outpatient and Retail Pharmacy

PROFESSIONAL EXPERIENCE

Director of Pharmacy

Seagull Valley Hospital, Salt Lake City, UT   **2005 to Present**

- Responsible for all aspects of hospital pharmacy department, including purchasing, medication distribution, clinical pharmacy, medication security, pharmacy policies, and procedures.
- Responsible for $18 million annual pharmacy budget.
- Implemented USP797 sterile compounding requirements for the inpatient pharmacy.
- Implemented PHS-340b program, which continues to save over $2.2 million annually in drug costs.
- Designed MS Office applications, which standardized nursing unit inspections, tracked pharmacist interventions, and maintained perpetual narcotic inventories.
- Responsible for pharmacy informatics, which maintained software libraries for several pharmacy applications (Meditech, Omnicell, PharmaServ, Hospira IV pumps).

- Responsible for orienting and training new hospital staff to the pharmacy department, including end-user training for Omnicell.

- Designed and relocated pharmacy department to new facility.

- Successfully opened and managed hospital outpatient pharmacy.

- Successfully completed two Joint Commission surveys.

- Managed 40+ department staff personnel.

- Co-chair, Pharmacy, Infection and Transfusion Committee (PIT) making formulary decisions for the hospital.

Pharmacist, Staff
Seagull Valley Hospital, Salt Lake City, UT   **1992 to 2005**

- Responsible for medication order review and entry into HCIS; performed medication review for patients in a 137-bed inpatient hospital.

- Worked routinely in oncology clinic, including review of complex medication orders and therapies.

- Functioned as informatics pharmacist responsible for software maintenance, including development of an outpatient prescription billing software application used to adjudicate prescriptions.

Head Pharmacist
UPharm, Salt Lake City, UT   **1990 to 1991**

- Responsible for all aspects of pharmacy functions for a large retail drug store chain, including purchasing, inventory control, pricing, customer service.

- Scheduled and managed all pharmacy personnel.

- Consistently exceeded pharmacy sales and contract compliance expectations within the pharmacy district.

Staff Pharmacist
Southside Pharmacy, Salt Lake City, UT   **1988 to 1990**
Community pharmacist serving local residents

OTHER
Contract pharmacist for Portal, a Washington State mental health program.
Instructor, Bellingham Vocational and Technical Institute, Bellingham, WA, 1988–1990.
  Vocational instructor for multidisciplinary students (pharmacy, nursing, E.M.T.).

EDUCATION
Master of Business Administration, Western Washington University, Bellingham, WA
Bachelor of Science in Pharmacy, University of Washington, Seattle, WA

PROFESSIONAL AFFILIATIONS
American Society of Health System Pharmacists (ASHP)
Washington State Pharmacy Association (WSPA)

PHYSICIAN ASSISTANT

Excellent résumé, as everything is laid out so you don't have to do extra reading to see this person's qualifications and duties.

WENDY SIMON, PA-C

Address   Phone #   Cell #

EDUCATION

University of North Carolina Medical Branch, Raleigh, North Carolina
Bachelor of Science in Physician Assistant Studies, August 2002
Accomplishments: Dean's List

University of North Carolina, Chapel Hill, North Carolina
Bachelor of Science in Psychology, May 1999; minor in Anthropology
Accomplishments: Magna Cum Laude, Dean's List, Psi Chi—National Honor Society in Psychology, Golden Key National Honor Society
Awards: Outstanding Service on a Psi Chi Committee, as a Psi Chi Committee Chair, and as a Psi Chi Officer

LICENSES AND CERTIFICATIONS

Certified by the National Commission on Certification of Physician Assistants, September 2002; recertified June 2009

Licensed by the Texas State Board of Physician Assistant Examiners, November 2002

Basic Life Support (BLS/CPR), Renewed February 2009

Pediatric Advanced Life Support (PALS), March 2009

PROFESSIONAL AFFILIATIONS

American Academy of Physician Assistants (AAPA)—since 2001

Texas Academy of Physician Assistants (TAPA)—since 2002
TAPA CME Committee—2009–2010

Texas Gulf Coast Physician Assistant Association (TGCPAA)—since 2003

Society of Dermatology Physician Assistants (SDPA)—since 2008

Physician Assistants in Orthopaedic Surgery (PAOS)—since 2009

WORK EXPERIENCE

University School of Medicine
Pediatric Orthopedics, Texas Main Hospital   April 2005 to Present

Dallas Orthopedics Sports Medicine Associates, Orthopedics   October 2003 to April 2005

Frisco Medical Group, Family Medicine   February 2003 to October 2003

Recent CME Conferences
6th Annual Fall Society of Dermatology Physician Assistants (SDPA) Conference, November 5–8, 2008; 32 hours CME
6th Annual Skin Curriculum Overview for Physician Extenders (SCOPE), May 15–17, 2009; 20 hours CME

Physician Assistants in Orthopedic Surgery (PAOS) Annual Conference, October 19–23, 2009; 32 hours CME

Upcoming CME Conferences
35th Annual Texas Academy of Physician Assistants (TAPA) Spring CME, February 23–26, 2012

7th Annual Skin Curriculum Overview for Physician Extenders (SCOPE), March 23–25, 2012

CLINICAL ROTATIONS
Pediatric Endocrine Team Elective: John Sealy Hospital

Pediatrics Diabetes Camp Elective: Texas Lions Camp

Orthopedic Surgery: UTMB Clinics & John Sealy Hospital (TDCJ)

General Surgery: John Adams Hospital (TDCJ)

Emergency Room: John Adams Hospital

Family Medicine: RGC Medicine Clinic

Internal Medicine: RGC Hospital

Occupational Medicine: Valley Diagnostic Clinic

Ob/Gyn: UTMB Clinics & John Sealy Hospital

Pediatrics: UTMB Clinics & John Sealy Hospital

Pediatric Emergency Room: Lyndon B. Johnson Hospital

Internship: Family & Occupational Medicine, Valley Diagnostic Clinic

RESEARCH EXPERIENCE
Baptist College of Medicine—Elder Abuse and Neglect—1998

M.D. Anderson—Smoking Cessation—1996

Résumés for the Legal Field

ATTORNEY AT LAW

This is an excellent résumé because of the following factors:

- Overall, it shows this as an exceptional candidate with an outstanding educational and professional history.

- It instantly identifies the candidate's specialty or area of practice.

- It details the candidate's educational history, inclusive of all degrees received, institutions attended, year each degree was received, honors, and GPA.

- The reverse chronological order identifies all employers, gives inclusive dates of employment, and mentions titles/positions held.

- It lists professional licenses, with inclusive dates.

- It specifies professional organizations to which the candidate belongs, with inclusive dates of membership and offices held.

Robert Hardy Falk, P.C.

Address   Phone #   Cell #   E-mail

AV-Rated Professional Intellectual Property Trial Lawyer

Experience in Management of Law Firms and Hands-On Experience in All Phases of Intellectual Property, Prosecution, Licensing and Litigation (Management, First and Second Chair), including Patents, Trademarks, Trade Dress, Copyrights, and Trade Secrets, and the Surrounding Areas of Unfair Competition and Antitrust Law. State and Federal Courts and the International Trade Commission; Foreign Oppositions and Cancellation Proceedings in Canada, the European Patent Office, the Commonwealth Countries and Japan.

EDUCATION

Juris Doctor, **University of Texas** at Austin (May 1975)
  Honors, GPA 3.5/4.00

  President of Patent, Trademark & Copyright Association; Board of Advocates (director and member); Assistant Editor, *Texas Law Review*; APLA Giles Sutherland Rich Moot Court Competition; Hildebrand and Geary Breis Competitions; and Phi Delta Phi

M.S., Chemical Engineering, **University of Texas** at Austin (August 1972)
  Salutatorian, GPA 3.80/4.00

B.S., Chemical Engineering, **University of Texas** at Austin (December 1971)
  Valedictorian, GPA 3.95/4.00; Tau Beta Pi; Phi Kappa Phi

B.A., Chemistry, **Austin College**, Sherman, Texas (January 1970)
  High Honors, GPA 3.79/4.00; Phi Beta Kappa

PROFESSIONAL EXPERIENCE

Falk & Fish, LLP, Dallas TX

Managing Partner   **June 1992–Present**

- Responsible for client procurement and development, as well as coordination of firm's resources as lead counsel for cases filed or defended on East and West Coasts of U.S., locally in Dallas, various other states including North Carolina, as well as Canada, Europe, and Japan.

- Have a range of legal responsibilities that run the gamut of litigation, licensing, and prosecution as managing partner in a boutique Intellectual Property firm, including supervision and construction of pleadings, motions, the taking of depositions, and trial testimony, including participation in same.

- Supervise the preparation and prosecution of chemical, mechanical, and electrical patent applications, and the preparation and prosecution of trademark and copyright applications.

- Supervise the litigation work of junior partners, salaried partners, associates, and paralegals, as well as foreign and domestic legal counsel and foreign patent agents.

- Appear in Federal District Courts in Texas, New York, Illinois, California, Arizona, and North Carolina.

Geary, Glast & Middleton, P.C., Dallas TX
Director, Intellectual Property Section　　　　　　　　**January 1992–June 1992**

- Responsible for client procurement and development, as well as litigation, licensing, and prosecution as head of an Intellectual Property department of a major Dallas law firm.

- Member of the Executive Committee of Geary, Glast & Middleton, P.C.

- Supervised one junior partner, six associates, and a number of paralegals.

- First- and second-chair responsibilities for the filing of several major patent suits, as well as suits involving trademarks and servicemarks.

- Responsible for worldwide prosecution of trademarks and servicemarks.

- Invoices to clients of Falk-originated clients during 5½-month period at Geary, Glast & Middleton, P.C. was in excess of $2 million.

Hubbard, Thurman, Turner & Tucker, Dallas TX
Equity Partner　　　　　　　　**March 1984–December 1991**

- Responsible for client procurement and development, as well as litigation, licensing, and prosecution responsibilities for a partner in a major firm in the Intellectual Property field; duties involved patents and trademarks and the surrounding antitrust and trade regulation areas.

- First-chair and second-chair responsibilities in numerous litigations, including Federal District Court litigation, Federal Appellate practice, State District Court and State Appellate practice, and the International Trade Commission.

- First-chair responsibilities in state trade secret, Deceptive Trade Practices Act (DTPA-Texas) in state antitrust actions.

- Co-author with William D. Harris Jr. of "The ITC as Patent Infringement Forum," lecture given before the Southwestern Legal Foundation, 28th Annual Institute on Patent Law, December 6–7, 1990.

Akzona Incorporated, Asheville NC
Division Patent, Trademark, and Licensing Counsel　　　**January 1977–February 1984**

- Representing Organon Inc. (pharmaceuticals and diagnostics—primary healthcare subsidiary of Akzona), Organon Teknika Corporation (dialysis equipment and supplies), formerly Info-Chem Project (thermometers and hospital disposable products—sold to the PyMaH Corporation of Somerville, NJ), and Akzona New Ventures (high-risk medical projects).

- Seven years' concentrated, intensive, broad Intellectual Property *inter partes* experience at Akzona, lead negotiating counsel of, as well as primary counsel for design and implementation of, the largest diagnostic licensing program (enzyme immunoassay) in the North American medical industry and other licensing programs.

- Lead counsel in a number of contested/opposed reissue and reexamination applications for patents involved in the program.

Pravel Wilson & Gambrell, Houston TX

Associate   **May 1975–January 1977**

- Extensive patent and trademark prosecution experience (average 20 U.S. originated and 12–15 foreign originated filings per year; since 1975, firm clients have procured over 40 issued patents.

- Assisted three partners as second chair with numerous pieces of patent, trademark, and trade-secret litigation, including travel to Austin, Texas; New York; and Boston.

Supreme Court of Texas, Austin TX

Clerk for Chief Justice   **November 1974–May 1975**

- Reviewed drafts of opinions circulated in Conference for Chief Justice and Other Justices.

- Extensive review of Texas and foreign laws and preparation of first draft of opinions as directed by Chief Justice.

Exxon Corporation U.S.A., etc., Houston TX

Process Engineer   **January 1970–August 1975**

- Summer work on platforms of drilling rigs for Superior Oil Corporation and seismographic boats as way of obtaining sufficient funds for completion of undergraduate studies at Austin College and University of Texas at Austin.

- Full-time work for Exxon Corporation in Baytown, TX, on Phenol Plant complex; designed 6 plants for Exxon Corporation during summer work.

LICENSES

Supreme Court of Texas (October 1975–present); Federal District Court for the Southern District of Texas (December 1975–present); Fifth Circuit Court of Appeals (January 1976); Court of Customs and Patent Appeals (January 1976–October 1982); Patent and Trademark Office (December 1975–present); District of Columbia Court of Appeals (December 1977–present); the United States Supreme Court (December 1978–present); Supreme Court of North Carolina (August 1979); Court of Appeals for the Federal Circuit (October 1982); Canadian Patent Office (January 1983); Court of Appeals for the Federal Circuit (October 1982–present); Fifth Circuit Court of Appeals (1988–present); Southern District of Texas (1989–present); Court of International Trade (1985–present)

PROFESSIONAL ORGANIZATIONS

Association of Trial Lawyers of America; America Patent Law Association (Committees on Awards, Antitrust Law, and Chemical Patent Law); America Bar Association; Licensing Executives Society; Dallas Bar Association; Dallas Patent Lawyers Association; Houston [Texas] Bar Association; Buncombe County [North Carolina] Bar Association; Houston [Texas] Patent Law Association; Houston [Texas] Junior Bar Association (former member); Texas Trial Lawyers Association; American Trial Lawyers Association (1983–present); Licensing Executive Society (1983–present)

Résumés for CEOs and Other High-Level Executives

Résumés for CEO and other high-level positions (CFO, COO, CTO, etc.) can be a bit more difficult to organize. More often than not, these high-level folks are "tapped" by executive recruiters rather than being in the position of "looking" for a job. Executive recruiters often are retained by the companies with the openings to fill.

So, the key is to have your "biography" available, online, and out there every other way possible when you are not really looking for a job. Then, when the job or recruiter "comes to you," the person usually will do so having seen your bio already posted (sometimes even posted on your present company's Web site).

This kind of résumé needs to be quick, informative, and—again—invite the "tell me more" response. A CEO or other such leader may have a more traditional résumé than what follows here, but this one is included for general awareness. These high-level résumés are as "personal" as business.

CHIEF EXECUTIVE OFFICER

Most CEO résumés are more like biographies, providing a sense of the person's character as well as accomplishments.

SHOUVIK BHATTACHARYA
Address   Phone #   E-mail

Shouvik is Chief Executive Officer of Adea. He has been with Adea for more than seven years, and has held leadership roles in strategy, delivery, and operations. He is responsible for leading the company to year-over-year profitable growth and for expanding global operations and sales. He has been instrumental in transforming the company in the last three years into a global consulting firm with diversified services in high-growth areas.

In April 2008, Shouvik was profiled among "12 Global Leaders for Tomorrow" in *Chief Executive* magazine. In January 2009, he received the Bharat Gaurav award, recognizing his contribution to the industry as a nonresident Indian. He was named "CEO with HR Orientation" by the Asia-Pacific HRM Congress in September 2009.

Prior to joining Adea, Shouvik was with Booz Allen Hamilton in New York, where he applied his management-consulting experience toward serving several industries, including oil and gas, telecom, energy utilities, financial services, and education, for clients in the United States, Europe, and the Middle East. Shouvik started his career with the Tata Group in India, working in engineering design and captive power plant operations. He subsequently held managerial roles in sales and marketing, supply chain, and information technology divisions. He then worked at InfoUSA Inc., in the United States, where he was Director for Offshore Operations.

In other management and technology consulting roles, Shouvik has implemented large-scale enterprise resource planning systems and customer-care solutions; he has redesigned supply-chain processes for global food and chemical companies, and has led consulting teams at Verizon Communications in strategy, planning, metrics, and program management.

Shouvik regularly speaks at conferences worldwide on various aspects of management, including the Global Offshoring conference in Xi'an, China; the MIT Venture Capital and Private Equity conferences in Boston; a CEO conference in Beijing; and the Minority Enterprise Summit in Dallas. He frequently speaks on the emergence of China and India in the world economy and reflects on implications of the "Chindia" concept.

Shouvik was a Sloan Fellow at the Massachusetts Institute of Technology and has an MBA from MIT's Sloan School; he is an alumnus of the well-respected Indian Institute of Technology. Recently, he has been involved in setting up a Merchant Bank in China, focused on cross-border mergers and acquisitions. His research interests include Entrepreneurial Finance, China's outbound investment market, and trends in India's BPO sector.

While growing up in India, Shouvik was actively involved in theater, sports, and music during the time he was receiving his education at Sherwood College, in the beautiful northern Himalayan hill station of Nainital. He was captain of a leading tennis team at university level, and played the Sarod, a rare Indian classical instrument, on Indian television. Shouvik is based in Dallas now, and often surprises his clients and employees by playing guitar and performing country western songs.

Résumés for Jobs with the Federal Government

The vast majority of résumés in this book are for positions in private industry. However, a résumé for a job with the federal government is different. According to Kathryn Troutman,* author of *Ten Steps to a Federal Job*, a good job with the federal government may be waiting for you.

Many jobseekers do not realize that the federal government is the largest employer in the United States, with almost 2 million employees, excluding the Postal Service—way more than the nation's largest private employer, Wal-Mart! The federal government is hiring now, and the pay and benefits often exceed what private industry is paying for equivalent work. You do *not* have to have security clearance to land a federal job. If the position requires clearance, the process will begin after you are hired.

The best place to begin looking for a federal job is at the official Web site of the government's Office of Personnel Management (OPM): www.usajobs.gov. Most federal jobs are listed there, though some of the intelligence positions (CIA, NSA, NGA, etc.) are posted on those individual agencies' Web sites. The U.S. Congress and Senate have their own Web sites with their own job listings.

You need to know, however, how to prepare a résumé for one of these government jobs. Here are a few points critical to first-time applicants for federal jobs:

1. Though your private-industry résumé will probably be two pages, the federal-government résumé should be longer—an average of four pages. The résumé must *prove* that you have certain experience; that's why it runs longer.

2. Though you can use the same résumé to apply to multiple specific jobs—for example, accounting specialist,

---

*Our thanks go to guest contributor Kathryn Troutman, who provided the advice given in this section. Kathryn Troutman is president of The Resume Place, Inc., a consulting firm for individuals seeking positions with the federal government, www.resume-place.com.

budget specialist, financial management specialist—you need to change the résumé slightly for each "occupational series."

3. Each federal job title requires a specific set of skills, knowledge, and abilities, with corresponding key words. These skills and key words should match the "occupational series." This means about a 15 percent change, mostly in key words.

4. The language you use has to match the language used in the USA JOBS vacancy announcements.

Applying for a federal job involves taking multiple steps. Ninety-five percent of all federal job applications are submitted online, and you begin by submitting your résumé into a "builder"; there are several résumé builders, and several automated job sites for identifying federal jobs. Be prepared to copy and paste your résumé into the résumé builder. At this time, you set up your account in USA JOBS so that you can see the entire application process. Next, you may have to answer some Assessment questions related to the position. You will be asked to fax some documents, such as a college transcript, military DD-214, or certifications to prove that you have certain professional designations. *If you do not follow the directions, you will lose consideration for the federal job.*

Vacancy announcements are a critical piece of information in writing your résumé. In these announcements, you will find the key words and required skills in the following sections: Summary, Mission, Duties, and Qualifications. The announcements are long and complex, but reading them thoroughly is essential to landing a stable, well-paid position with excellent growth opportunities. Your first federal application may take several hours to research and write.

The format most recommended is a modified *chronological résumé*. This format allows you to feature the most important skills for the job within the context of previous jobs. The book *Ten Steps to a*

Federal Job contains 24 samples using this format (called the "outline" format in the book) for preparing a federal résumé. This format has been highly successful, and federal human resources (HR) specialists appreciate how easy it is to read.

The skills and key words found in the vacancy announcement should be featured in ALL CAPS in the outline format. An HR specialist may receive 300 to 1,000 résumés for an opening. The USA JOBS system is not an artificial-intelligence system, and so an actual person will read and review your résumé to determine if you are qualified for the job. The Assessment questionnaires are automatically scored, then the résumés are reviewed by staffers. That's why the résumé *must* be easy to read, with the most important skills featured.

Your Accomplishments are critical, too. If your résumé is referred to a supervisor, then the listing of accomplishments can help make the résumé stand out, so that you can land an interview.

The Knowledge, Skills, and Abilities narratives are being eliminated soon in this process, according to John Berry, director of the Office of Personnel Management, who is determined to simplify the federal hiring procedures (great idea!). However, the short essays and examples within the Assessment questionnaires may or may not be eliminated. You may see requests for writing samples. Be prepared to give examples of your work experience that demonstrate specific skills. These are pre-interview questions and are important in the application.

Your federal application is basically an examination, and it is scored. The résumé and your answers to the Assessment questions are scored. The highest score for a nonveteran is 100. You can ask the HR specialist for your score; usually you have to ask for it. Veterans receive 5 to 10 extra points for serving their country. Thus, if you get a score of 100, a veteran can get a score of 110.

The federal job-search process is faster now than it has been in years. The OPM has made recommendations to the agencies that they should hire in 90 days. We have seen that the hiring can be much faster than that.

For information on résumé writing or on completing the Knowledge, Skills, and Abilities sections of your résumé, visit www.resume-place.com. There, you will also find information on government salaries, official job titles, and position descriptions, plus some articles on federal jobs. The following sites also have information on federal jobs:

U.S. Army civilian jobs: www.cpol.army.mil

Other federal agencies: www.avuecentral.com

Department of Defense jobs, including Pentagon: www.whs.mil

U.S. Navy civilian jobs: www.donhr.navy.mil

SAMPLE RÉSUMÉ FORMAT FOR FEDERAL JOBS

This format makes it easy to copy and paste your résumé into the USA JOBS résumé builder and other automated résumé builders.

KATHY BARROW
Address
City, State, Zip
Phone # home
Phone # cell
<u>E-mail Address</u>
SSN: xxx-xx-xxxx
U.S. Citizen
Not a veteran

WORK EXPERIENCE

BRANCH OPERATIONS COORDINATOR   September 2005–Present
Department of Corrections Credit Union
40–50 hours per week; Salary: $63,000 per year (includes car allowance)
Supervisor: Ellen Dunn, Chief Operating Officer, 225-342-6618, extension 205. May contact.

Manage and Direct the Operations of 8 Branches Statewide and the main office operations with assets of $65 million. As part of the Management Team, perform strategic planning, budget functions, implement new products and services, and conduct marketing activities. In the absence of the Accountant, work with the CFO to complete tax liens, accounts payable, prepaids, fixed assets, and more (4 months in 2005–2006 and again for 6 months in 2008).

Supervise, Develop, and Monitor the Performance of 29 Employees. Plan and assign work, create schedules, set goals, and devise action plans. Appraise performance, recognize achievers, and provide disciplinary action as needed. Recruit and hire managers and employees. Staff branches.

Travel Statewide to Visit Branches. Provide technical advice and oversee operations. Communicate orally to provide briefings and branch updates to Branch Managers, Tellers, Member Service Reps, and Loan Officers; updates on Branch progression for Board reports; training for Board Members on the Bank Secrecy Act; and other varied oral and written briefings and updates.

Prepare Written Reports such as summaries for loan and teller transactions, performance appraisals, training for employee files, OFAC reporting, FINCEN reporting, Currency Transactions Reporting; review 5300 call report for Office of Financial Institutions, cash over/short reports, ATM reports/outages, and more. Prepare compliance audit/report findings, consumer complaint investigations, noncompliance audit/report results, and briefing packages for senior management.

Use Automated Systems for accounting functions, customer account management, communication, and more. Includes Microsoft Office (Excel, Word, PowerPoint, and Outlook), Computer Marketing Flex System, Online Banking Setup, and Audio Response Setup. Knowledgeable about Windows XP and Vista and in-house computer network configuration. Administrate user accounts, manage security profiles, and manage backup operations.

Continuity of Operations Planning. Member of Disaster Recovery Team involving policy writing, generator installation, alternate IBM AS400 hot site, personnel placement, transition of duties for staffing for continuance of electronic transmissions, and Visa ATM, debit, and credit cards with third-party vendors.

Loan Approval Authority. Independently approve loans up to $50,000 and supervise approval of loans for Branch Manager/Loan Officers. Assess credit risks and work with high-risk borrows. Member of In-house Loan Committee review board.

Coordinate with State Examiners, Supervisory Auditors, and external parties for compliance issues. Perform cash audits for tellers and vaults, audit key/combinations security breaches, and investigate cash over/short/outages for embezzling. Present documentation on compliance issues (such as training and disclosures) to auditors and examiners. Provide technical advice and guidance to subordinate Branch Managers with regard to consumer regulations including FACT act and Privacy of Consumer Information.

Regulatory Oversight. Assistant Compliance Officer in charge of compliance with and programs related to Community Reinvestment Act, fair lending, consumer regulations, and more. Perform internal audit functions and serve as a key contact for external audits and exams. As part of the management team, involved in all OFI (Office of Financial Institution) exams, participating in 3 annual exams during this tenure.

Key Accomplishments

- Oversaw the build-out and opening activities of the last four branches.
- Developed and updated policy manuals for tellers, branch managers, member service reps, lending, personnel, ATM policy, internal security, and first IT policy.
- Developed training materials and standard operating procedures for lending, tellers, and member services.
- Reduced staff and expenses by utilizing Web-based online loan and new account applications; promoted online banking and bill pay services.

CHIEF EXECUTIVE OFFICER   December 1996–September 2005
Maple Federal Credit Union
50+ hours per week; Salary: $40,000 per year
Supervisor: Barry Daigle, Board President, 337-873-6815 (home). May contact.

Hired to Transform Small City-Employees Credit Union and position for growth and expansion. Supervised up to 7 employees and guided the work of a 7-member Board of Directors plus a 3-person Supervisory Committee and a 3-person Loan Committee. Created full-service financial institution from organization previously focused on savings and small loans.

Implemented Significant New Programs, including checking accounts, Debit/ATM cards, Electronic Transmissions (ACH, share draft, debit card), and Visa card program. Developed CRA-type loan programs for low income and underserved members, providing affordable rates and repayment options.

Developed Policy and Procedures. Recruited, hired, trained, and developed new employees. Oversaw payroll and performed other administrative tasks.

Directed Expansion and Build-Out of Second Branch. Chose location by demographic member base, prepared rough designs for architect, coordinated with builder/contractor, paid all bills. Coordinated and tracked building structure materials, landscaping, new computer installation, furniture, banking equipment, security equipment, and the amortization schedules for assets. Coordinated computer upgrade, security system upgrade, and move to new location.

Security and Compliance Officer. Ensured compliance with all federal government rules and regulations and instituted compliance procedures as new electronic products and services became available. Performed internal audit functions and worked with external auditors and examiners. Improved NCUA CAMEL rating from 2 to 1 for five consecutive years. Assisted federal examiners and Supervisory Auditors for internal reviews that involved the FACT (Fair and Accurate Credit Transactions) act, privacy of consumer information, and other compliance issues; gathered preexam documentation. Participated in 9 annual exams during my tenure. Ensured employees were trained and in compliance with all of these and provided follow up action for audit/exam areas of recommendation.

Prepared Financials and Board Reports. End of Year report filing to regulatory agencies and other internal reports. Prepared monthly financials (P&L) for board report, monthly board package, Annual Meeting financial report, credit committee report, supervisory committee report, and annual election of board and credit committee reports. Coordinated annual meeting including reports, food, elections, door prizes, and minutes for all committee/board meetings.

Oral Communication and Public Speaking. Presided over all Board meetings, presented updates and briefings, facilitated discussion on business before the Board, acted as parliamentarian, and made formal and informal presentations in an official capacity. Addressed groups of up to 50 to convey member services and grow membership.

Key Accomplishments:
- Increased assets from $2 million to $10 million, creating full-service financial institution.
- Successfully designed and executed build-out of new location.
- Facilitated major technology upgrades, including upgraded IBM AS400, all PCs, software configuration, assisted with installation of hardware, coordinated with Phone Company for IP addresses and installation of phone system, and new system training for employees.
- Challenged problem-solving skills during the process for business contingency.

COMPUTER SKILLS

Personal Computer and Networked Systems, Microsoft Office (Word, Excel, and Outlook), WordPerfect, TRW Credit Data, Equifax and Trans Union credit reporting

PROFESSIONAL TRAINING & CERTIFICATIONS

Notary Public, since 1984 (current)
Banking coursework includes: Principles of Banking, Accounting, Law and Banking, Supervisory Management, Commercial Lending, Consumer Lending, Check 21, OFAC, Various Louisiana Credit Union League seminars for Federal rules and regulation updates

PROFESSIONAL PROFILE

20+ year banking and financial career. Consistent career growth in branch operations and lending. Strong background in institutional development, new product development and customer service.

- Proven ability to function in high-pressured ever-changing environment, interacting effectively with all levels of support staff, management, and customers.

- Excellent interpersonal skills, coalition building, and collaborative partnerships. Ability to communicate orally and in writing, including technical and financial reports, and persuasive client/vendor interactions.

- Strong analytical and problem-solving skills; excellent decision maker.

- Maintain up-to-date knowledge of banking/financial industry and governmental policies and regulations.

- Adept at using automated systems for data entry and retrieval. Ability to sort data and develop reports.

COMMUNITY ACTIVITIES

Acadiana Security Association, Secretary (1992–1998)

Consumer Credit Association (former member Board of Directors) (early 1990s)

Branch Coordinator, Running of the Ducks (top seller 5 years) (1993–1998)

Sertoma Air Show Volunteer (1998–2002)

Better Business Bureau, Membership Drive Volunteer (early 1990s)

Coordinated Kidney Association Walkathon (late 1990s)

8

E-Mailing Résumés, Cover Letters, and Attachments

Increasing the Chances Your Résumé Will Get Read

ALWAYS KEEP in mind that your goal in sending your résumé is to set up an interview with the hiring authority. Nothing else matters! This book so far has shown you how to develop a winning résumé; now you need to consider how to get that résumé into the hands of the hiring authority. This chapter explains just how to do that—in other words, what works and what doesn't work, especially in this world of electronic communication. Should you use a cover letter? How do you get employers to open up your e-mail? Should you send a hard copy? Let's get started.

Ninety percent of the time you're going to deliver your résumé to an employer by e-mail. It is best to make your résumé an attachment, rather than a part of the e-mail itself. It is easier for the reader to open the résumé as an attachment, read it, and print it.

You want to send your résumé to a hiring authority. If you send your résumé to a company's general Web address in response to a job posting, it isn't likely to get into the right hands—that is, the hiring authority feeling the "pain," or the person who truly needs to hire someone.

E-Mailing Your Résumé

In today's job market, résumés are often e-mailed rather than sent via snail mail (information on snail mail follows later in the chapter). Therefore, it is important to know how to craft an e-mail message that will get your résumé *read*. Once again, the point of delivering a résumé to prospective employers is to obtain an *interview*. That's true whether you use e-mail or snail mail.

If your résumé is sent via an e-mail message, there's a good possibility *it may never get read*. In reality, the time of day that the e-mail arrives in the recipient's inbox, the number of other e-mails the person receives, the person's concerns at the moment, and his or her mood at the time will determine if your e-mail is opened and actually read. If there is urgency in hiring someone, all the e-mails with résumés might be opened. But if the hiring need is low, or if a higher priority has arisen, your e-mail might be ignored or even get deleted. The hiring urgency can ebb and flow, big time. Therefore, your e-mail communication must be *short* and *personal*. You need to send an e-mail that addresses the personal needs of the prospective employer in a concise manner. Here are some tips for sending an attention-getting e-mail message.

GRAB ATTENTION WITH THE SUBJECT LINE

Unless you are responding to an online application, put something compelling into the *subject line* of your e-mail to a prospective employer. Remember that you are communicating directly with the hiring authority—that is, the person with the "pain"—so write something on the subject line like the following:

Exceptional candidate

200% performer

Personally referred by [the person you know]

Proven track record

A stable, solid, consistent performer

Or, you can use a phrase or expression that will catch the reader's eye. For example, use a Latin phrase that might be recognized or pique curiosity, such as *"non illegitimus carborundum," "carpe diem,"* or *"omnia mutantur, nos et mutamur in illis."* If you use this kind of device, though, be sure to briefly explain it in the body of the e-mail, showing how it applies to the position being sought. Similarly, use a short quote from a famous person, followed in the body of the e-mail with an analogy to your experience.

Indeed, the subject line of an e-mail is a chance for you to be creative. Treat it like a newspaper headline or an advertisement. In any event, the subject line should grab the reader's attention enough to get him or her to open the e-mail and read it. Be careful, though, that the subject line message isn't so "out there" that the message gets deleted as annoying. For example, "Greetings from your cousin in Zimbabwe," or "News about your inheritance," won't get your e-mail message read.

Try different approaches, too. Different personalities respond to different kinds of messages. For instance, a comptroller or a V.P. of Finance may not be teased into reading an e-mail with a subject line of "Hire a 200% performer," but a V.P. of Sales would. Use your good judgment, but be mindful always of your objective: to get your e-mail résumé opened. For help with understanding the different kinds of personality types you'll encounter in the interview process, see www.thejobsearchsolution.com.

Remember, and this is important, that you are trying to motivate *the recipient* of the e-mail message. It's possible that, within reason, what you might personally be uncomfortable doing may be just the thing that can get you an interview. Over the years I have recommended that candidates do some fairly aggressive things, either to get an interview or to be remembered after an interview. Some candidates say things like, "Tony, it's 'just not me' to be that aggressive. I'm *uncomfortable* doing that."

The obvious question is, Are you more uncomfortable with being *out of work* and not being able to feed your family, or with doing something aggressive that's necessary to find a new job? If what you're doing isn't getting you the interviews, then you may *have* to do things that are uncomfortable. You are not being asked to betray your basic beliefs; you are simply trying to get an interview.

I have personally placed over 8,500 people in new jobs, sometimes by recommending that they do things they feel are either inappropriate or too aggressive. Obviously, this suggestion often works. The point is that you need to look beyond your own needs and consider the recipient's needs, his "pain." Writing a subject line like, "An exceptional candidate needs a job" does not communicate empathy or interest in what the employer *wants*. Hiring authorities don't care what *you* want. They only care about what *they* want. Now, if you can get what you want by helping them get what they want, everyone is happy.

MAKE THE E-MAIL MESSAGE A QUICK READ

The body of your e-mail message should have the same qualities as a cover letter: short, personal, and to the point. Consider the recipient and the number of e-mails he or she receives. I personally get between 100 and 150 e-mails a day. If the subject line grabs me, I quickly scan the body of the e-mail. But if the message is more than two or three sentences, I may not read it. The biggest mistake candidates make when e-mailing their résumés is to write a long introduction about themselves in an e-mail message.

Here is an example of an e-mail that is *way* too long:

```
Dear Hiring Manager,
As someone who has worked in a variety of indus-
tries, I believe my expertise in a broad category of
fields may be valuable to your firm. I have enclosed
my résumé, which outlines my accomplishments and
```

experience for your review and consideration. As a business professional, I have consistently maintained the highest standards. I have developed and continually refined many of the personal attributes, skills, and capabilities that would prove very beneficial in assisting you to achieve your business objectives in a timely and professional manner.

I am flexible and able to adapt to changing business environments. I have developed my capabilities to communicate effectively in both verbal and nonverbal situations. I have maintained solid working relationships with my superiors, coworkers, clients, vendors, and outside consulting groups. I have also effectively managed and motivated employees, successfully implemented projects minimizing the cost of operations and maximizing incoming profits, and presented information on multiple subjects. I am confident the skills, knowledge, and expertise I have developed, coupled with my personal initiative and quality goal setting, would be of direct and continuing benefit to your organization.

I have successfully created and/or enhanced HR departments from start to finish while sitting in an active HR role and searching for an in-house HR Director various times throughout my career. I have worked in large HR departments as well as small ones. I have led teams as well as been a good follower.

Realizing that this summary and my résumé cannot adequately express my communications in-depth to you, I would appreciate having the opportunity to meet with you and members of your staff to explore possibilities of how I might fulfill your employment needs and to discuss my career objectives.

Please note I have both worked in a home-based environment and as a commissioned Recruiter and have been successful in both settings.

I look forward to continued discussions with you regarding this employment opportunity.

Thank you for your consideration.

Sincerely,

Instead of going on for paragraphs about your qualifications, tie the body of your e-mail to the subject line in a way that's short, personal, and to the point. Here are a few suggestions:

Re: "I have lost almost 300 games"--Michael Jordan

Michael Jordan stated, "I have missed more than 9,000 shots in my career. I have lost almost 300 games. On 26 occasions I have been entrusted to take the game-winning shot and missed. I have failed over and over and over again in my life. And that is why I succeed." Like Michael Jordan, I know how to succeed. My résumé is attached.

I would like to meet with you and explain my personal "Michael Jordan experiences" and how they would be of value to you and your firm. I will call you tomorrow at 3:00 p.m. to see when we might get together. Or feel free to reply back and tell me when your schedule might allow us to meet.

Sincerely,
Tony Beshara
214-823-9999

Re: "Never, never, never quit"--Winston Churchill

Churchill was right. I don't quit.

I understand you and your firm are seeking a quality accountant [salesperson, engineer, office manager, etc.]. I would like to share with you the success I've had and how it will be of value to you and your company.

My résumé is attached. I will call you tomorrow
at 10:00 a.m. to see when it would be convenient
for us to get together. Feel free to reply back
with a time when your schedule might allow us
to meet.

Sincerely,
Tony Beshara
214-823-9999

Re: Winners do the things losers fail to do

All good companies and leaders are looking for winners. You and your company were referred to me by
_____. He said you were an expert in
_____ [profession] and a great teacher and
mentor.

I do the things losers fail to do. At this point in
my career, I need a great teacher and mentor.

My résumé is attached. I will call you tomorrow at
1:00 p.m. to see when we might meet. Or, feel free
to reply back with a time when your schedule might
allow us to meet.

Sincerely,
Tony Beshara
214-823-9999

Re: The 200% return

The story of how my employer got a 200% return on
his investment in me is a great one. I can do the
same thing for you.

My résumé is attached. When might we be able to
meet? I will share with you my story and show how
it can apply to you and your firm.

I will call you tomorrow at 10:00 a.m. to arrange a
time we might meet. Or, feel free to reply back
with a time that is good for you.

Sincerely,
Tony Beshara
214-823-9999

Re: non illegitimus carborundum

Don't let your board or investors grind you down!
You need a hard-working, determined, proven production engineer [bookkeeper, financial analyst, or
salesperson] who can withstand the daily grind and
the pressure *you* are under.

My résumé is attached. I will call you tomorrow at
3:00 p.m. to see when we might be able to meet. Or,
feel free to respond to this e-mail with a time
that would be convenient for you.

Sincerely,
Tony Beshara
214-823-9999

Another approach along the same lines is to cite information
you might have about the individual or the company you have
researched or discovered, thereby implying that you would be a
unique candidate for the company. A recent expansion, or need for a
turnaround, promotion, or even bankruptcy might make you stand
out from the crowd.

Re: Your company's reorganization under Chapter 11

Reorganization and Chapter 11 are difficult things
to deal with. As a financial specialist, I've
helped three companies successfully reorganize.

Your company may need my extensive experience. My
résumé is attached along with press releases of

the successful Chapter 11 reorganizations that I
have led.

I will call you tomorrow morning to see when we
might meet.

Sincerely,
Tony Beshara
214-823-9999

Re: Congratulations on your promotion

I read the announcement of your promotion. From my
research, I understand it is well deserved.

Often, when there are changes within a company,
"new blood" may be needed. I have been hired in
similar situations three times in my career and
have helped leaders, like yourself, be tremendously
successful.

I will call you tomorrow to see if there's a
time we might meet so I can share with you how I
might help you and your organization reach new
heights.

Sincerely,
Tony Beshara
214-823-9999

Cover Letters, If You Must

The survey we conducted regarding cover letters revealed that they
are nowhere near as important as a lot of résumé experts and
acclaimed résumé writers will tell you. We found that most cover letters are read only when the hiring authority has already read your
résumé and wants to know more about you.

Remember, since your résumé is going to get read in ten to thirty
seconds, you can assume that your cover letter isn't going to get much
more attention and probably less. You are trying to sell the potential

employer on the idea of granting you a face-to-face interview, not on hiring you. Even if your cover letter gives all the reasons you ought to be hired, you're going to have to get interviewed anyway. So, it is important to sell yourself only one step at a time—in this case, your cover letter *and* your résumé are written to secure the interview.

Remember the principles for Web communication as stated by Facebook's founder, Mark Zuckerberg: seamless, informal, immediate, personal, simple, minimal, and short. The cover letter, therefore, should have the following characteristics:

- Be short and to the point (especially if you send it electronically)

- Encourage the hiring authority to interview you

- List your accomplishments that apply to the specific job opening

- Use bullet points to attract attention

- Be personally signed (with an electronic signature, if necessary)

- Always have a postscript that is an "action item" (it will get read before the body of the letter does)

I can't tell you the number of résumés I receive with a full-page cover letter that will rarely, if ever, get read. Remember, the screening or interviewing authority has, on average, sixty of these résumés and cover letters to review (even *after* sorting through 100 or more). You have to make an impact *quickly*, with specifics that say: "You need to interview me." Here are three sample cover letters.

COVER LETTER #1

If possible, have a personal phone conversation with the hiring authority and then send your résumé with a brief cover letter to act as a reminder. In this case, you've established rapport and your letter and résumé will more likely get read. A typical cover letter of this type should look something like this:

Dear_____,

Thank you for the time we spent on the phone. Based on what we discussed, I would be an excellent candidate for the position of _____.

Attached is my résumé. You stated you were looking for someone who:

- Was a CPA with 10 years of experience in the insurance industry
- Has managed a staff of at least 5 accountants
- Has experience with P & C, as well as life, accident, and health
- Has a clear track record of making difficult decisions

As you can see from my résumé:

- I've been a CPA and have 12 years of experience in the insurance industry
- I have managed as many as 4 degreed accountants; overall, there was a staff of 10 people
- I've had 3 years of P&C, as well as 8 years of life, accident, and health
- I have a clear track record of making difficult decisions, especially in the firm I worked for last; we had to close 5 offices and lay off 35 people in order to be profitable

Sincerely,

Tony Beshara

Tony Beshara
214-823-9999

P.S.: I will call you tomorrow at 1:30 p.m. about meeting with you this week.

It's that simple. Don't make your cover letter any more complicated or longer than this sample. Use three or four short bullet points with as many quantifiable statements as possible. Then ask for an appointment.

COVER LETTER #2

If you don't have the luxury of a phone conversation beforehand, you might use the information you gathered from a job posting or just plain old common sense. Your letter might look something like this:

Dear_____,

I understand you are searching for a general manager for your building products distributorship. Attached is my résumé. As you can see:

- I've grown a building-products distributorship from $10 million in sales with a 2% pretax profit to $100 million in sales with a 5% pretax profit
- I started out on the ground floor in sales, then moved to sales management, then to general management over a period of 15 years
- I offer stability; I've had only 2 employers in those 15 years
- The owners of my previous firm will testify that they were able to successfully sell the organization because of my leadership

Sincerely,

Tony Beshara

Tony Beshara
214-823-9999

P.S.: I will call you tomorrow at 1:30. We can make an appointment to meet.

P.P.S.: Enclosed [or attached] are the results of a psychological profile our company did on all of its managers. You can see that I scored in the upper 2% of all managers the consulting firm surveyed on a worldwide basis.

Again, this letter is short and to the point—easily done once you get the hang of it. Also, remember that it never hurts to include some type of *numbers* in your cover letter. Numbers, statistics, percentages—any quantitative fact that says "I'm good!" helps you get interviewed.

COVER LETTER #3

I think it is always best to actually *telephone* a personal referral or someone you have something in common with *before* you send the person a cover letter and résumé. But if for some reason you cannot, or you have left a number of messages and not received a call back, you can write a cover letter to accompany your résumé. It would be something along this line:

Dear_____,

A mutual friend of ours, John Smith, recommended that I forward you my résumé. He said you and I have a lot in common, particularly when it comes to hard work and success.

I would like to meet with you to discuss any opportunities either with you and your company or any others that you might know of. John said you were the kind of guy I should get to know.

My résumé is attached. I will call you tomorrow morning to see if there might be a convenient time that we can meet.

Sincerely,

Tony Beshara

Tony Beshara
214-823-9999

It is important to begin the first paragraph with something personal. Remember, *do not focus on your needs!* Saying anything like, "I need a job," won't help you. Hiring authorities care only about getting what they want. Now, if you can get what you want at the same time, things might work out for you. So, to insert a personal note, begin the first paragraph with something you might have in common, such as:

We both graduated from Notre Dame . . .
We were both members of Sigma Chi . . .
We both worked at ABC Corp . . .
We both know . . .

Other Attachments to Your Résumé

Some job candidates send other attachments with their résumés that further substantiate their success. As with the résumé and cover letter, these should be relatively short and obvious. At a glance they should communicate, "My résumé and cover letter state that I am a very successful businessperson—here is proof of that."

What kind of information might you attach? You might include a positive performance or salary review; previously published documents of former employers ranking your performance as high; personal psychological evaluations that show high rankings in leadership; personality surveys that indicate you are a strong salesperson or analytical thinker; news releases of recognition and honors; or 30-60-90-day plans you have developed in the past or would implement if you got hired. Any objective document that substantiates your success, as long as it is concise and clear when viewed, will work. Often these attachments get viewed *before* the résumé is read.

A few of our candidates, not having this kind of objective "proof" of their skills, have gone online and taken self-administered psychological tests, intelligence tests, and aptitude tests. They pay for these tests and get formal-looking results. If they perform well, they attach the results to their résumés. I had one candidate who took two intelligence tests showing he was in the upper 2 percent of the surveyed population regarding intelligence. He also took three sales-aptitude tests that proved he was in the upper 5 percent of sales performers and a "leadership" survey that proved he was a real leader. He got tons of interviews because of these attachments.

Anything that separates you from the average candidate can be attached. One of our candidates "attached" a link to the Amazon.com page of her published book of poetry.

Sending Your Résumé by Snail Mail

These days, most of us don't get much mail delivered by the Post Office. The rapid response that e-mail and the Internet foster has made snail mail pretty much a thing of the past. Nevertheless, there may be times when you want to send your résumé as a hard copy. If so, print it on slightly off-white paper with matching envelope—almond color works best. Avoid dark colors, fancy paper, or any frou-frou paper or envelope; those aren't appropriate for business.

Communication Strategies That Get You Attention

You've probably caught on by now that e-mailed résumés to anyone *other* than a hiring authority feeling the "pain" aren't likely to get read. If a third-party screener or HR person reviews your résumé (and a hundred others), you won't get a response unless you are an absolutely perfect match (yeah, right!). All of the earlier e-mail examples are most effective with direct hiring authorities. That attention-getting or interest-catching e-mail subject line will not work if you are dealing with a company Web site that asks you to submit your information.

AVOIDING THE BLACK HOLE

If you do e-mail your résumé to a company Web site, and many candidates consider this sending a résumé down a black hole, you're also not likely to get attention by sending it more than once. In other words, you're probably going to be eliminated the second, third, fourth, and fifth times as quickly as you got eliminated the first time. However, if you have access to the hiring authority's direct e-mail address, you can increase your chances by sending your résumé, e-mail message, and cover letter more than once.

So, you say, "Well, if they tell me I have to send my résumé to their employment Web site (i.e., the black hole), how do I get the hiring authority's e-mail address?" Come on! You're smarter than that.

You can (a) call the company, ask who the [department] manager is, and what his or her e-mail address is. Twenty percent of the time, you'll get the information. Or, you can (b) go to the company's Web site, find out the names of the department heads, figure out what their e-mail addresses are likely to be, and use them. Some of your mail may come back, but others are likely to hit pay dirt.

CAPITALIZING ON HIRING PATTERNS

If you have very narrow experience and very narrow skills that apply to a very narrow sector of a business, you know there aren't many other people out there like you. That's good! If a hiring authority is looking for someone with that narrow experience, you know they're not getting very many résumés. On the other hand, if you know in your heart that there are many other people with the same experience and the same background, you realize that the hiring authority is receiving a lot of résumés. If you're a salesperson, for instance, who knows you can sell just about *anything*, you aren't unique; there are hundreds of people just like you.

Similarly, when you send your résumé to an organization seeking someone with specific experience and you don't have that experience, you know—especially in today's market—that the company is being bombarded by other people just like you. Your résumé is going to go into the deleted file along with the others.

So, you need to plan your strategy. For instance, you might send your résumé to a direct hiring authority, using a different subject line or message three or four times over a four- to five-week period. Along with this, you might call the hiring authority to evoke interest—a topic I speak about in Chapter 9.

Consider the typical hiring scenario. When an organization first starts looking for a person, it often gets a surge of résumés, and you might assume that the position will be filled quickly. However, a company's search for the perfect candidate can drag on a long time, for all different reasons. If e-mailed a bit later than the initial posting, your résumé may show up right after a candidate has been offered the job and turned it down, or it arrives the Monday morning after the candidate they hired on Friday failed to show up for the first day of work. Timing can be everything.

Don't hold your breath, waiting for this kind of thing to happen. But it does happen often enough for you to consider sending your résumé and making a phone call three or four times over a period of four to five weeks. After that time, if you still haven't found a job and you remain interested in the company, send the résumé every month or so.

USING CREATIVE WAYS TO DELIVER YOUR RÉSUMÉ

Sending your résumé via e-mail or snail mail isn't the only way to get it into the hands of someone who will ask to interview you. Here are some of the more imaginative ways I've seen candidates deliver their résumés:

▮ Sent via FedEx to the employer

▮ Waited in the company's lobby so as to hand it to the hiring person as he or she passes

▮ Had it delivered along with a bottle of the person's favorite wine, a gift certificate for a dinner, or another token of appreciation (i.e., a book on golf, fishing, or other hobby)

▮ Packaged so that a bunch of colored sticky stars fell out when opened, along with a cover letter with "HIRE A STAR" on top

▮ Put under the windshield wiper of the hiring authority's car

▮ Printed on a slightly oversized poster board

Other candidates have been similarly creative. For example, one candidate showed up at the hiring authority's favorite Starbucks in the morning; another rode up in the elevator with the person on the way to the office; yet another waited in the lobby for the individual when he left in the evening or arrived in the morning (do this only once—you don't want Security to escort you out). In each case, they introduce themselves and hand-delivered the résumés. Several candidates have called the senior administrative person of the hiring authority (we used to call them secretaries) and asked about the executive's likes, dislikes, and preferences before sending the résumés. One of my candidates had a unique approach. She would buy a pair of baby shoes, put one in a box along with her résumé, and send it to the hiring authority. A note in the box stated, "Just let me get my foot in the door." When she was called in for an interview, she would bring the other shoe with her, and the conversation would always get off on the "right foot."

You have to be careful, however. Some candidates, unfortunately, go a little over the top and it backfires. One man had his résumé delivered by a fellow in a gorilla suit. Another had his résumé delivered along with a singing telegram. They got attention, but it irritated the hiring authority and, needless to say, the candidates did not get interviewed.

In short, there are probably a limitless number of attention-getting ways of delivering your résumé. Whatever technique might separate you from the hordes and get you that interview is worth considering, as long as it doesn't go overboard. Frankly, you have nothing to lose. As Babe Ruth said, "Don't let the fear of striking out get in your way."

9

Leveraging Your Résumé

THE MOST IMPORTANT thing you can do in a job search, next to actually getting a job, is to get job interviews. No matter how good your résumé might be, unless it helps you get face-to-face interviews with hiring managers—that is, the hiring authorities who are feeling the "pain" (the urgent need to hire someone), your efforts are wasted.

Getting interviews is hard work. It requires tenacity, persistence, determination, and courage to thrust yourself upon people, even if that doesn't come naturally for you. Most people are not comfortable convincing others to interview them, even when there's the possibility of being hired. It can be a daunting, burdensome, and excruciating task.

Especially, no one likes being rejected, yet this risk accompanies the interview process. The sooner you face this reality and prepare for rejection, the sooner you will be able to find a job. To repeat: a perfect résumé doesn't do you any good unless it gets you interviews.

So, how do you make that happen? There are multiple ways of leveraging your résumé, of identifying opportunities that will move you closer to that invitation to interview. This chapter discusses how to expand your network of contacts, harness the Internet to find job openings, and use social media to develop your personal brand. Also included here are sample scripts to follow for telephone inquiries to known contacts and cold calls, plus methods for hand-delivering your résumé when that's appropriate. All of these methods are given an evaluative slant, so your efforts can be directed toward the most productive results—getting job interviews.

Expand Your Network

The most effective way for you to get an interview is to pick up the telephone and call anyone and everyone you can, whether you know them or not, so as to find people who might grant you an interview. When you call those people, most of them are going to ask to see your résumé. Bingo! With the help of this book, you now have an excellent résumé to send and a reason to follow up in 30, 45, and 60 days.

This is the power of networking. It's estimated that 60 percent of people who find jobs have located them through networking. Of course, this depends on how you define the word *networking*. If you view networking as calling only the people you know personally, that 60 percent is probably an exaggeration. But if you consider networking to be calling anybody and everybody with whom you're somewhat familiar, then the statistic is probably close to accurate. Sending your résumé to hundreds of people, without establishing any personal connection to them, is a waste of time: Your odds are about the same as winning the lottery. So, your goal is to expand your network of contacts as rapidly and widely as possible.

MAJOR NETWORK SOURCES

To expand your network, think of people to call whom you've never thought of before. If that idea seems scary, consider that you'll have a script to follow that will remind you of what to say, as well as a system for following up on any leads. In my books *The Job Search Solution* and *Acing the Interview*, I emphasize how *managing the process* of looking for a job is the key to successfully finding one. Developing a system for contacting people and presenting yourself to them is an integral part of that process.

Sit down by yourself, then with a spouse or friend, and start thinking of all types of people—friends, colleagues, relatives, and more. *The Job Search Solution* provides an expanded explanation of networking, but for any attempt your first task is to start making a list of people's names—some obvious, some not so obvious, and some you have not considered before.

▮ **Previous Employers, Peers, and Subordinates.** Think of anybody and everybody you ever worked *for* or *with*, even those you may have supervised. If you didn't keep track of them all, ask people who might know about those you worked with and how to contact them. Keeping up with former colleagues is easier now with social networks like LinkedIn, Facebook, Twitter, Plaxo, and probably a few others by the time you read this. The point is, you want to contact as many people as possible; it doesn't matter what your past work relationship was.

▮ **Family.** The bigger your immediate and extended family is the better. You should call every member of your family—brothers, sisters, parents, uncles, aunts, first cousins, second cousins, third cousins, in-laws, cousins-in-law, and their cousins as well. "Family" can extend further than you think. I know of one candidate who got a good job through his brother's wife's father's brother. Write down the name of everyone you can think of and then think of even more names. Some people are embarrassed to call their family members when they're either out of work or looking for a new job. Get over it!

▪ **Friends.** Talk to your friends just as you would talk to your relatives. Here, too, the pool could be larger than you think when you consider friends of friends. Your friends will often put you in contact with people they know whom you don't know.

▪ **Acquaintances.** These are different from friends. They're people you know, but not that well. People in your church, athletic club, neighborhood, social club, tennis club, volunteer organizations, parents of children who are friends with your children, even acquaintances of your spouse or friends of family members who might be able to help you.

▪ **Competitors.** You know who your competitors are in business. Capitalize on your knowledge of your markets and call them. Candidates often tell me they know *everything* about their competitors and they would not want to work for them. This usually stems from an organization's painting their competitors as people with horns and tails. The truth is that most of us don't really know much about our competitors except in relation to competitive situations. You need a job—call anybody who might hire you. Competitors probably are a good fit for your skills and experience.

▪ **Customers, Clients, Suppliers, Distributors, Partners, Dealers.** Think about everyone you ever interfaced with in business. They're all potential employers or know other people who are. *Caution:* If you are presently employed, *do not*—I repeat—*do not* contact these people. No matter how confidential you think the information might be, the probability of your job search getting back to your present employer is almost a hundred percent. I can't tell you the number of candidates I've interviewed over the years who have lost their job because they were indiscreet.

▪ **Trade and Professional Associations.** Some professions and trades have more active associations than others. Most of them have membership directories that can be a good source for networking. Some even publish job opportunities for their members.

▪ **Alumni Associations, Fraternity and Sorority Members.** Some school alumni associations are very strong and very active in the business community. Don't hesitate to take advantage of any contacts you might have with these organizations. Also, don't forget old high school mates. No matter how "old" they are, if they even vaguely remember you, call them.

▪ **College and University Placement Offices.** It doesn't really matter how long ago you graduated from your college or university; the placement office would still like to help you. MBA and graduate schools of most universities keep a running list of organizations that approach them from time to time about graduates. It's simply another source.

OTHER SOURCES OF NAMES AND INFORMATION

In addition to direct networking, you can obtain names and contacts from civic organizations, local businesses, and professional services. For instance:

▪ **Job Fairs.** Job fairs are more popular when the employment market is strong. They're designed so that candidates can visit several employers at the same location and the employers can interview many people in one day. If you are presently employed, do not go to a job fair. I've known a few employed candidates looking for a job who attended a job fair, only to discover their own organization was represented. This can both be embarrassing and lead to termination. However, if you're not currently employed, a job fair—if you are able to find one in a slow market—can be a good source of leads and contacts.

▪ **Religious, Community, and Social Organizations.** It is important for you to let people in these kinds of organizations know you are looking for a job. Common values are one major criterion most people use in hiring others. We all have a tendency to hire people we like, and we tend to like people whose values and beliefs are similar to our own.

▪ **Bankers, Loan Officers, Venture-Capital Firms, Lawyers, CPAs.** These groups of people are a surprising source for many opportunities that lead to the job you need. Bank and loan officers, especially in small communities, know about businesses that are expanding and looking for people, simply because they lend money to these organizations. Small businesses make up 99 percent of the employers in this country, and their relationships with bankers and civic groups help them expand when they need to.

For example, venture capital firms provide money for startup companies of all sorts. It is not uncommon for them to impose one of their own members on a company to ensure that their investment is protected. You may have to have an "insider" connection to a job this way, but it is possible.

Attorneys whose clients include medium to small companies, who handle labor law, or who have other kinds of business-related specialties often know which organizations are expanding. Managers at medium to small businesses sometimes speak to their CPA firms about needs they want met in their accounting or bookkeeping area. If your background is in finance, you already know lots of these people.

▪ **New Companies in Town.** Subscription services and business newspapers often publish news of companies that are expanding, contracting, and building new offices. It is easy to find this information and give the companies a call.

In short, you really, really have to "kiss a lot of frogs" to find a prince. But that search can be a successful endeavor. The take-away message here is: Leave no stone unturned.

A BRAINSTORMING TOOL FOR BUILDING NETWORKS

On the next page is a simple form to help you brainstorm the names and telephone numbers of previous employers, peers, subordinates, family, friends, acquaintances, etc. Use it to brainstorm and come up with the names of at least 200 people.

Calling Your Contacts

The telephone is your primary job-search tool. You need to develop good telephone skills, if you do not already have them.

Name_____ Company_____

Relationship_____ Phone_____ e-mail_____

Name_____ Company_____

Relationship_____ Phone_____ e-mail_____

Name_____ Company_____

Relationship_____ Phone_____ e-mail_____

KEEPING RECORDS OF YOUR CALLS

Keep a record of who you call and what they say. Most candidates will agree that they *should* contact all of the people on their brainstorming list. However, because they fear rejection, most will simply e-mail their résumés to the people they want to contact. This won't work.

If you want your contacts to be effective, *pick up the phone* and call these people . . . and then call them again. You want to call them at least three times, if not more. Unless you get very lucky, calling people just one time won't do any good. Most contacts won't become engaged in what you are sharing with them until at least the third call. They are busy, distracted by other things; that's why you need to call every 30, 45, and 60 days. Leave a very nice "What I can do for you" voice mail.

WHAT TO SAY ON THE PHONE

Here is what you need to say when you call the contacts on the list you have compiled. Please, please do not deviate from the script.

> "Hello, [person's name]. This is [your name]. I know you from [having worked with you before . . . we met at school . . . I'm your third cousin . . . we met at my wife's sister's girlfriend's cousin's wedding . . . my uncle mentioned that I should call you . . . I was referred to you by _____]. I

am presently looking for a new job. I called to ask you if you might know of any job opportunities available with the firm you are with or any other job opportunities you might know about. For the past [period of time] I've been working at [name of company or what you have been doing]. I am presently looking for a job as [position]. Can you think of anyone who might need what I can offer?"
[Very long pause . . .]

Most likely you will hear an immediate "no." You should expect that! If you hear no, then you say:

"I really appreciate your time. I'd like to e-mail you my résumé, and if you can think of anyone who might be interested, please let me know, so I might call them. . . .

By the way, I'm not sure how long my search will take; I'd like to call you back in a month or so to see if you might have thought of anyone who might be interested. Would that be all right?"

Keep a record of exactly what the person says. Make a note on your calendar about calling the individual again in 30 days. And when you follow up, be sure the person has received your résumé and confirm again that you'd like to call back in another 30 days. Most people will not "connect the dots" to your needing a job with any job opportunity they might know about on the very first call. It often takes two or three calls for people to remember that you are looking for a job. (Please don't get frustrated with this reality!)

Remember: Your needing a job is a very high priority *only to you.* The people you speak with show empathy—*for the moment.* But once you hang up, they are going to go about their business and your priority is no longer in their mind. When you call back two or three or four times, though, they might suddenly remember that you need a job and, coincidentally, remember that they know of one that might fit your qualifications.

CALLING OUTSIDE YOUR NETWORK

You can also use your résumé to get an interview with people you don't know. Most people call this a cold call, but I prefer to use the term *warm call*. It's simple and direct, and the results are immediate. That is, the warm call will either result in an interview or it won't.

When you make a warm call, you are trying to get an interview regardless of whether there is a position open or not. In essence, you are selling an interview, not necessarily selling the idea of giving you a job. It is extremely important that you recognize this difference. The purpose of the warm call is to get you in front of the prospective employer so you can sell yourself and your skills. You ask for a meeting—without asking if there is a need.

Many people are uncomfortable being this forthright—or pushy. They're uncomfortable because they fear being immediately rejected. Well, if you practice what I suggest, this approach becomes very natural and easy. But it does take guts. For those who claim the method is pushy, or just not them, let me ask: "Which is more uncomfortable? Being out of work or experiencing a little rejection?" It's up to you.

WHOM TO WARM-CALL

If you don't know the name of the hiring authority at the company when you call, simply ask for the name of the manager of the department you would normally report to. For example, if you are an accountant, ask for the name of the controller. If you are a controller, ask for the name of the vice president of finance or the CFO; if necessary, talk to anyone who is in charge of the finances for the company. Similarly, if you are a salesperson, ask for the sales manager, the regional sales manager, the vice president of sales, and so forth. If you are an administrative person, ask for the administrative support manager. In short, when you call, ask for the manager of the kind of department where your skills and ability fit best. It's that simple.

If you have skills that can transfer from one industry to another, you can call just about anyone in the organization. Any kind of administrative experience, accounting experience, bookkeeping experience, sales experience, and so forth can carry over to a lot of different businesses. So you can warm-call from just about any reference book that might provide the names of companies and their telephone numbers. Don't overlook the telephone book itself.

I do not recommend calling Human Resources unless you're seeking a job in that department. Most of the first-line screeners in an organization are taught to send anyone inquiring about a job to HR. The people in Human Resources are usually mid-level record keepers. In 97 percent of the companies in the United States, the HR department is not going to help you find a job in the company. HR will not normally interview people unless there is a specific opening, and even then will look for candidates who fit the opening perfectly. Remember, the HR (i.e., Hiring Roadblock) department's underlying, unwritten motto is, "We don't want to look bad." So don't get relegated to the HR department; it is a waste of your time.

WHAT TO SAY WHEN YOU CALL

For most calls you will be told that there is no opening but you can send your résumé. Here's the script for handling that call and response.

> "Hello, who is your [controller, vice president of sales, IT director, CEO, etc.]? Fine, let me speak with [name].
>
> [transfer of call]
>
> "Hello, [name], my name is [name] and I am [an accountant with 15 solid years of experience . . . a salesperson with 10 years of over 100 percent quota production . . . a production supervisor who has successfully managed 25 people and hasn't missed a day of work in 10 years . . . a bookkeeper who has won awards for precision and accuracy. . . an engineer who graduated with excellent grades and has 10 years of experience in your business]. I have a great track record and make an excellent employee. I would like to meet with you to discuss my potential with your company. When might we be able to get together?"

For our purposes, let's assume you are stymied in just about every way and are told to e-mail a résumé. Make sure you get the proper e-mail address of the person. Then you end the conversation by saying, "I will e-mail it to you right now and follow up tomorrow to be sure that you got it. Please read it closely because I am an excellent employee."

You then e-mail the résumé. A day or so later, you call the hiring authority and say something like, "Mr. or Ms._____, I wanted to be sure you received my résumé. I also wanted to see if there is a time in the near future that we might get together."

If you conclude that you simply are not going to get an interview, then there really isn't any risk in asking if you can call back in 30 days to see if the company's needs may have changed by then. You'll also ask if the individual knows of anybody else who might need someone with your skills. You'll be amazed at the number of job opportunities that you can uncover this way. Controllers know other controllers. Vice presidents of sales know other vice presidents of sales. Engineering managers know other engineering managers.

Most people you speak with will agree to let you call back. Great! That gives you another future possibility.

IT'S A NUMBERS GAME

In today's job market, out of every 100 calls you make using this method, you are going to reach about 10 hiring managers. This average depends on the kind of hiring managers you need to get hold of, of course. Vice presidents of sales are not in their offices as much as are accounting managers, controllers, and so forth. On average, you will discover one opportunity for every 30 to 40 managers you speak with, though this again depends on the level of job you are seeking—engineering manager positions are a lot harder to find than design jobs. However, this statistic is about right, so figure you're going to have to make about 300 calls to get one interview. That's what it takes to be successful getting interviews this way. So, do yourself a favor and don't complain about it. If that's what it takes to be successful, then that is what you have to do. (As the economy gets better, the ratios will get better, too.)

HANDLING VOICE MAILS

It is important that you know how to handle voice mails. Since the advent of this technology, many employers, and people in general, rarely or *never* answer their phones. They let everything go to voicemail and then return only the calls of those they wish to talk with. This is especially true for "nonpeople" types like engineers, information technology folks, accountants, and most analytical people. This situation can pose a real dilemma for the job seeker.

As a professional recruiter, I make more than a hundred calls a day. The vast majority of the time, I make warm calls for the candidates I represent. Here's what I have found works regarding voice mail. I call the potential hiring authority, and if I get a voice mail, I leave a scripted, compelling fact about the candidate that's intended to evoke a return call.

For the candidate calling directly, leaving a brief scripted message on the voice mail gives you the opportunity to make a compelling statement about yourself. Your message is not much different from what you would say if you were speaking face to face, and it could go something like this:

> "Mr. or Ms. [name], my name is Tony Beshara. I am a design engineer with fifteen years of experience. I'm stable, have not missed a day of work in ten years, and have won awards for speed and accuracy with two of the firms that I have worked for. I am a difference maker and I am looking for a new opportunity. Your company was referred to me as an excellent organization to work for. I can be immediately productive and am asking less than market value in compensation to work for a quality firm like yours."
>
> [brief pause]
>
> "I'd like to meet with you as soon as possible. Please call me at 214-823-9999. Again, that is 214-823-9999. I look forward to hearing from you."

Be sure you practice your message before you leave it for an employer. Write it out and have it handy. Even record yourself and listen to it. Then make the presentation slowly and distinctly, and be sure to repeat your phone number twice at the end of the message v-e-r-y s-l-o-w-l-y so the hiring authority can grab a pen to record it.

When leaving a voice-mail message, you need to come across as confident, moderately enthusiastic, direct, and to the point. It takes practice—lots of practice. Most phone systems have a recording feature. Use it to practice your presentation and listen to it. Practice until you get it down perfectly.

Now—and this may come as a surprise—don't expect a call back after having left only one voice mail. It can happen, but the probability isn't great. So, follow up with another voice mail in a day or two, with something like this:

> "Mr. or Ms. [name], this is Tony Beshara again. I'm that experienced design engineer who called the other day and left you a message about my availability. I am an excellent and efficient employee. Please call me at 214-823-9999; again 214-823-9999."

Now, you're going to ask me: "Tony, how many times should I call like this?" I suggest you call and leave a message like this at least four or five times. If you know there definitely is an opening in an organization, then leave as many as eight or ten voice mails similar to this.

"My goodness! That is terribly pushy!" you say. "I don't have the nerve to do that. Besides, what if I make them mad?" Well, do you need a job? What is more uncomfortable? Leaving five, six, seven, or ten messages like this or not feeding your family? I assure you, if you give this message nicely, no one is ever going to get mad at you. Employers may not call you back because they simply don't have a need for what you have to offer, but they're never going to get angry with you for trying to find a job.

You then ask, "Why would I leave that many voice mails for the same thing? If they have a need for what I do, they're going to call me right back after the first one, right?" Wrong. The answer is, "No, they aren't!" Well, they might, but it isn't very likely. Here's why: Looking for a job is *your* highest priority. But a hiring authority has many priorities. Hiring someone may be a top priority one day, and it drops to priority number 22 the next day. If at the moment the hiring authority gets your voice mail filling that position is a number 1 priority, you will get a callback. If it isn't, you won't.

What is going through that hiring authority's mind? It likely is, *Damn, I really need to fill that job . . . fire Leroy and hire someone else . . . get ready for the surge of business we're going to have . . . replace Rhonda because she is going on maternity leave . . . get rid of Ralph because he's late all the time . . . replace Susan because she is transferring to another department. But, I'm late for that meeting. I'll call that Tony guy back later today.* However, "later today" never comes around. About the third time you leave a message for the hiring authority, you make it really easy for him to pick up the phone and call you back.

There is a tendency for job seekers to think that when a company needs to hire someone, it does it in a 30-day period or so. People think, *Well, they had an opening a few weeks ago . . . they must have filled it.* Based on my work in this field since 1973, I guarantee you that it takes more like 120 to 150 days to fill most positions—even when the hiring authority says it's a priority. Candidates get offered jobs, say they'll take them, then the day before they are supposed to show up, they decline. Or, candidates accept the job, show up, and a week later another opportunity they were considering comes along and is better, so they leave the first job.

That's why companies interview a group of candidates over a period of 30 days, then start all over. They change their criteria, don't like what they have seen, or have any number of other reasons. The hiring process is always longer than anyone thinks.

Remember: You have everything to win and absolutely nothing to lose. Even after five or six of these messages, you can call the hiring authority back in 30 or 45 days and leave at least one final message. If your experience is very narrow and there are only a few organizations that would hire you, after the third or fourth voice mail, you would leave a message like this:

> "Mr. or Ms.[name], this is Tony Beshara again. You may not need anyone of my experience and background right now. Would you know of anyone in our profession who might need someone of my experience and background?"

Obviously the hiring authority didn't need anyone like you or he would have called you back. So, no big deal! Ask for a referral. Notice how you should emphasize the collective *our* profession. It communicates that you are all in this together. And if you don't get a courtesy call back from the hiring authority, don't take it personally.

Delivering Your Résumé in Person

One of the most effective ways to get the attention of the hiring authority and possibly obtain an interview is simply to show up at his or her office with your résumé. I mentioned this approach briefly in Chapter 8, but it is important enough to consider here, too. This technique of résumé delivery is especially effective if your experience is narrow and specific to a field of business.

When presenting yourself unannounced, ask the administrative person if you can have a few moments of the hiring authority's time. Then wait in the office or waiting area until he or she agrees to see you. Once you meet the person face-to-face, even if just for a brief moment, you can state the following and hand the person your résumé:

> "Mr. or Ms. [name], if you are like most forward-thinking employers, you're looking for an excellent candidate in the position of [job] all of the time. I am an excellent candidate, and I'd like to discuss my qualifications with you. Do you have a few moments?"

Do not expect to get an interview right then and there. That happens very, very rarely. If the hiring authority says he or she does not have time right then, ask if there would be a better time as you hand over your résumé.

I know this is a bold approach, but you have everything to win and nothing to lose. When I first recommended this and other aggressive strategies in my book *The Job Search Solution*, some reviewers commented negatively, saying the advice was too pushy. Okay, not everyone likes or appreciates some of these strategies, but *these techniques work*. Not every time, but enough times to make them worth trying.

Using the Internet to Find Job Openings

The Internet has revolutionized the way people go about looking for a job. However, it is nowhere near the magic tool those in the Internet business would like you to believe. When I first got into this profession, résumés were delivered by mail. Résumé delivery was then speeded up by faxes—do you remember those? (In 1983, I placed a salesperson with the Burroughs Corp., hired to sell fax machines for $100,000 each. Technology has certainly changed.)

In Chapter 8, I discussed the use of e-mail to get your résumé into the hands of hiring authorities. But there are a number of other ways you can use the Internet to job-hunt, including social networking. At the end of this chapter, I describe the results of a survey we conducted regarding candidates' use of Facebook, Twitter, MySpace, and LinkedIn. It was revealing of the great impact the Internet has had on the job search process.

By the time you read this, there will be new innovations involving the Internet that will be helpful in your job search. However, please understand that the Internet is only one tool to be used in your job search. For instance, the Internet cannot conduct your interviews for you, though if used right, it may help you get interviews. The Internet isn't going to "sell" you any better than you can sell yourself. As before, getting the interview is the most important thing you can do in the job search—*provided* you sell yourself well.

COMPANY AND PEOPLE RESEARCH

The most effective use of the Internet for a job seeker is to research companies and locate individuals who might interview you. For example, you can use a search engine like Google to find out about any hiring authority you may speak with. You can visit the Web sites of organizations to obtain information that even the people you interview with may not know about their companies. The more extensive research you do about individuals and organizations you are going to speak with, the more likely you will interview well.

There are hundreds of ways you can use the Internet to promote your résumé, as well. However, the return on investment relative to the time you spend is low. Skillfully using the Internet to research companies, the people who work in them, the hiring managers you will speak with, their competitors, and anything else you can find of interest still yields the best return on time invested.

Everyone, objectively, knows to research the organizations and people they may interview with, but some stop with the basic information even when there's that little something extra out there that can be helpful in the interview. For example, we have placed a number of people with a CEO who has written a couple of books about his favorite hobby. If you Google his name, you will find out about his avocation; nothing impresses this guy more than a candidate who asks about the books he has authored. So use the Internet to research *everything* you can about the organizations and about the people who might interview you. You never know what information you uncover may prove useful.

INTERNET SCAMS AND SOLICITATIONS

If you post your résumé on the Internet, you really need to be extremely careful about giving out information to anyone who contacts you as a result. Identity theft and fraud account for almost a billion dollars a year, and much of it comes as a result of job seekers posting résumés on job boards. Scammers pose as potential employers and dupe candidates into revealing personal information.

These schemes can be very sophisticated, and they may not always involve outright theft of your money. It recently happened in our organization. Some scam artist ran an ad on Craig's List for a proof-reader/transcriptionist. The individual used an e-mail address similar to that for our company, Babich & Associates. A woman responded to the ad and corresponded three or four times with an individual who made an agreement with her to work on a contractual basis. He vaguely referred to our firm. She was to work out of her home, editing and rewriting technical information. She received the material by e-mail, edited and rewrote it, and returned it by e-mail. She agreed to $10 an hour as compensation, and she was told she would be paid every two weeks. After two weeks' worth of work—90 hours, to be exact—the payday rolled around and she received nothing.

When she called the listed phone number, no one answered. She e-mailed the address she had been sending the work and received no response. Once she realized she had been cheated, she called our organization, and it became clear that the whole thing was a scam. This kind of thing is hard to imagine until you experience it.

The news is full of stories of people who unknowingly either e-mail or in other ways give out private information like their Social Security numbers, credit card numbers, and so on. For job candidates who have posted their résumés on job boards, the scam involves being contacted by "potential" employers who claim they have to do a background check before the interview. They ask for all kinds of private information and often get it.

You can assume that your personal information, either on your résumé, on a personal Web site, or on social network sites like LinkedIn, Facebook, MySpace, or Twitter, will float around in cyberspace, readily available for just about anyone to use or see. So, you might want to consider using a different e-mail address while looking for a job; you can easily cancel the address if this kind of stuff gets out of hand.

However, it is very simple to avoid these problems. Just don't give any personal information to anyone until you have interviewed with someone face-to-face and you know you are dealing with a legitimate business. Even when the person sounds legitimate, verify the facts. A number of years ago, a prospective employer called our organization.

He told us he was an executive with a company that was going to establish an office in the Dallas–Fort Worth area. He told us he was flying into town and wanted to meet a number of potential office managers at the hotel where he was staying. It was our long-time experience as recruiters that signaled this as fishy. We called the corporate office of this supposed new client to find out an executive's briefcase had been stolen. Someone was using his identity and credit cards, pretending to be him. So, even if the person sounds good, don't provide personal information until you are certain you're giving it to a legitimate person with a legitimate business.

If you are requested to do something that appears odd, be suspicious. A legitimate organization interested in you as an employee is going to follow traditional steps. If you don't get a face-to-face interview after a few conversations, be leery. Check on the legitimacy of the opportunity and the company.

It is easy to say, "Come on, can't people figure out when they might be duped?" But when a person is desperate for a job, suffering emotional "disease," and receives come-ons like this, he or she might think, *Maybe this is okay . . . I need help.*

Expect also to get legitimate franchise and business investment opportunities, insurance solicitations, credit card offerings, and the like as a result of your résumé's being posted on the Internet. I guess that's part of free enterprise. This can be irritating, and it has led many job seekers to avoid posting their résumés or to respond only to specific opportunities and specific people. But if you're careful, and can put up with a few unwanted solicitations, posting your résumé on the Internet should not be a problem.

JOB BOARDS

There are basically four types of job boards on the Internet: national job boards, like Monster.com, HotJobs.com, and CareerBuilder; regional job boards, which focus on your state or metropolitan area; profession-specific boards, which cover one profession or industry; and company job boards, which are specific to an individual company. There are also some job boards that link many job boards together; you can save some time by posting your résumé on one of those.

There are hundreds of job boards. In fact, there are now Internet services that post your résumé for you on hundreds of sites. You post your résumé once, and for a fee the service distributes it to hundreds of job boards. There are even Web sites that send your résumé to over 8,000 recruiters—for a fee.

Many job boards are going to ask you to reformat your résumé to conform to their format. You may not have much choice in this if you decide to post your résumé on those particular job boards. Different job boards keep your résumé active for different periods of time, so you should check with each one so you know how long your résumé will be posted. How often you update your résumé is up to you, but don't confuse this activity with productivity.

Most job boards provide key-word searches for their users. That is, if you are a specific type of engineer, or specific type of accountant, most job boards will produce your résumé for those users who use those key words. General résumé submittal forms may work for you; however, by using them you may limit yourself to an ideal job or an ideal company. The same holds true for indicating any preference for company size. Try to be as open as possible to various situations so that your résumé appears in any company's search for a suitable applicant.

Expect to get a ton of junk e-mail responses to your résumé posting; pyramid schemes and multilevel marketing organizations are going to attack you. Don't ever respond to these solicitations by providing your Social Security number or any other personal information.

Post your heart out, but don't expect a big return on your investment. Studies show that only 2 to 5 percent of candidates receive a worthwhile response from an Internet posting. I've seen this go as high as 10 percent, but that depends on how one defines a "worthwhile response." If a company calls you because it found your résumé posted, and it asks about your skills or availability, is that a positive response? If you get a call from a recruiter who finds your résumé on a job board, but you never hear from that recruiter again, is that a positive response?

The results from Internet job board postings are often over-rated. Every year, the employment consulting firm CareerXRoads conducts a survey of human resources managers at large companies. The 2009 survey showed that just 13 percent of recent external hires were found from job boards, while 27 percent were found through referrals—that is, people who work at the company. In fact, the percentage of external hires from job boards has averaged between 12 and 13 percent since 2005.

This won't come as a surprise to most perennial job seekers, but when the market is flush with candidates, as it has been for the past few years, employers or recruiters with job opportunities call even less. Your attitude may be, "Well, I only need one good opportunity." You're right! The hard part is finding that good opportunity.

WEDDLE's is a leading publisher of print guides to the 100,000+ job boards now operating on the Internet. It has conducted a poll since 2004 regarding the best online employment job boards; here are WEDDLE's top finishers for 2011:

WEDDLE's 2011 User's Choice Awards: The Elite of the Online Employment Industry

6FigureJobs.com	EHSCareers.com
Absolutely Health Care	ExecuNet
AfterCollege.com	FlexJobs.com
AHACareerCenter.org	Hcareers.com Network
AllHealthcareJobs.com	HEALTHeCAREERS
AllRetailJobs.com	HigherEdJobs.com
CareerBuilder.com	HospitalDreamJobs.com
Climber.com	Indeed.com
CollegeRecruiter.com	Job.com
CoolWorks.com	JobCircle.com
Dice.com	JobFox.com

Jobing

Monster.com

National Healthcare
Career Network

SimplyHired.com

SnagAJob.com

TopUSAJobs.com

VetJobs.com

WSJ.com/Careers

ADVANCED GOOGLE SEARCHES AND OTHER SEARCH ENGINES

You'll be amazed at the number of local companies and job opportunities you will uncover using this simple Internet search tool. A Google search, or entering the key words that relate to your situation, will produce company names. Other search engines like Indeed.com are specific to job searching. When you find organizations that may need the skills you have to offer, pick up the phone and call them.

By the way, if your search engine work uncovers the news that a particular organization is expanding in one area, don't assume it may not be expanding in other areas as well; it may need the kind of expertise you offer. If a company is hiring three or four inside salespeople, for instance, the business may very well be in need of an accountant, bookkeeper, or administrative person also. "Bodies in motion tend to stay in motion"—and that goes for companies that are expanding as well.

Responding to Web Site Job Postings

Applying directly to a company that has posted a job opening can be one of the most frustrating experiences you will have. There's a tendency to think that if a company posts a job opportunity, it has a real opening. Well, at the time someone posts the opportunity, maybe the company does—but maybe it doesn't.

DON'T HOLD YOUR BREATH

Don't assume that there is really an opening; 25 to 30 percent of the time, companies post these openings just to be able to say they did it. They're going to promote from within, and they knew this to begin with, or the nephew of the V.P. of sales was already told he would be hired. Why do companies do this? They need to justify their internal or "brother-in-law" hire by saying, "Well, we searched all over the place for qualified candidates and couldn't come up with anybody better than the person we hired!"

At least 20 percent of the time these companies never hire anybody at all, even when they start out needing an employee and post the job opening. I know this because, as a recruiter since 1973, I have experienced this over and over. Our clients give us a search assignment, expend effort in interviewing candidates, and then claim they're not going to hire anyone. Happens all the time. Job opportunities are posted on company career sites for all kinds of business and political or legal reasons.

There's no question it is frustrating to be looking for a job, see a job posting you know you are well qualified for, apply for it, and never hear a word. You probably will apply three or four times and never hear a word. You will get frustrated and angry, as well as downright disheartened, about the whole experience. The problem is, you have no idea if the job is really open, why it was posted in the first place, and the quality of the 473 other candidates who have applied for it. So, respond to postings on company Web sites, but don't hold your breath waiting for a response.

CALL THE COMPANY

The specific questions that companies ask on a Web site posting may very well eliminate you right away. Most of the time, you are forced to enter on the Web site the money you have earned before. You know the likelihood of being eliminated is great if you put down the wrong figure; and the money you earned in the past really has nothing to do with the money you would consider today, especially if you've been out of work for any length of time. Unfortunately, if you leave this entry blank, your application often will be automatically eliminated.

Most people who advise on job hunting and résumé preparation will tell you not to call the company or the appropriate individual. Don't buy this advice. You need a job. The ad will say, "Do not call."

Well, I can't tell you how many times I have earned thousands of dollars in fees when I was told not to call and I called anyway.

So, you say, "Well, what if I make them mad?" First, hiring authorities who really need to hire someone—that is, those who have a great deal of "pain"—don't really care how they find the best candidate. The HR people are trying to protect their jobs and keep a hiring authority from having to answer the phone, so they dictate the "Do not call" order.

You say, "Well, I really don't know whom to call." Cut it out! If you're a salesperson, you call a sales manager. If you're an accountant, you call the comptroller. If you are a comptroller, you call the CFO. If you're the administrative assistant, you call the office manager. You know who to call—don't use that wimpy excuse! Pick up the phone and find the hiring authority with "pain" and call that person. Tell him or her you would make an excellent employee, and you need to interview as soon as possible.

Your odds of getting an interview this way are much greater than if you take the passive route. You can either believe me now or believe me later, but you will eventually come to this conclusion. Yes, you may make five or ten calls to a hiring authority and never get a call back. Okay, that's life. I didn't say it was going to be easy. But I absolutely guarantee you'll get more interviews doing this than if you apply online and wait for someone to call you.

BREAK THROUGH THE HR (I.E., HIRING ROADBLOCK) BARRIER

You might be pleasantly surprised to find out how frustrated hiring authorities are with the ridiculous "recruiting" process their company has likely burdened them with. Yes, you read that right. Most hiring authorities don't like the recruiting process that the HR department imposes on them. How do I know? I talk to tons of these folks every year. They want to find quality candidates, quickly. Most company recruiting processes don't work very well because hiring people isn't the primary job of the HR folks. They are primarily record keepers; they perform an administrative function.

I have been referring to HR departments as Hiring Roadblock departments. I know that is strong and there are some HR folks who are really good at what they do. But most of their processes and procedures center on what is good for them rather than what is good for you as a candidate or the direct hiring authority who has "pain." Most hiring authorities would rather manage the interviewing and hiring process themselves. They are as stuck with the HR department as you are. And most of them will admit that, off the record.

I know this because I have spoken to thousands of direct hiring authorities since 1973. Just know that if you get relegated to the HR department, your odds of getting an interview, let alone a job, are drastically reduced.

That's just the way it is!

Also, remember that the average company in America has sixteen employees! Fortunately, most companies don't have an HR department. Even the ones that do don't recruit very well. So, pick up the phone and call someone at the company who can get you an interview. Be relentless! You're the one who's looking for a job!

For example, suppose you go to the company Web site for a business in your local area and see who their employees are. Maybe you know some of them; if you do, call them! (LinkedIn is great for this, as you will see later.) Ask them about the job and the hiring authority, and find out how they might help you get an interview. Don't be bashful. And if you don't know anyone directly, you may know someone who knows someone who works there, especially if you are in the same or a related business. This is a great way to use your second and third levels of contacts through LinkedIn or another social/business network. Call the person and ask for an introduction to the hiring authority.

Again, don't be shy. Don't worry about irritating anyone. If you are professional and pack a powerful message—that is, why you would be a good employee—the person won't be irritated. And, in the back of his or her mind, the person may recognize that the roles may be reversed somewhere down the line and he or she may be calling you in the future.

Develop Your Own Brand

You can go well beyond the process of posting your résumé on job boards, following up with people you know, and calling people you don't know to try to get interviews. Now, you can build your own professional "brand." This ability is an outgrowth of the powerful Internet, coupled with the reality that, on average, people change jobs every two and a half to three years. In other words, you need to be prepared to look for a job at any time. Developing and sustaining a personal identity, a brand, will make that easier.

Alison Doyle's *Internet Your Way to a New Job* provides a good foundation for establishing your personal brand. The concept is that you, as an individual, *create* a professional presence on the Internet, *market* yourself, *connect* with others who can help you find a job, and *help* prospective employers find you. The goal is to create an online presence that sells you as a candidate, much like a consumer product or service is marketed. People, especially prospective employers, are able to locate you through online media and, therefore, know what you can do for them.

This concept is fascinating, and represents a new approach to the job search, but unless you have the time (are looking for a job full time and can also devote time to developing the brand), its effectiveness is questionable. If you have the time, it certainly can't hurt.

Caution: If you are looking for a job while you still have one, think twice about having a large online presence. I recently had a candidate who, while still at his job, began to look for new one. He updated his LinkedIn contacts to include me. Alas, his boss was also one of his contacts, and when he saw that I was newly added, he asked my candidate if he was looking for a job. Of course, my candidate denied that he was looking for a job, but their relationship was strained. So, if you are presently employed, be careful what you post or what contacts you add!

Here are some ways you can develop your online brand. By the time you read this, of course, there may be dozens of other possibilities.

POWERPOINT RÉSUMÉS

I have personally received a number of these. They involve ten or twelve PowerPoint slides with creative images, pictures, and graphics about the candidate, which take the place of a traditional résumé. The concept is simple and can be done very creatively. The major problem is that when 123 other candidates are also submitting traditional résumés, the hiring manager, although amused, may not really know what to do with this. Reviewing the PowerPoint presentation may be interesting, but if the reader, as most do, decides to print out some of the résumés of people to pursue, he or she is going to think twice about printing out a lengthy PowerPoint presentation. And it is unlikely the printed version is anywhere near as effective as the online presentation.

A PowerPoint presentation is most effective as a follow-up communication with prospective employers and hiring authorities—after an initial interview. My candidates have had excellent responses to their candidacy when they developed creative PowerPoint presentations based on information they gleaned during the initial or follow-up interviews.

For example, a hiring authority is impressed with a well-done PowerPoint presentation on "Why You Should Hire [Your Name]." A creative slide PowerPoint summary of your features, advantages, and benefits is a killer follow-up to any interviewing situation.

VIDEO RÉSUMÉS

Traditional résumés can carry add-ons such as videos, links to projects, or Web sites, or be totally video as posted on YouTube. Again, these can be creative and somewhat entertaining. Some Web sites provide a service that helps you create these kinds of visual résumés. They can be produced and easily updated, as well as connected to LinkedIn, Facebook, Twitter, and Plaxo—in fact, to any of the social media you might think of.

If you are going to develop a video résumé, consider the following tips:

▮ Keep it short—under three minutes . . . sixty seconds is better.

▮ Make it professional looking and demonstrate your skills, features, advantages, and benefits.

▮ Be sure you are photogenic.

Again, if you are presently employed, posting a video résumé may not be a good idea, even though many of these sites will tell you they are secure. Video-sharing sites are often available to the public (Yahoo Video, Metasafe, Buzzquest, etc.). Another disadvantage of video résumés is that employers are busy. If they take only 10 seconds to read a traditional résumé, who is going to take 60 to 180 seconds to review a video résumé?

People under age 24 might be comfortable with hazy, fuzzy pictures and clips from an iPhone. These are social! Video résumés are supposed to be *professional*. Google "video résumés" and look at a bunch of them. Most are awful. These people could practice for years and never look or sound any better. Would you be encouraged to interview any of them?

I consulted long-time friend, and America's first career columnist, Joyce Laine Kennedy. She has been writing for four decades about careers, has a syndicated column *Careers Now*, and has published seven books about careers, changing jobs, résumés, and interviewing. Her take on this new buzz is about the same as mine. The only people who may get ahead are the ones who are charging a job candidate for making the video résumé.

Consider how you really look on a video; it may not be complimentary. In fact, most people are not that photogenic. Unless you really look good, reconsider. Until it becomes more "traditional and practical," most employers may not give video the time of day. In fact, I don't know of any companies that use them; the survey mentioned in Chapter 3 bears this out. Even if they present a candidate well, the major problem with video résumés is the same problem educational TV had in the 1960s and online video training has now: there is *no* personal interaction between people and no feedback exchange between candidate and employer. Things may change, but as of this writing, the time, money, and effort to produce a video résumé may not be worth it.

FACEBOOK AND MYSPACE PROFILES

Keeping your Facebook profile up to date, especially for professional reasons, will help you build your brand. Keep in mind, however, that whatever you write on Facebook, or any other type of Web site, is going to be there forever, even though you may think you are editing it as you go along.

As of this writing, I'm not convinced you need a Facebook presence to launch a quality job search. We have had candidates whose profiles on Facebook were a little racy. In doing their due diligence, employers often review a person's Facebook profile. Even though the profile is intended to be "social," it does say something about you.

When a job market is really, really tight, potential employers are looking for just as many reasons *not* to hire you as they are reasons to hire you. Don't give them the ammunition to eliminate you. So, if you insist on having a Facebook presence, make sure it is professional. Don't give me that nonsense about, "That is my personal life and has nothing to do with my professional life." In case you haven't caught on, how you present yourself personally is just as important to a prospective employer as how you present yourself professionally. So, don't put anything on there you wouldn't be proud to show your mom, your present or future spouse, or your present or your future children.

The developers of Facebook and MySpace claim that these sites are excellent tools to help you find a job. Read the survey results later in the chapter and draw your own conclusion.

TWITTER ACCOUNTS

You already know about Twitter. By the time you read this, there may be other rivals. There are now ways of tweeting your résumé, as well as keeping in contact with recruiters and hiring authorities. Again, read the survey results later in this chapter and draw your own conclusions.

PERSONAL WEB SITES

If you are presently employed, you certainly can't develop a Web site announcing that you are looking for a job. However, if you are looking for a job full time, you may have the time to develop your own personal Web site. This is another way of building your brand. You can create a pretty compelling profile of yourself. Be sure, though, that everything is businesslike and professional, including your picture (make sure it is professional—you are not trying to get a date). It goes without saying that you need to be careful with what you put on your Web site.

Don't put all of your faith in your Web site to get you a job. I've had candidates who have developed their own Web sites and *assumed* that interested companies and hiring authorities would automatically visit it. Think about it: When a hiring authority is receiving 140 and 150 traditional résumés, he or she may not take the time to visit your personal Web site, no matter how good you think it is.

BLOGS

A blog, or Web log, is another popular way to build your brand and share your credentials with the world. Like your personal Web site, it can take a lot of time to prepare. Maintaining it is fairly easy, once you get the hang of it.

You can connect your blog to your Web site, LinkedIn, and Twitter, as well as including its address on your traditional résumé. If you are going to write a blog, though, you better have something to say that's worth reading, and it had better be information the reader can't get any other way. If you don't have expertise on what you are writing about, and a prospective employer reads it, you won't look very professional. Having a blog just to say you have one isn't going to help you get a job.

The Value of Social Media for Getting a Job

The Internet has expanded the opportunities to locate job openings and publicize your availability for work. Only time will tell how effective these various options are.

WEB SITES AND BLOGS

I'm not convinced that either a personal Web site or a blog will necessarily help you get a better job. I recently had a candidate who had a personal Web site and a blog, which he directed readers to by noting the addresses at the bottom of his résumé. A company I referred him to was interested in hiring him, so one of the administrative personnel visited his Web site. His Web site communicated that he was a very devout Christian. In fact, on his blog, he continually wrote about how no one would be saved without having Jesus Christ in his or her heart.

The owner of the company was sympathetic to the candidate's belief, but after the information about the candidate's Web site was passed around to a number of people in the company, several employees warned that they did not want a "bible beater" in the company who was going to try to convert them. The employer decided not to hire the candidate, simply because he didn't want to create any more hassles than he already had to deal with.

The lesson is clear. If you are looking for a job, you cannot afford to have anything floating around in cyberspace that might get in your way. For those of us who are Christian, this is a sad commentary. I read the guy's Web site, and I admit that it was rather judgmental; it made clear the writer was convinced Jesus Christ is the only way to salvation. However, that doesn't mean the candidate would try to convert everyone to his persuasion. The owner could have checked the guy's references and bluntly asked previous employers if the guy was on a mission to convert folks and if he made people uncomfortable at work. But the employer just didn't want to go to that trouble and, more important, did not want to run the risk of making his present employees uncomfortable. So stay away from controversial stuff.

OUR SURVEY ON FACEBOOK, MYSPACE, AND TWITTER

Because there is so much hype about these social media, I decided to do a quick survey of job candidates and determine their success in using these three tools to get a job.

We asked 4,000 local candidates who registered with our firm over the last few years; 1,650 of them responded to our survey. The group represented just about all generational levels, from recent graduates to boomers. They ranged widely in profession, from sales and accounting to information technology, healthcare, and administrative support. Earnings varied from $25,000 to $250,000 a year. Also, 60 percent of them were currently employed and 40 percent were looking for a job full time. Some have been looking to change jobs for as long as two years, while others have just started looking. Without being too scientific, they represented a valid cross section of solid employment candidates.

Now, don't shoot the messenger, but only *one* of the 1,650 people surveyed said he had found a job through any of these social media—and it was through Facebook. *Three* of them reported that they secured interviews as a direct result of being on Facebook. That was it! Many others stated that they had contacted people via Facebook about a job *after* they knew their names. Three people said they found contract/freelance jobs by using Twitter and Facebook.

These results are a bit surprising, since the Internet resources proclaim how lots of people get jobs as a result of using the media. The vast majority of respondents stated that these social media helped them get jobs by being able to make new contacts through existing contacts. But as far as actually getting a job directly from one of these contacts, or being contacted by someone offering a job, none of these media seemed to work for anyone except the three previously mentioned. So, you may feel you have to use these tools, but don't get too hopeful you are going to land a job by using them.

Here is a quote from one of the respondents that sums up our conclusions. Asked the question, "Has Facebook, Twitter, or MySpace helped you get an interview or a job?" he answered, "No. Facebook,

Twitter, or MySpace have not yielded me any interviews nor my friends. After seven months of looking for a job, my thought is they simply create false, busy activity—not meaningful connections."

It seems to be a matter of hype rather than reality. Here are some other responses:

> "I keep my social life *social* and my *professional* life professional—I don't have the time for this kind of stuff."

> "I use Facebook and MySpace and Twitter extensively . . . but I haven't found a job through any of these—I guess they are just social."

LINKEDIN: A TRUE RESOURCE

Unlike Facebook, MySpace, and Twitter, the network LinkedIn actually *does* seem to help people in their job searches. It is very easy to create a profile on LinkedIn and begin linking to many new contacts. You can update your profile regularly and get recommendations from colleagues, previous bosses, and clients. You can find out where people with your kind of background are working, determine where people came from, see if a company is hiring, and most important, find out who the hiring manager (the one with "pain") might be.

We surveyed more than 2,100 people in our company's database over the last five years—both candidates and hiring authorities. A full 500 of these people were also surveyed about Facebook and Twitter. We asked these two questions:

1. Has LinkedIn made your job search easier? How?

2. Is LinkedIn simply another tool to get interviews or does it really enhance your job search and make it more effective?

A full 61 percent of respondents said that LinkedIn definitely helped them in their job search and made it easier. Fifteen percent of the respondents were employers who said LinkedIn helped them in the hiring process. Only 10 percent of the respondents said they actually found a specific job as a result of being contacted directly by either an employer or a recruiter from their LinkedIn profile.

However, having said that, it appears that LinkedIn is extremely useful in helping people get jobs or employers find good candidates. Being "discovered" for a specific job opportunity by a specific person may be rare, but LinkedIn enhances your job search in a number of ways. Here are quotes from some of the 61 percent of the respondents who said LinkedIn helped them:

> "I connect with former associates and let them know I am looking for a new opportunity."

> "I can review who's been looking at my profile and get an idea of who is doing their homework on me prior to an interview."

> "Savvy users continue to provide updates of their progress in a company. I can see who is moving 'up' and know who to call."

> "I can do research on companies and individuals I wish to target, to see if they know someone I know."

> "I can link an online résumé to my profile and therefore get more exposure."

> "Look at recommendations—you can tell how something is written if the person is leaving or has left the company. I do this for companies I'm interviewing with to look for previous RIFs that can't turn over."

> "I look at current and former employees to see if I know anyone. If someone has recently left, it may indicate an opening before one has been announced. I look for new hires in management; it may indicate a change is coming and there may be openings."

> "I can find the names of hiring managers more easily."

"I can find internal company contacts, second or third person, and get them to refer me to the hiring authority."

"By researching old company teammates you can find out where they landed and add these companies to your job search."

"I can use InMail to communicate and follow up on positions that I applied for."

"The job board has posted positions not found elsewhere that appear to be of higher quality."

"Recruiters find you more easily."

"As an employer, if anyone is referred to me, I can find out about them by finding common connections."

"LinkedIn is another tool to enhance my personal branding but I think it's important to complete your profile 100%. I note my profile is constantly being visited and I get frequent contacts."

"The recommendations have given potential hiring managers a short reference from my peers, managers, customers, and partners."

"Prior to LinkedIn, I would only be able to contact people one phone call at a time. LinkedIn makes it easier because it runs 24/7/365 and can be multithreaded."

"LinkedIn discussion groups have allowed me to informally meet many contacts who have led me to interviews."

"I search not only for people but for jobs as well. I've been able to search for jobs by keyword and e-mail the key contact for each matching job."

"I connect my ACT database with my LinkedIn connections. My goal, when I am looking for a job, is to 'touch' my context a variety of times—the magic number is six, for a number of different channels."

"I came across an opportunity as a director of marketing for a financial firm. It mentioned the position reports to the VP of marketing. I went to their Web site, found the VP's name, and went to LinkedIn to learn more about him."

"Since 80 to 90 percent of jobs come from people you know, it makes sense to expand your personal network and use it to find new opportunities. I was pursuing a company earlier this year and did a LinkedIn search to find out who I knew inside the organization in order to make a personal connection. As a result, I was able to get an interview and position myself as an 'insider.'"

"I haven't found employment directly from LinkedIn, but it has contributed to landing interviews."

"When looking for a job, I used LinkedIn's company search. It gave me an overview of my target company and a list of LinkedIn members who work there."

"LinkedIn was the catalyst that allowed me to secure a V.P. of sales position in the worst job market in my lifetime. I applied for a V.P. position online. Within a few days I received an automated rejection notice electronically signed by the search consultant. I immediately invited him to join my LinkedIn network and called to offer my assistance for any searches he was conducting in the Dallas/Ft. Worth area. I kept in touch and communicated with the recruiter from time to time via LinkedIn. During one of our conversations I asked him if he was working on any other V.P.-level positions. He said, 'Never in Dallas, but I have one in the Pacific Northwest.' I ended up with the position I was looking for in Seattle."

Although LinkedIn may not outright get you an interview, it certainly seems like it can enhance your job search efforts. It is a tool to help you find a job, not an end in itself.

ACTIVITY CONFUSED WITH PRODUCTIVITY

In the final analysis, creating an online presence and branding yourself might be good tools, but they are just that—tools. I had a candidate a few months ago who kept trying to send people to his LinkedIn profile, his Web site, and his blog. He spent all kinds of time and effort doing this, but he wasn't getting many interviews. He asked me what might be the problem. It turns out that he simply wasn't asking for interviews. He was assuming his online presence would sell him into the interviews and then get him a job. This wasn't going to happen.

Looking for a job is an emotionally difficult thing to do. After death of a spouse, a child, or a parent, or divorce, it is the most emotional thing we do. People don't like being rejected. They often spend all kinds of time writing a résumé, building an online brand, and doing any other job-search activity that appears to be of value as a way of avoiding rejection. They confuse activity with productivity.

One respondent said that he thought all of this Internet activity would eventually lead to "Internet overload." He might be right. Can you imagine getting 125 or 130 tweets a day while monitoring LinkedIn, managing a Web site, writing a blog, getting interviews, and still being able to do your job? Could you do that even if you're looking for a job full time? Unmanageable for most of us.

None of these activities matter unless you get interviews and perform well during the interview. Any technique that lands you an interview and helps you perform well is of value. Anything that doesn't get you an interview and help you perform well is a waste of your time.

10

How to Handle Common Résumé Problems

(Too Many Jobs, Employment Gaps,
Changing Careers, Relocating, etc.)

There are certain common résumé challenges that can cause problems if you don't handle them properly. They will raise red flags in the minds of hiring authorities and may keep you from getting an interview or will lead to questions during the interview. Obviously, you will have to answer questions concerning these problems, but it is preferable to answer them in person, at the interview. You certainly don't want to be eliminated before you even get in the door. None of these problems is insurmountable; it's all in your presentation.

Too Many Jobs in Too Little Time

As you can see from the survey mentioned in Chapter 3, one of the things most employers look for in potential candidates is stability. There's a natural assumption on the part of a screening or hiring authority that if you've had three jobs in the last three years, you're going to be at your next job for only one year.

This is one of the biggest challenges that professional recruiters like me have to deal with. It doesn't seem to matter that the average job in the United States lasts only two and a half to three years, or that companies expand and contract more these days than they ever have in the past. The implication is that employees should be more stable than the companies that they work for.

It is logical for you to ask what the definition is of a "stable work history." Job stability may be different for different professions. Regardless, in any profession, one job a year for three or four years in a row is always going to raise a red flag. On average, two jobs in five years in most professions is kind of a tipping point. Thus, I cannot give you a blanket definition of what job stability might be in your particular profession or line of work, but you probably know what it is!

The important point is, *Don't try to justify your perceived lack of stability*. I hear excuses all the time along the lines of, "Well, looking at everybody else, considering the economy, my stability is not so bad . . ."; "There are good reasons for it, so let me explain . . . blah, blah, blah." It doesn't do any good to make excuses. If you've had a number of jobs in the same year, or three jobs in five years, the person reviewing your résumé is going to be concerned. You probably already know this because you've been told by a prospective employer or a recruiter that you've had too many jobs.

There is an online video by a "career coach" that advises people to say that "tenure doesn't matter . . . what matters is the quality of your work." Don't buy that! It is junk. Every hiring authority is concerned about stability. But take heart; it won't always be this way. When the market is flush with people, hiring authorities have lots of candidates to choose from, so they will eliminate you and others for all kinds of reasons. But this situation will eventually change (we hope, in the near future) and, as with the recovery from recessions in the late 1980s and late 1990s, companies will again have fewer candidates to choose from and they won't eliminate people as easily.

However, you have to deal with this problem now if you want a job now. There are a couple of ways to handle this problem on your résumé so that you can be able to at least get to the interview. The first solution is to lump two or three jobs into one span of time—something like this:

2009–2011   **ABC and XYZ Companies, Dallas, TX**

Sold business forms to the insurance industry for ABC. **Ranked #2 of 48 salespeople** in the western region of the United States. The company was sold. XYZ is an independent oil company and investment firm. Successfully raised more than $1 million from individual investors via telephone and personal contacts. **Ranked #3 of 20 salespeople.**

Psychologically, this format is more successful than delineating the two jobs in two years. Another way of doing this is to use one job title for more than one job:

2007–2111   **Mechanical Design Engineer, Allentown, PA**

Design engineer of turbine engines for LMN Corp. Received recognition for accuracy as well as high performance. Designed HVAC systems for PQR Corp., receiving "Rookie of the Year" award. Designed machine tools for EFG Corp. and was promoted to Customer Services Manager in six months.

You are still going to be questioned about the number of jobs in such a short period of time, but you're more likely to get an interview using this format.

If you have had one or two long periods of employment with one company, those periods of employment should show up on the *first page* of your résumé. In other words, if you have three positions that lasted less than a year, preceded by one or two positions that were four years or more long, put the longer stints on the first page of your résumé to "counterbalance" the short stints.

Reentering the Workforce

If you are reentering the workforce after a number of years, you face a real challenge. Whether you like it or not, most employers are concerned about hiring someone who has been out of the workforce for any period of time. They worry that, for whatever reason, you will leave again, either for the same reason or for another reason.

You say, "Wait, Tony, I have to work. I can't afford not to work. Why would anyone think that?" Well, it's like this. The employer has ten or twelve or fifteen candidates to choose from. They all have some risk factors. You have one more risk factor the others don't have. You can sit there and complain about it being unfair—and you're right. It is unfair, but that's the way the hiring authority sees it.

So, in order to get the interview, you need to explain why you are reentering the workforce *as well as* communicate the fact that you are serious about keeping a new job. You want to assure the hiring authority that employing you is not a risk.

If you are a woman reentering after the birth of a child, make sure you state on your résumé that you have excellent child care. Hiring authorities are always a bit nervous about women in the workforce who have children at home. They think that, without good child care, the mother will be absent a lot from work, especially when the child is ill. So, you need to state something on your résumé like, "Returning to the workplace after the birth of a child. Fortunately, I have excellent child care, so missing work is not an issue."

Don't give me that, "That's none of their business" stuff. Regardless, this is the way hiring authorities are going to think, whether they admit it or not. Just remember: You're trying to get a job.

Gaps Between Jobs

Having a big gap—a year or more—on your résumé is a difficult matter to deal with. People currently employed—that is, hiring authorities—

have a tendency to think that finding a job is easier than it really is unless they also have been recently unemployed. So, even though many folks have been looking for work for a very long time, most hiring authorities are not going to empathize with a long period of unemployment.

If they've been out of work for a while, many candidates fill the gap by claiming that they are or have been a "consultant." When interviewing or hiring authorities see this, most of them automatically think it is just a fancy way of saying you have been out of work. So, if you're truly going to be a consultant, you'd better have on your résumé the names of people you've consulted for and the duration of each engagement, as well as a description of each project. I even recommend offering the names and phone numbers of people who can verify the work you did.

Some candidates write on their résumés that they've been on a sabbatical. Dumb, dumb, dumb! Don't let anybody kid you. This is not academia. Unless you work for one of those rare companies that offer employees a leave of absence, don't put this down. An interviewing or hiring authority will think, "If this person can afford to take a sabbatical in this market, and I hire him, and he doesn't like the job for whatever reason, he will simply go back to his sabbatical."

I had a candidate not too long ago who had been out of work for almost a year. He put on his résumé that he was the CEO of his own video production company. To make matters even worse, the dates he was the CEO of his company overlapped with his previous employment by fifteen years. So, it appeared he had been the CEO of his own production company while he was working for his previous employer. Whew! It's bad enough to try to convince someone to hire you when you have been a CEO, but it's even worse when it appears you have been working two jobs. No hiring authority is going to be interested in someone who is running his or her own company, no matter how small, while "working" for them. (Actually, this candidate had been videotaping weddings, bar mitzvahs, events at his church—anything he could do to make some money while he was looking for a job. He barely made any money at it; it was a hobby. I got him to rewrite his résumé, reflecting for the past year that he had been doing video free-lance work. We took the CEO title off the résumé.)

Being out of work for a protracted time is not as great a stigma as it used to be. The problem is that it may be very difficult to explain on your résumé. Do your best to quell any fears on the part of the interviewing or hiring authority that you are a risk; do whatever you can to ensure that you will be a steady, dependable employee. (A funny, but sad, story: One of my candidates had been out of work for eight-een months. He finally found a job as a manager at an equipment com-pany. He called to ask for help in finding a salesperson for his company. We discussed a number of candidates. With a straight face, he told me not to send him anyone who wasn't presently employed. In his opinion something was wrong with a person if he was out of work. I reminded him of his own recent fate; he had the gall to say that *it was different with him*. Go figure!)

So, if you have been out of work for an extended time, don't hide or minimize the gap. However, don't underplay it with the attitude that, "It's no big deal." It is a very big deal, especially to a hiring authority. It is likely you will get asked about the gaps in your résumé. Do not be defensive or nervous about them. Simply tell the truth—something like this, with humility but factual:

> "I've been actively looking for a job for the past nine months. As you know, the market is very difficult. I've had two job offers [*only if this is true*] that came in the very begin-ning of my search. Frankly, I had no idea it was going to be this difficult. I've had a number of opportunities [*be specific about the number, if you can*] where I've come in second in the interviewing process. Even though I have outrun a number of candidates, I still haven't found a good opportunity.
>
> [pause]
>
> "I've learned from being in the workplace that everyone's number two candidate is someone else's number one candi-date, and that's why I am speaking with you today. Even

though the market is difficult, I've been an excellent employee before and I will be again—I hope for a quality organization like yours."

[pause]

"My track record . . ."

Then proceed to talk about your track record and how it applies to the specific needs of the hiring authority. It's that simple! But you do have to practice this presentation. You must deliver it with confidence and conviction. If you come across weak, apologetic, defensive, angry, or even emotional when you give this presentation, you will be passed over. Practice! Practice! Practice!

Your Name

This is a sticky issue, but I must address it. If your name makes it obvious that you are of a member of a minority group or are foreign born, you may want to consider changing it for résumé purposes only. Now, you probably will respond with horror: "Well, that's discrimination! People shouldn't decide on interviewing me based on my name." You're absolutely right! It is discrimination. All hiring is discriminatory. Some of it is legal, and some of it isn't. But remember that you are trying to get job interviews, not change the world. If you're uncomfortable doing this, don't do it.

We're all familiar with the studies done of two identical résumés, one with the name Sharonda and the other with the name Sharon. Sharon gets more interviews. So if your name is Janeka, Lee-Ron, Kareem, Kamal, Aadarsh, Dipti, Akbar, Abdul, Yan, Li, Mei-li, or Hala—in short, any name that immediately identifies you as a minority or as foreign born, consider altering it on your résumé.

Now, even if you alter your name and all of your degrees are from the India Institute of Management, it may not make a big difference. In some professions, like information technology, sciences, or healthcare, being foreign born doesn't seem to matter as much. But the majority of businesses in the United States are concerned about cultural "fit"—the ability to communicate, and so on. Let's face facts: The sales résumé of Pol Ying is not likely to get the same attention or interest as Paul Young.

I'm trying to get you interviews. You don't want something on your résumé to keep you from getting those interviews, especially your name. I recently had a sales candidate with the first name of Kamar and a last name similar to Cole. It was obviously a Middle Eastern name. When he altered the name on his résumé to Kenny Cole, he increased the number of interviews he received. Interestingly enough, his nationality didn't hinder him at all. Once he got into the interviewing cycle, no one seemed to care.

Again, don't shoot the messenger! If you don't feel comfortable doing this, don't do it. Use your own judgment. Just remember that you don't want to be eliminated from an interview by what is on your résumé, if you can easily avoid it.

Changing Careers

Though the idea of changing careers might be appealing, this is one of the most difficult things to do, especially when unemployment is high. There are boatloads of books about how to change careers. Most of them make it appear easy to do. Don't believe it! *Changing careers is very difficult!* Unless the hiring authority is a family member or someone you know who will overlook the fact that you don't have any experience in what she needs done, you are competing with experienced people in this new field.

Since 1973, I've interviewed thousands of candidates who have wanted to change their careers. For one reason or another, they want to get out of what they're doing and into something else. About 98 percent of the time, they still need to earn the same kind of money that they have been earning in their present field. Neat trick.

I hear things like, "My neighbor is the president [or comptroller, vice president, or whatever] of a big company. He is a schmuck. He's a lousy husband and father, and everybody knows he is an idiot. I know

I can do a better job than he can. So I want a job like that." Or, I hear things like, "Well, you know the green movement is really catching on and I hear there's a lot of money in it. I've been really successful in everything I've done, so find me a job in something that has potential in green technology."

Most of the books on career change aren't realistic. They give examples that are the exceptions to the rule rather than the common situation. If you are going to try to shift into any career that's even reasonably competitive, it's going to be an uphill battle. Michael Jordan was a great athlete—the best basketball player in the world—but when he tried to play baseball, he was not as successful. In spite of his hard work and natural athletic ability, he was competing with guys who were solid baseball players. They may not have been as good an athlete as he was, but they were better baseball players. So, when the big leagues were looking for documentable baseball skills, Michael Jordan wasn't at the top of the list. He went back to basketball.

What most of the career change "experts" neglect to mention is that the further away you get from your documented skills or demonstrated knowledge, the harder it is to get hired. Unless you're willing to either start over at the bottom or take a drastic cut in pay—and even then it is difficult—changing careers is a near impossibility. Why do you suppose lots of career-changing folks start their own business? Because they have a hard time getting a job with someone else!

Once in a while a sector of business emerges for which there is very little "like kind" experience among job seekers. Back in the mid-90s, when computer technology was being developed for business, there were few salespeople who had experience in the profession of selling hardware and software solutions. So companies recruited good salespeople from payroll services, real estate, and just about any other field involving sales. We're now, however, in our third or fourth iteration of technology. Many of these software and hardware firms have contracted, merged, or gone away. Advanced technology has made many of these solutions a commodity. And as the technology has advanced, the opportunity to make a lot of money in selling software or hardware has diminished.

We still get candidates who claim that, since they're very good at selling insurance, or real estate, or whatever, they want to change careers and sell software because it is more lucrative. They say, with a straight face, "I saw a job you advertised where the earnings are $250,000 per year. I need to make that kind of money, so get me the interview." They have no idea that they're competing with experienced salespeople who got into the software and hardware business years ago. Why would a company hire an unproven person when people with documentable skills and successes are available?

Those people who want to change careers say things like, "But I know I can do it." Okay, maybe you can, but it is going to be rare for a company to take a chance on you when it can hire a person with direct experience. And when unemployment is high and the market is flooded with all kinds of people having all kinds of experience, getting hired to do something you have no documented skills in and also making reasonable earnings is going to be even harder.

Most people who successfully change careers either go into a profession not saturated at the time, like teaching or healthcare, or they open their own business and run the risk on themselves. But, similarly, most career-change books don't tell people how hard it is to run a business. A lot of new businesses fail because the people who start them have absolutely no idea how to run a business.

What to do? If you are considering changing careers, first get tested to see if you have the aptitude to do what you have in mind. For instance, if you want a career in playing music but find out you are tone deaf, you may want to reconsider. We all know people who thought they were good at a particular hobby, but once they tried to turn that hobby into a business, they failed. So, for a first step, assess your skills and aptitudes to see where your strengths are. And don't rely on cheap online programs to do this assessment. The Johnson O'Connor Foundation, a nonprofit organization, does an excellent job of giving people an assessment of their aptitudes.

Be prepared to start at the bottom, no matter what you decide to do. Even if you can get someone to hire you in a business you know absolutely nothing about, you're still going to have to prove yourself. The probability of your being hired in a business you know nothing about, by someone who doesn't know you, at a decent salary, isn't very high.

A book with good, grounded advice about changing careers is *Strategies for Successful Career Change*, by Martha Mangelsdorf. She encourages you to consider the logistical realities of a career change, such as finances, health insurance, and family obligations. Simply thinking you should "Do what you love and the money will follow" is folly. In fact, Mangelsdorf does not find any strong correlation between passion and money. She reviews four significant elements that do tend to determine how much a job pays: "People willing and able to do the job, the specialized skills the job requires, the unpleasantness of a job, and the demand for services the job fulfills" (p. 90).

So, to change careers you're most likely going to have to make it a good business deal for a prospective employer—worth the risk involved in taking on someone without proven experience. You'll have to say something along the line of, "Look, I've been a successful accountant for the past fifteen years, but I want be a real estate appraiser. I'm working on certifications. I'm willing to go to work for half of what you would normally pay an appraiser. I am willing to start out at the bottom and work my way up. I am a good employee. I will make the risk worthwhile for you."

Your résumé is not likely to get you this kind of interview. You are going to have to call and push your way into a face-to-face inter-view. Then you're going to have to sell yourself very, very hard. Only a personal contact is likely to get you the interview.

Relocating

Since our firm works primarily in Texas, and we have a more business-friendly atmosphere than most other states, we get hundreds of résumés weekly from people in other parts of the country who want to move here because the economy is better. They are having a difficult time finding employment in California, New York, or Florida, and they want to go where the economy is better and find a job.

With the economy as it is (and it may be this way for the foreseeable future), companies are reluctant to relocate candidates from other parts of the country. Nor are they keenly interested in hiring people who are willing to relocate if they get hired. This is the case for the following reasons.

First, there are already lots of people in the area. Except for very rare types of positions and experiences, most hiring authorities believe that there's plenty of talent right where they are. Even though they may find a perfect candidate somewhere else in the country, they say, "Well, surely there's somebody locally who can do this job." This may not be true, but they still think it: "With all the unemployed out there, we surely should be able to find someone without having to consider somebody who doesn't live in the area."

Second, with the economy as it is, most firms don't want to take on the expense of relocating someone from another part of the country unless they absolutely have to. So you say, "Well, I'll pay for my own relocation." Fair enough, but the issue isn't just the expense of having to pay for your relocation, even though a prospective employer might tell you that.

Third, when the economy turns around and a job is easier to find in your home state, the company might feel that you will return, leaving the job it hired you to do.

When the economy is slow and unemployment is high, employers tend to think this way. They don't want to go to the expense of relocating someone, or running the risk of having their new hire leave them to "go back home" in the future. In the early 1970s and early 1980s, when many Texas businesses were expanding, lots of people moved here. Some stayed and some didn't.

On the other hand, there are times when an employer simply can't get its people locally. For a plastics processing company here in Texas, we searched for over eight months to find a person with the exact experience and personality needed. We finally found a qualified candidate in Ohio. Even in 2010, in the middle of a recession, the company hired him and, reluctantly, paid part of his relocation costs. This, however, was an exception.

So, if you live in an area where you can't find a job and you're going to have to relocate, go to that place and start looking for a job. If you can't move there and have to search from a distant location, know that this is going to be extremely difficult. We hear this all the time: "Gosh, I can't move to [Dallas]; I have a job where I am and can't move. But if I can line up a few interviews at a time, I can come for a few days or maybe a week." Alas, it doesn't work that way. Lining up "a few interviews" at a time is hard. In fact, getting one interview is tough enough—more than one is a bonus.

If you're set on relocating nonetheless, here are some recommendations:

∎ Be prepared to pay your own relocation costs for the place where you desire to live. Lots of companies did away with paying relocation expenses a long time ago. You may be able to negotiate this once you have secured an offer, but don't bank on it.

∎ If you live far away from where you're trying to find a job, take your physical address off the résumé. If you have a friend or relative in the proposed city, ask to use that address on your résumé. I've known candidates who rented P.O. box numbers in the desired city and had friends or relatives pick up the mail.

∎ Use the addresses of corporate headquarters in the body of your résumé. You can work for J.C. Penney and similar large companies in all kinds of cities. Don't worry if your cell phone does not have an area code that corresponds to the desired city; people keep cell phone numbers from place to place.

∎ Don't tell a prospective employer *before* you've interviewed that you are not in the area. Eventually you're going to have to explain to a hiring authority that you don't live in the area and that you need to relocate. But you're going to do this *after* you've had a chance to sell yourself.

In short, I'm not suggesting you deceive prospective employers; I am just telling you to remove potential barriers to getting interviewed. Concerns about relocation on the part of a prospective employer shouldn't be a bigger problem than if you were fired from your last three jobs or if your references are awful. Location may wind up being a deal killer, but you don't want the issue to keep you from getting the interview.

The Top Ten Rules (You Now Know) of Résumé Writing

Having completed this book, you should know and follow these ten guidelines for writing unbeatable résumés:

1. You'll never overestimate the value of your résumé. You realize that your résumé is a tool to help you get the most important event of the job search—the interview.

2. You know that your résumé is going to get initially read in less than a minute. So, your résumé is short, direct, and to the point.

3. You know how many résumés the hiring authority is reviewing. You are going to have to do many other activities to separate yourself from the pack and augment the impact of your résumé.

4. You know that your résumé will be reviewed and screened by many people who don't know what they're looking for. This is another good reason to keep your résumé simple but direct.

5. You write your résumé clearly and concisely with straightforward content. Your résumé should be written so a high school senior can understand it.

6. Your résumé format is attractive and encourages people to read it. Your résumé should be pleasant to look at, catch the reader's eye, and draw him or her into reading it, whether you are providing it online or as a hard copy.

7. Your cover letter is short and gets read. Realize the limited value of a cover letter so when you write one, it has impact.

8. You customize a number of different résumés. Customize your résumé for specific positions you are applying for. One size does not fit all!

9. You are aware of the proper length of and the items that should appear on your résumé. Also know what employers and hiring authorities like and dislike on a résumé.

10. You have the right "strategy" for your résumé. Realize your résumé is simply a tool and part of an overall strategy of getting face-to-face interviews. You now know what to do to get that face-to-face interview.

Good Luck! And God Bless!